Stitch by Stitch

Volume 18

TORSTAR BOOKS

NEW YORK · TORONTO

Stitch by Stitch

TORSTAR BOOKS INC.
300 E.42ND STREET
NEW YORK, NY 10017

Knitting and crochet abbreviations

approx = approximately	in = inch(es)	sl st = slip stitch
beg = begin(ning)	inc = increas(e)(ing)	sp = space(s)
ch = chain(s)	K = knit	st(s) = stitch(es)
cm = centimeter(s)	oz = ounce(s)	tbl = through back of
cont = continue(ing)	P = purl	loop(s)
dc = double crochet	patt = pattern	tog = together
dec = decreas(e)(ing)	psso = pass slipped	tr = triple crochet
dtr = double triple	stitch over	WS = wrong side
foll = follow(ing)	rem = remain(ing)	wyib = with yarn in
g = gram(s)	rep = repeat	back
grp = group(s)	RS = right side	wyif = with yarn in front
dc = half double	sc = single crochet	yd = yard(s)
crochet	sl = slip	yo = yarn over

A guide to the pattern sizes

		10	12	14	16	18	20
Bust	in	32½	34	36	38	40	42
	cm	83	87	92	97	102	107
Waist	in	25	26½	28	30	32	34
	cm	64	67	71	76	81	87
Hips	in	34½	36	38	40	42	44
	cm	88	92	97	102	107	112

Torstar Books also offers a range of acrylic book stands, designed to keep instructional books such as *Stitch by Stitch* open, flat and upright while leaving the hands free for practical work.

For information write to Torstar Books Inc., 300 E.42nd Street, New York, NY 10017.

Library of Congress Cataloging in Publication Data
Main entry under title:

Stitch by stitch.

Includes index.
1. Needlework. I. Torstar Books (Firm)
TT705.S74 1984   746.4   84-111
ISBN 0-920269-00-1 (set)

98765432

© Marshall Cavendish Limited 1984

Printed in Belgium

ISBN 0-920269-18-4   (Volume 18)

Step-by-Step Crochet Course

Step-by-Step Knitting Course

Contents

Crochet / COURSE 79

*Crochet mittens
*Working a mitten without a thumb
*Working a mitten with a thumb
*Patterns for boot cuffs, mittens and beret

Crochet mittens

Simple crochet mittens can be made by working a tubular shape (see Volume 4, page 11), making a seamless fabric which can be shaped to make the mitten.
Patterns vary in shape and style, depending on the yarn and stitch used. In this course we show you how to work a basic mitten, with and without a thumb. The pattern can be used as the basis for many different styles, since by changing the yarn, working striped patterns in bright colors, using odds and ends of yarn for the mittens, or working a different stitch,

you can alter the appearance considerably.
Once you have practiced working the basic shape, you should have no difficulty in adapting the pattern to the size and style you want.
To decide the size of the mitten and to ensure a good fit., measure the hand around the widest part—that is around the knuckles with the hand laid flat. Make a stitch gauge sample in the yarn and hook of your choice and calculate the number of stitches needed for the circumference

of the mitten. When making a thumb opening, also measure the hand farther down, going around the base of the thumb. Subtract the knuckle measurement from this measurement to calculate the number of stitches needed for the thumb opening.
Measure the hand from the top of the middle finger to the wrist bone to determine the length, remembering that room must be left at the top for movement and that additional length can be added at the lower edge if desired.

Working a mitten without a thumb

In this simple shape, stitches equivalent to the circumference of the hand are worked in a straight piece of tubular crochet until the fabric measures $\frac{1}{2}$in (1.5cm) less than the completed length for a small mitten, to approximately 1in (2.5cm) less than the completed length for a larger mitten, before shaping the top. Variations can be worked, using the basic pattern as a guide, by choosing different stitch patterns or using different yarns. A simple shell pattern could be worked at the base of the mitten before the hand is worked in a plain single crochet or half double fabric to make a baby's mitten.

1 Refer to Volume 4, page 11 on how to work a tubular fabric. Work the mitten in a sport yarn using a size E (3.50mm) hook. Make 26 chains. Join into a circle with a slip stitch. If necessary work the foundation chain with a larger hook to ensure a loose edge.

2 Make 2 chains. Work 1 half double into each chain all around. Join into a circle with a slip stitch. 26 stitches. Continue to work a tubular fabric in this way until mitten measures $4\frac{1}{4}$in (11cm) from foundation chain, or $\frac{3}{4}$in (2cm) less than finished length.

3 Begin to shape top. Work 2 chains, then 1 half double into next stitch. Now work next two stitches together to decrease one stitch. Continue to decrease a stitch by working every 2nd and 3rd stitch together all around. Join with a slip stitch.

4 To complete shaping on next round, work 2 chains, then decrease by working two stitches together all around fabric so that only 9 stitches remain.

5 Break off yarn and thread through remaining stitches. Pull stitches together tightly to complete top. Thread ribbon or crochet chain through stitches at wrist as shown here to complete mitten.

Working a mitten with a thumb

Our basic mitten has been worked in an Aran-style yarn using sizes G and H (4.50mm and 5.00mm) hooks to achieve the correct shape. To work the same pattern in a different yarn or stitch, make a stitch gauge sample in the yarn and hook of your choice and use this sample to calculate the number of stitches needed for the circumference of the mitten, measuring the hand around the knuckles and the thumb joint.

To make sure that you get a loose edge on your fabric, it is a good idea to use a larger hook when working the foundation chain, changing to a smaller hook for the wrist section of the mitten.

1 Using larger hook make 28 chains. Change to smaller hook. Make 1 chain, then work 1 single crochet into each stitch all around, joining with a slip stitch to first chain. Work 1 in (2.5cm) in single crochet for wrist section. Change to larger hook and continue in single crochet until fabric measures 3¼in (8cm) from foundation chain.

2 Now make thumb opening. For the left hand work 22 stitches including turning chain. Make 6 chains. Skip next 6 stitches and join last chain to first with a slip stitch. For right hand alter position of thumb by making 7 chains at beginning of round, skip first 6 stitches and then continue in pattern to end.

3 For a larger opening leave 8 or 10 stitches unworked and make appropriate number of chain. On next round work a single crochet into each stitch and chain worked in previous round so that you have left an opening in the fabric for the thumb as shown here.

4 Complete the main part. Continue in single crochet without shaping until mitten measures 4¼in (11cm) from thumb opening or ¾in (2cm) less than finished length. Fabric should reach top joint of middle finger at this point.

5 Make 1 chain, work 1 single crochet into next stitch. Work next 2 stitches together to decrease one stitch. Continue to decrease thus by working every 3rd and 4th stitch together all around, ending with 1 half double worked into each of last two stitches. 20 stitches remain.

6 Work another decrease round in same way, but working one stitch between each decrease instead of two. Repeat last round once more, ending by working 2 single crochets together. Join with a slip stitch in the usual way.

7 On the final round work 2 stitches together all around, so that you are left with a narrow opening at top. Break off yarn, thread through remaining stitches and draw the stitches tightly together to complete top. Fasten off and sew end of yarn to inside of mitten.

8 Return to thumb opening. Rejoin yarn to center of upper edge. Now work around opening as follows. Make 1 chain, work 1 single crochet into each stitch along top edge, 1 stitch into corner, 1 stitch into each stitch along lower edge, 1 stitch into corner and 1 stitch into each stitch to end. 14 single crochets.

continued

9 Work two rounds without shaping. On next round shape thumb by working 2 stitches together at each corner. 12 single crochets.

10 Work 2 more rounds. Decrease 1 stitch at each corner as before on next round. 10 single crochets. Continue without shaping until thumb measures 2¾in (7cm) from base. It should reach top of thumb at this point.

11 Shape top by working two stitches together all around. Break off yarn and thread through remaining stitches. Pull yarn tightly through stitches to complete top.

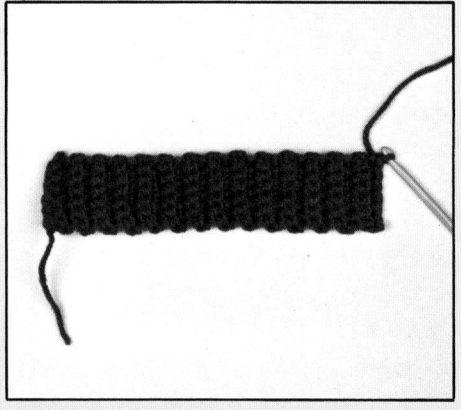

12 To work an alternative to the single crochet edging at the bottom of the mitten, use a size G (4.50mm) hook to make a strip of single crochet ribbing (see Volume 12, page 30), so that number of rows is equivalent to wrist measurement. Here we have worked 28 rows with 6 stitches in each row.

13 Change to a size H (5.00mm) hook and work across top of ribbing, increasing stitches if necessary across top so that there are 28 single crochets worked across top.

14 Join last stitch to first chain with a slip stitch and then continue to work the mitten as before, omitting wrist section. When the mitten has been completed, overcast the two ribbed edges together on wrong side.

Beret, mittens and boot cuffs

Coordinated accessories will give a sporty look to your fall separates. If you use two different yarns, one textured and one plain, you will get a fashionable tweedy look too.

Sizes
Beret To fit average size head.
Mittens Width around hand above thumb 8in (20cm).

Materials
Sport yarn
Beret *2oz (50g) in 1st color (A) tweed*
2oz (50g) in 2nd color (B)
Mittens and boot cuffs *2oz (50g) in 1st color (A) tweed*
2oz (50g) in 2nd color (B)
Size F (4.00mm) crochet hook

Gauge
19sc and 22 rows to 4in (10cm) worked on size F (4.00mm) hook.

Beret

To make
Using size F (4.00mm) hook and B, make 4ch, sl st into first ch to form a circle.
1st round Work 8sc into circle.
2nd round Work 2 sc into each sc all around. 16 sc.
3rd round *2 sc into next sc, 1sc into next sc, rep from * all around. 24 sc.
4th round *1 sc into each of next 2 sc, 2 sc into next sc, rep from * all around. 32 sc.
5th round *1 sc into each of next 3 sc, 2 sc into next sc, rep from * all around. 40 sc.
Cont to work in this way, working 8 more sc on every round until there are 136 sc. Work 11 rounds without shaping.
Next round * 1 sc into each of next 15 sc, work next 2 sc tog, rep from * all around.
Next round * 1 sc into each of next 14 sc

work next 2 sc tog, rep from * all around.
Cont to work in this way, dec 8 sc
on every round, until 88 sc rem.
Cut off B, join on A.
Work 7 rounds in sc firmly.
Sl st into each of next 2 sc. Fasten off.
Using eight 10in (25cm) lengths of A tog
make a twisted cord and knot one end.
Draw folded end through the hole at
center of beret. Sew ends of knot inside.

Mittens

Left hand
**Using size F (4.00mm) hook and A,
make 33ch, sl st into first ch to form a
circle.
Base round 1 sc into each ch all around.
Next round 1 sc into each sc all around.
Rep last round 7 times more.
Join on B.
Next round With B work * 1sc into each
of next 5sc, 2sc into next sc, 1sc into
each of next 6 sc, 2 sc into next sc, rep
from * once more, 1 sc into each of next
5 sc, 2 sc into next sc, 1sc into last sc.
38 sc.
Work 2 rounds in sc without shaping.
Cont in sc working in stripes of 1 round

A, 2 rounds B, 1 round A, 2 rounds B,
1 round A and 3 rounds B.
These 10 rounds form stripe sequence.
Work 4 more rounds. **
Next round 1 sc into each of next 29 sc,
6 ch, skip next 6 sc, 1sc into each of last
3sc.
Work 24 rounds in sc, working 1sc
into each of the 6 ch in first round.
Next round * Work next 2 sc tog, 1 sc
into each of next 2 sc, rep from * to
within last 2sc, work last 2sc tog. 28 sc.
Cut off B.
Next round 1 sc into each sc all around.
Next round *1 sc into next sc, work next
2 sc tog, rep from * to within last sc, 1sc
into last sc. 19 sc.
Next round * Work next 2 sc tog, rep from
* to within last sc, 1sc into last sc.
Fasten off leaving a long end. Thread end
through each sc, pull tightly and secure.

Thumb
With RS facing return to the 6 sc that
were left unworked, join B to first sc
with a sc, 1sc into each of next 5 sc, 1 sc
into side of next sc, 1sc into each of
next 6ch, 1sc into side of sc in previous
row. 14sc.

Cont in sc and stripes to match glove,
work 11 rounds.
Next round With A work (2 sc tog) all
around. 7 sc.
Fasten off leaving a long end. Thread end
through each sc, pull thread tightly and
secure.

Right hand
Work as for left hand from ** to **.
Next round 1 sc into each of next 3sc,
6ch, skip next 6sc, 1 sc into each sc all
around.
Complete as for left hand.

Boot cuffs (make 2)

To make
Using size F (4.00mm) hook and A, make
36ch, sl st into first ch to form a ring.
Base round 1 sc into each ch all around.
Next round 1 sc into each sc all around.
Rep last round 6 times more.
Join on B.
Cont in sc working in stripes of 3 rounds
B, 1 round A, 2 rounds B, 1 round A, 2
rounds B, 1 round A, 3 rounds B. Cut off
B. Work 10 rounds in sc.
Sl st into each of next 2sc. Fasten off.

Crochet / COURSE 80

Crochet flowers—chrysanthemum

In this course we show you how to make flowers by crocheting in rounds, building up the petals while you work.

The flowers can be worked in a variety of yarns, and by combining contrasting colors or different kinds of yarn, you can achieve a variety of different effects from one pattern.

Texture can also be introduced into the flower patterns by using bobble or cluster stitches or crochet loops for the flower centers or petals.

The pictures show you how to work a small chrysanthemum, employing the same technique of working in rows and then rounds to form the petals, as is used to make the large flower pillow cover on page 13.

To alter the size of the flower, work more rounds at the center before making the petals. The length of the petals can be altered by changing the number of chains worked each time, and the width is changed by working single crochet for a narrow petal, or half doubles or doubles for wider petals.

A round of single crochet or half doubles worked between each petal round creates a tightly bunched flower, while doubles worked between each petal round make a much more widely spaced flower.

Work the chrysanthemum in a knitting worsted yarn and size F (4.00mm) hook, so that you can see clearly how the shape is made; finer yarns and textures can be used once the technique has been perfected. Our flower has been worked in several colors so that you can see how each round is worked.

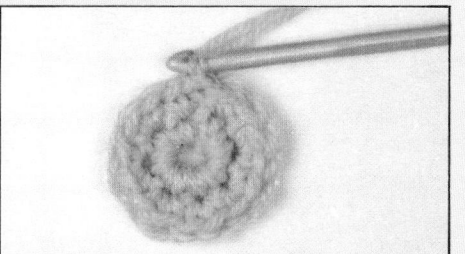

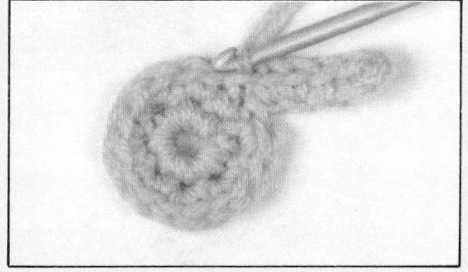

1 Make 4 chains and join into a circle with a slip stitch. Work 1 chain, then 7 single crochets into circle. 8 single crochets in all. Work one more round, working 2 single crochets into each stitch. 16 single crochets.

2 Make the petals by working in rows around the center disk, working into the **front** loop only of each stitch. Slip stitch into first stitch. Make 6 chains. Work 1 single crochet into 3rd, then into each chain back to center. 5 single crochets. Now slip stitch into front loop of next single crochet in center disk.

3 Continue to work petals all around center in same way, moving petals around the circle by working into front loop of next stitch on center disk each time. Join last petal to back of first petal with a slip stitch. 16 petals.

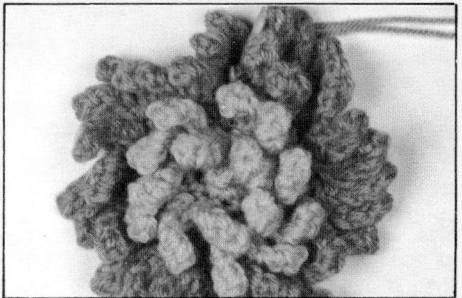

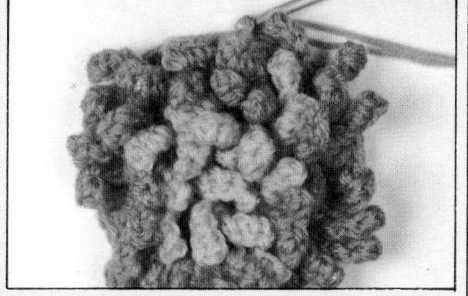

4 Now make 3 chains and work a double into stitch at base of these chains. Fold petals forward so that you can see back loop of stitches worked in previous round and work 2 doubles into back loop of each stitch all around, thus pushing petals forward. Join with a slip stitch to turning chain.

5 When changing color pull new yarn through in the usual way at the end of a round. Work a 2nd round of single crochet petals in exactly the same way as before, working into front loop of double made in previous round. 32 petals.

6 Work another double round as before, but work two doubles into every 4th stitch to increase around circle, instead of every stitch (3 doubles between each increase) so that there are 40 stitches in all at the end of this round.

continued

Mike Berend

9

7 Make 6 chains, 1 single crochet into 3rd chain from hook and into next chain. Complete petal by working one half double instead of a single crochet into each chain to center, making a wider petal.

8 Slip stitch into each of next **two** stitches. Make another petal in same way as before. Continue around flower in this way so that each petal consists of two single crochets and three half doubles, with two slip stitches worked between each. Join with a slip stitch to the **back** of the petal as before.

9 Work another double round, working 4 doubles between each increase so that the size of the flower is gradually increased.

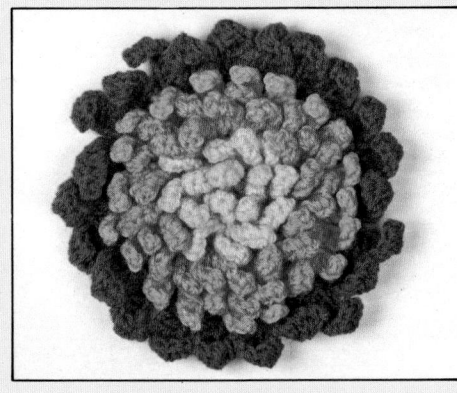
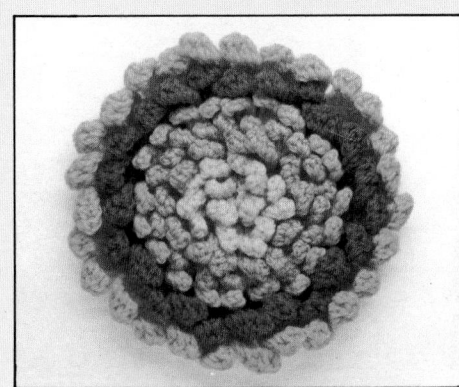

10 Make 9 chains. 1 single crochet into 3rd chain from hook and next chain. Work one double into each chain to center, making a wider petal than before.

11 Slip stitch into each of next two · stitches and work another petal as before. Complete the round with slip stitches and petals worked in same way all around the flower.

12 To make a larger flower work alternate double and petal rounds, working one more double between increase on plain double rounds each time.

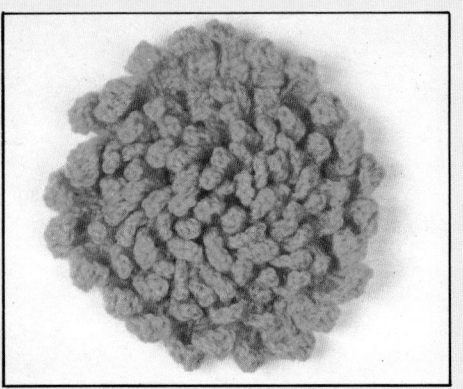

13 Here we show you the same flower worked in one color qnly, using a size C (3.00mm) hook and soft sport yarn to obtain a smaller flower.

14 To make a much tighter-looking flower, work in same way as before, working single crochets around each layer of petals. Work the first three rounds as shown in steps 1 to 3, so that you have made one round of single crochet petals at center.

15 Work 1 chain to count as first single crochet, then a single crochet into stitch at base of chain. Now work two single crochets into back loop of stitches made in previous round, folding the petals forward in the same way as before so that you can see the back loops of each stitch clearly.

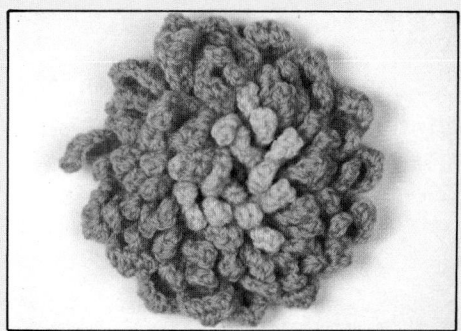

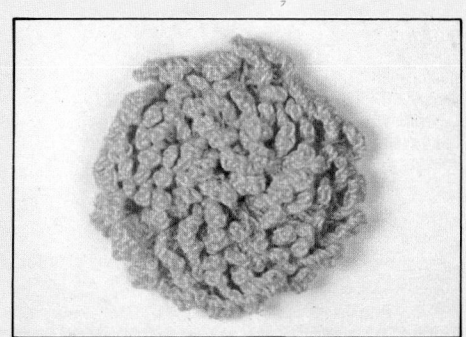

16 Work one more single crochet petal round to obtain a tight center, which could be worked in a contrasting yarn as shown here. For a really tight flower work each petal round in single crochet.

17 Complete the flower with one half double, then one double petal round in same way as before, but with single crochet rounds between each petal round, increasing stitches in same way as when making larger flower.

18 Here the same flower has been crocheted in a medium-weight mercerized cotton with a fine hook to obtain a smaller, lighter flower.

Stitch Wise

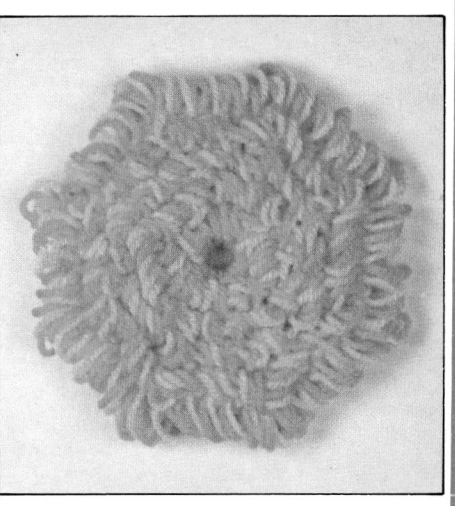

Mike Berend

Picot-edged double flower

Use two colors, coded A and B.
Using B, make 4 ch. Join into a circle with a sl st.

1st round (RS) 2ch to count as first hdc, 19hdc into circle. Join with a sl st to top of ch. 20hdc.

2nd round Turn so that WS is facing. 2ch to count as first sc, insert hook into next st, draw yarn through, taking yarn from underneath index finger (see Volume 13, page 11, step 10), drop loop, yo and through all loops on hook—called loop 1 sc—, work 1 loop 1 sc into each st to end. Join with a sl st to 2nd of first 2ch. Break off B. Join in A.

3rd round Turn so that RS is facing. 2ch, 1hdc into each of next 3sc, turn and work first petal on these 4 sts, *2ch, 1hdc into each of next 2hdc, 1hdc into turning ch, turn, 1ch, 1sc into each of next 2hdc, 1sc into turning ch, turn, 1ch, (insert hook into next st and draw through a loop) twice, yo and draw through all loops on

hook—called dec 1sc—, 1sc into turning ch, turn, 1ch, dec 1sc, ** (first petal completed), sl st down side of petal and into st, at base, 1hdc into each of next 4hdc *, turn and work 2nd petal as before, working from * to *. Cont to work 3 more petals in same way, working from * to * each time. Join last petal with a sl st to first ch. Break off A. Join in B.

4th round Using B, work around each petal as foll: 1ch to count as first sc, 2ch, 1sc into same place as 1ch, (1sc into next row end, 2ch, 1sc into same place) to top of petal, (1sc, 2ch, 1sc) into top, (1sc, 2ch, 1sc) into each sl st down side of petal, (1sc, 2ch, 1sc) into first row end of next petal. Join with a sl st to first ch. Break off B. Join in A.

5th round Using A, work from back of flower, rejoin A around stem of 2nd hdc in first row of first petal, 2ch to count as first hdc, *6ch, 1hdc around stem of 2nd hdc in first row of next petal, inserting hook from back around front and to back again, rep from * 3 times more, 6ch. Join with a sl st to 2nd of first 2ch.

6th round Sl st into first 6ch loop, 2ch to count as first hdc, work 3hdc into same loop, turn and complete petal on these 4 sts as before, working from * to ** in 2nd round, sl st down side of petal and into same 6ch loop, sl st into next 6ch loop, 2ch, 3hdc into same 6ch loop. Complete 2nd petal as first. Work 3 more petals in same way. Join with a sl st to first ch. Break off A.

Looped flower

Make 6ch. Join into a circle with a sl st.
1st round (RS) 2ch, 15hdc into circle. Join with a sl st to first ch. Turn.

2nd round Join in 2nd color. Use 2 strands of yarn tog from now on. 1ch to count as first sc, insert hook into st at base of ch, draw yarn through next st, taking yarn from beneath index finger (see Volume 13, page 11, step 10) to make first loop, drop loop, wind yarn around hook and draw through both loops on hook—called loop sc—, * loop sc into next st (loop sc into next st) twice, rep from * to end, loop sc into last st. Join with a sl st to first ch.

3rd round 1ch, 1 loop sc into st at base of ch, * loop sc into each of next 2 sts, (loop sc) twice into next st, rep from * to last 2 sts, loop sc into each of next 2 sts. Join with a sl st to first ch.

4th round 1ch, loop sc into st at base of ch, * loop sc into each of next 3 sts, (loop sc) twice into next st, rep from * to last 3 sts, loop sc into each of next 3 sts. Join with a sl st to first ch.
To increase size of flower rep 4th round, working 1 more loop sc between each increase.

Flowery pillow covers

Crochet a large flower pillow cover or work a plain cover and add flowers and leaves made separately in colors to match your decor.

Chrysanthemum pillow cover

Size
18in (46cm) in diameter.

Materials
A knitting-worsted weight yarn
    7oz (160g) in rust (A)
    6oz (140g) in brown (B)
    4oz (80g) in yellow (C)
Size F (4.00mm) crochet hook
18in (46cm)-diameter pillow form

Front
Using size F (4.00mm) hook and B, make 4ch, sl st into first ch to form a circle.
1st round Work 8 sc into circle.
2nd round Work 2 sc into each sc. 16 sc.
3rd round Working into the front loops only of each sc on 2nd round, *sl st into next sc, 5 ch, 1 sc into 2nd ch from hook, 1 sc into each of next 3 ch, rep from * all around, sl st into same place as first sl st. 16 petals.
4th round 3ch, 1 dc into back loop of same st as last sl st, working into back loops only of sts on 2nd round (i.e. behind petals) work *2dc into next st, rep from * all around, sl st into top of first 3ch. 32 sts.
5th round As 3rd. 32 petals.
6th round Change to A and work 3ch, working into the back loops behind last row, work 1dc into each of next 2dc, 2dc into next dc, *1dc into each of next 3dc, 2dc in next dc, rep from * all around, sl st, into top of first 3ch. 40 sts.
7th round As 3rd. 40 petals.
8th round Using B, work as 6th round but work 4dc between incs. 48 sts.
9th round As 3rd. 48 petals.
10th round Using A work as for 6th round but work 5dc between incs. 56 sts.
11th round As 3rd. 56 petals.
12th round Using B work as 6th round but work 6dc between incs. 64 sts.
13th round As 3rd. 64 petals.

14th round Using A work as for 6th round but work 7dc between incs. 72 sts.

15th round As 3rd. 72 petals.

16th round Cont in A work as 6th round but work 8dc between incs. 80 sts.

17th round Working into the front loop only of each st work *6ch, 1sc into 2nd ch from hook, 1sc into next ch, 1hdc into each of next 3ch, sl st into next 2 sts, rep from * all around, sl st into base of first 6ch. 40 petals.

18th round As 6th round but work 9dc between incs. 88 sts.

19th round As 17th. 44 petals.

20th round As 6th round but work 10dc between incs. 96 sts.

21st round As 17th. 48 petals.

22nd round As 6th round but work 11dc between incs. 104 sts.

23rd round As 17th. 52 petals.

24th round As 6th round but work 12dc between incs. 112 sts.

25th round As 17th. 56 petals.

26th round As 6th round but work 13dc between incs. 120 sts.

27th round Working into the front loop only of each st, work *8ch, 1sc into 2nd ch from hook, 1sc into next ch, 1dc into each of next 5ch, sl st into next 2 sts, sl st into next st, rep from * all around. 60 petals.

28th round Change to C, working into the back loop of each st, work 4ch, 1tr into each of next 8 sts, 2tr into next st, *1tr into each of next 9 sts, 2tr into next st, rep from * all around. 132 sts.

29th round As 27th. 66 petals.

30th round Change to A and work as 28th round working 10tr between incs. 144tr.

31st round As 27th. 72 petals.

32nd round Using A, work as 28th round but work 11tr between incs. 156 sts.

33rd round Using C, work as 27th round.

78 petals.

34th round Using A, work as 28th round but work 12tr between incs. 168 sts.

35th round Using C, work as 27th round. 84 petals.

36th round Using C and working into the back of each st work 1sc into each st all around, sl st into first sc. Fasten off.

Back

Using size F (4.00mm) hook and B, make 3ch, sl st into first ch to form a circle. Work as given for white pillow cover until circle measures 17in (43cm) in diameter. Fasten off.

To finish

Press out petals on front.
With WS tog join pillow cover working 1sc into each st, through double thickness, leaving an opening. Insert pillow form, then join opening.

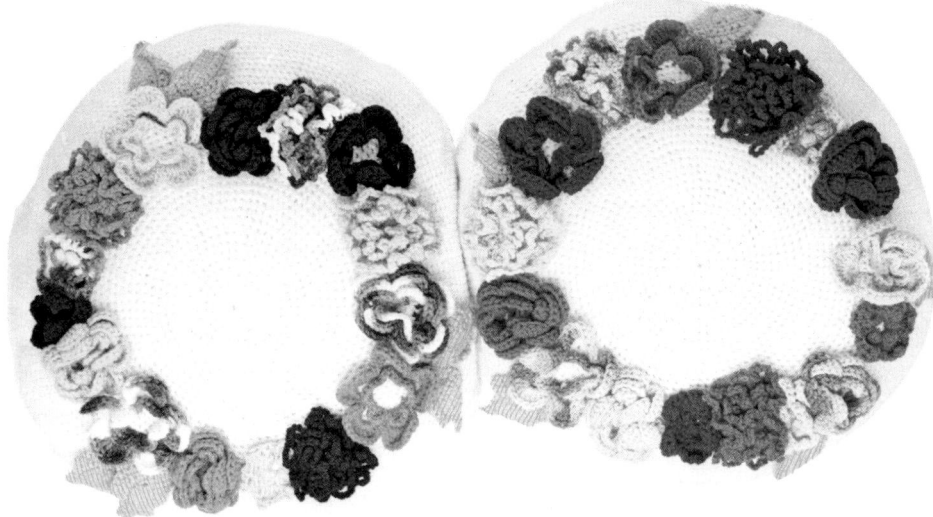

Flowery pillow covers

Size
18in (46cm) in diameter.

Materials
*A knitting-worsted weight yarn
8oz (200g) in main (background)
    color (A)
2oz (40g) in·green for leaves (B)
1oz (20g) in a variegated color (C)
    and 1oz (20g) in each of three
    shades of pink or blue for flowers
    (D, E and F)
Size C (3.00mm) crochet hook
18in (46cm)-diameter pillow form*

To make
Using size C (3.00mm) hook and A make
3ch, sl st into first ch to form a circle.
1st round Work 8sc into circle.
2nd round 2sc into each sc all around.
3rd round 1sc into each sc all around.
4th round (1sc into next sc, 2sc into
next sc) 8 times. 24sc.
5th round (2sc into next sc, 1sc into
each of next 2sc) 8 times. 32sc.
6th round (1sc into each of next 3sc,
2sc into next sc) 8 times. 40sc.
7th round (2sc into next sc, 1sc into
each of next 4sc) 8 times. 48sc.
8th round 1sc into each sc all around.
Cont in this way, inc 8sc on 3 rounds,
then working 1 round without inc, until
circle measures 17in (43cm) in diameter.
Fasten off.
Make another piece in the same way.

Loop flower
Using size C (3.00mm) hook and C make
5ch for first circle, sl st into first ch.
1st round 1ch to count as first sc, 15sc
into circle, sl st into first ch. 16sc.
2nd round *4ch, sl st into next sc, rep
from * to end. 16ch loops.
3rd round Sl st into each of first 2ch of
next loop, sl st into center of same loop,
5ch, *sl st into center of next ch loop, 5ch,
rep from * to end, sl st into sl st at center of
first loop.
4th round Sl st into each of first 3ch of
next loop, sl st into center of same loop,
6ch, *sl st into center of next 6ch loop,
6ch, rep from * to end, sl st into sl st at
center of first loop.
Fasten off.
Using size C (3.00mm) hook and C make
5ch for second circle, sl st into first ch.
1st round 1ch to count as first sc, 17sc
into circle, sl st into first ch. 18sc.
2nd and 3rd rounds As 2nd and 3rd
rounds of first circle. Fasten off.
Sew second circle to center of first circle.
Make 3 more flowers in each of D, E and F.

Picot daisy
Using size C (3.00mm) hook and C make
6ch, sl st into first ch.
1st round 3ch, *(yo, insert hook into
circle, yo and draw a loop through)
5 times, yo and draw through first 10
loops on hook, yo and draw through
rem 2 loops—cluster made—, 3ch, rep
from * 3 times more, sl st into top of first
3ch.
2nd round 3ch, *1sc into circle between
next 2 clusters working over 3ch made in
previous round so drawing these 3ch
down, 3ch, rep from * 3 times more, sl st
into first 3ch.
3rd round Sl st into first 3 ch loop, 1ch to
count as 1sc, (1hdc, 1dc, 1tr, 1dc, 1hdc
and 1sc) all into same loop, sl st into next
3ch loop, (1sc, 1hdc, 1dc, 1tr, 1dc, 1hdc
and 1sc) all into next loop, sl st into next
3ch loop, rep from * 3 times more,
working last sl st into first ch. 5 petals.
4th round *1ch, 1sc into next hdc, dc and
tr, 2ch, sl st into last sc worked—picot
formed—, 1sc into next dc, hdc and sc, sl
st into first ch in next petal, rep from * 4
times more, working last sl st into first ch.
Fasten off.
Make 3 more flowers in each of D, E and F.

Double rose
Using size C (3.00mm) hook and C make
8ch, sl st into first ch.
1st round 6ch, *1dc into circle, 3ch, rep
from * 4 times more, sl st into 3rd of first
6ch. 6 spaces.
2nd round Into each sp work 1sc, 1hdc,
3dc, 1hdc and 1sc. 6 petals.
3rd round *5ch, inserting hook from back
to front work 1sc around next dc on first
round, rep from * ending with 5ch, join
with a sl st to first ch.
4th round Into each sp work 1sc, 1hdc,
5dc, 1hdc and 1sc.
5th round *7ch, 1sc into next sc on 3rd
round working around stem as before,
rep from * ending with 7ch, join with a
sl st to first ch.
6th round Into each sp work 1sc, 1hdc,
7dc, 1hdc, and 1sc. Fasten off.
Make 3 more flowers in each of D, E and F.

Single rose
Using size C (3.00mm) hook and C make
15ch, sl st into first ch.
1st round *6ch, 1sc into circle, rep from
* 4 times more, omitting last sc and
joining with a sl st to first ch.
2nd round Into each 6ch loop work 1sc,
1hdc, 1dc, 8tr, 1dc, 1hdc and 1sc, join
with a sl st to sp formed by original ring
at base.
3rd round Into each sp at base of 2nd
round, work 1hdc, 5dc and 1hdc.
Fasten off.
Make 3 more flowers in each of D, E and F.

Leaves
Using size C (3.00mm) hook and B make
11ch.
1st row 1sc into 2nd ch from hook, 1sc
into each of next 8ch, 3sc into last ch,
do not turn but work along other side of
ch, 1sc into each of next 6ch. Turn.
2nd row 1ch, 1sc into each of next 6sc,
3sc into next sc, 1sc into each of next
7sc, turn.
3rd row 1ch, 1sc into each of next 7sc,
3sc into next sc, 1sc into each of next
5sc, turn.
4th row 1ch, 1sc into each of next 5sc,
3sc into next sc, 1sc into each of next
6sc, turn.
5th row 1ch, 1sc into each of next 6sc,
3sc into next sc, 1sc into each of next
4sc, turn.
6th row 1ch, 1sc into each of next 4sc,
3sc into next sc, 1sc into each of next
5sc. Fasten off.
Make 5 more rose leaves in the
same way.

To finish
On one section of cover, measure half the
radius and run a thread all around as a
guideline for sewing on flowers. Place
flowers all around guideline and space
leaves at intervals. Sew in place. With WS
tog join pillow cover, working 1sc into
each sc through the double thickness,
leaving an opening.
Insert pillow form, then slip stitch the
opening edges together.

Shoestring

Bright angles

Make an attractive pillow cover from three harmonizing fabrics arranged in a pleasing triangle patchwork design.

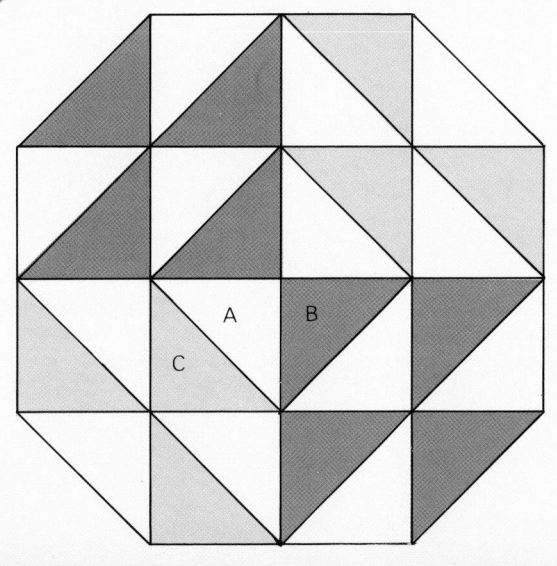

Brian Mayor

Finished size
16×16in (40×40cm).
A seam allowance of $\frac{3}{8}$in (1cm) has been included throughout.

Materials
$\frac{1}{4}$yd (.2m) of 36in (90cm)-wide solid-color cotton fabric (A)
$\frac{1}{4}$yd (.2m) of 36in (90cm)-wide dark, floral-printed cotton fabric (B)
$\frac{1}{2}$yd (.5m) of 36in (90cm)-wide lighter, floral-printed cotton fabric (C)
$\frac{1}{2}$yd (.5m) of 36in (90cm)-wide feather-proof cambric or other closely-woven cotton
Matching thread; stuffing
Small piece of thin cardboard

1 Make a cardboard template for the triangle. Draw a $4\frac{3}{4}$in (12cm) square on the cardboard. Divide this square diagonally, from corner to corner. Cut apart the resulting triangles, discard one and use one as the template.
2 Using the template cut out 6 triangles from fabric C, 8 triangles from fabric B and 14 triangles from fabric A.
3 Following the diagram, stitch the triangles together to form the vertical strips that make up the pillow cover front. To begin, place 2 triangles together, matching connecting sides and points. Pin, baste and stitch. Press seams open. Continue stitching the triangles together in the same way until each vertical strip has been completed.
4 Pin, baste and stitch the vertical strips together, following the diagram, to form the pillow cover front. To begin, position the first two strips together, matching edges and points. Pin, baste and stitch. Continue stitching the strips together in the same way until the pillow cover front is complete.
5 Press all the seams open. Trim away any excess fabric.
6 Using the patchwork pillow cover front as a pattern, cut out one piece of fabric C to make the pillow cover back.
7 Using the pillow cover back as a pattern,

Malcolm Robertson

cut two pieces about 1in (2.5cm) larger from feather-proof cambric to make the pillow form.
8 Place the pillow pieces together with right sides facing and edges matching. Pin, baste and stitch together around the edges, leaving a small opening in one side. Trim seam and turn pillow right side out.
9 Stuff pillow firmly. Turn in opening edges and slip stitch them together.
10 Place back and front covers together with right sides facing and edges matching. Pin, baste and stitch around leaving an opening in one side.
11 Trim seams and turn pillow cover right side out.
12 Place pillow form inside pillow cover. Turn in opening edges and slip stitch them together.

Crochet / COURSE 81

*Appliqué crochet flowers
*Wired crochet flowers
*Pattern for a shawl with appliqué flowers
*Patterns for wired flowers

Appliqué crochet flowers

Petal and leaf shapes made in fine crochet cotton can be sewn on a plain crochet background to decorate it.

By grouping individual petals together, you can make large flowers or sprays, using leaves and stems to complement the petals and complete the design.

The best results are achieved by making simply shaped, flat petals of differing sizes in a fine or medium-weight crochet cotton — fine mercerized cotton for example — using single crochet to obtain a firm, closely woven fabric, with half doubles and doubles used to shape the fabric. Small individual bobbles could be used as flower centers to give added texture to your appliqué design, using the method for making small crochet buttons shown in Volume 7, page 10.

Leaf shapes normally used in Irish crochet designs could also be applied to the fabric to create a complete flower pattern, using different colors, shapes of petals, leaves and simple crochet stems to embellish the background fabric in various ways.

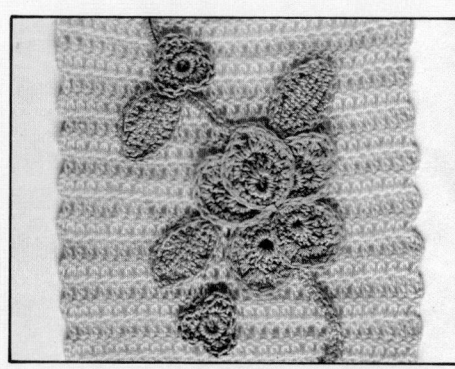

1 Use a fine crochet cotton and No. 7 (1.50mm) hook to make the petals, leaves and stems for your design. Baste each piece in place on your background fabric so that you can achieve a well-balanced design, making sure that the flowers complement each other in both style and color. To prevent a bulky looking fabric, try to lay the petals side by side, overlapping at the center only if absolutely necessary.

2 To sew the pieces to the fabric, use sewing thread in a color to match either the petals or the leaves and use either buttonhole stitch or satin stitch to sew the pieces to the fabric. Make sure that the stitches are worked closely all around the crochet to hold each piece firmly in place. If the appliqué is to be added to a garment, make sure that it is attached firmly to the background fabric so that it will withstand frequent washing or dry cleaning.

Wired crochet flowers

Petals and leaves can also be built up to form individual flowers. By using florist's wire and green florist's tape with crochet petals made in a fine crochet cotton, you can create a number of different flower heads and sprays. The wire is incorporated around the edge of each petal by working single crochet around the edge, covering the wire at the same time. By working in this way, you can mold each petal into shape once it has been completed.

The florist's tape is used to bind the exposed wires together at the base of the flower head and to make the stems. Additional leaves or flowers can also be added down the stem, using the wire and tape to fasten the pieces to the main stem. Our pictures show you how to make the rose featured on page 22, but the same technique can be used to make any number of flowers.

1 To make the petals for the rose, follow the instructions on page 21. Wherever possible, work over any spare ends of yarn to eliminate the need to darn in loose ends once the petal has been completed. Because of the fineness of the work, the chain made at the beginning of each row does not count as a stitch as it would normally.

2 To incorporate the wire, curve a piece around the edge of the petal.
If necessary, you can make a loop at the working end to prevent the wire from pulling through the stitches while you work.

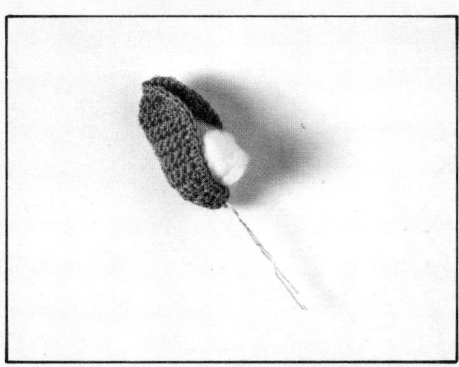

3 Rejoin the yarn to the lower edge of the petal and work single crochet around the edge and over the wire at the same time. Work the stitches as closely as possible so that the wire is completely covered, working into each row end or stitch all around. Work around each petal in same way.

4 To make the rose, wrap one of the small leaves around a small piece of absorbent cotton, which should be approximately the same size as an acorn.

5 Take the 2nd small petal and wrap it around the first, taking it over the edges of the first petal so that the cotton is completely covered and you have made a firm, rounded center for the flower. Twist the wires together at the base.

6 Wrap the medium-sized petals around the two center petals, overlapping the petals each time and molding them into shape. Use the wire to make a good rose shape. Twist the wires together at the bottom to hold the petals in place each time.

7 Now take the last three, large petals and construct the rest of the rose, overlapping each petal to achieve the correct shape. Twist the wire together at the bottom to hold the petals in place each time.

8 To complete the flower and make the stem, twist the strands of wire around a piece of thicker stem wire so that the stem is strong enough to support the rose.

9 Wind the green tape around the stem, starting at the top of the flower and overlapping each layer all the way down the stem so that the wire is completely hidden. Stretch the tape slightly as you wind it around the wire.

10 To add leaves work them as described on page 22, working in single crochet over the wire at the base to make a stem for each leaf.
To make tightly closed buds, use small petals only and twist them into shape on a wire stem as before, then work single crochet down stem in same way as when working a leaf.

11 Twist the leaf wire around the long stem of the main flower and then bind the tape around the finished stem to complete the rose.

Shawl with appliqué flowers

Delicate picot lace and flowers for your romantic moments.

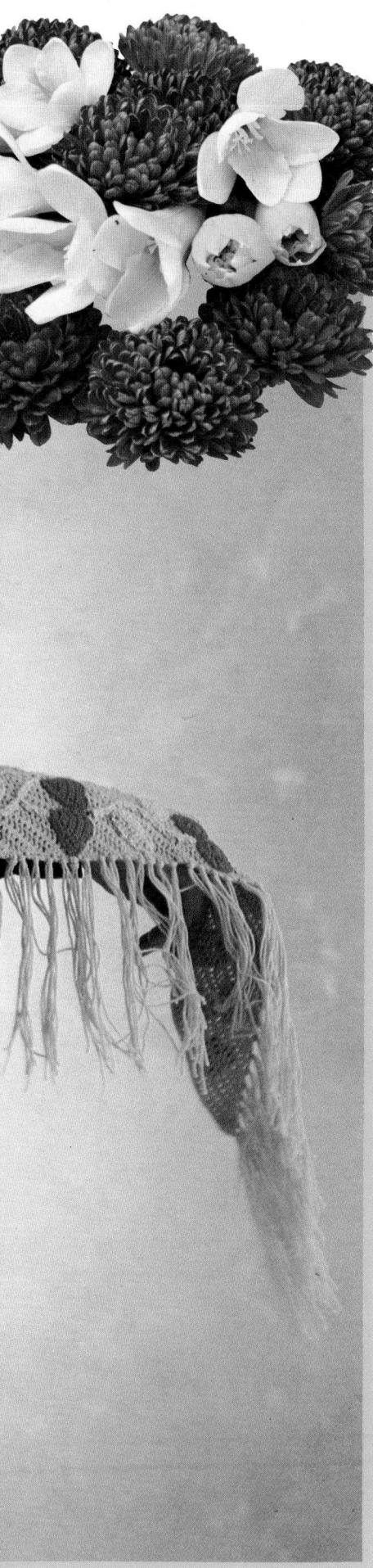

Size
27in (68cm) long, measured at center.

Materials
Sport yarn
8oz (200g) in main color
2oz (50g) in each of four contrasting
colors for flowers
2oz (50g) in green for leaves
Size D (3.25mm) crochet hook

Shawl
Using size D (3.25mm) hook and main color make 2ch.
Base row 1hdc into 2nd ch from hook. Turn.
1st row 2ch, 2hdc into next hdc. Turn.
2nd row 2ch, 2hdc into each of next 2hdc. Turn. 4hdc.
3rd row 2ch, 2hdc into next hdc, 1hdc into each of next 2hdc, 2hdc into last hdc. Turn. 6hdc.
4th row 2ch, 2hdc into next hdc, 1hdc into each of next 4hdc, 2hdc into next hdc. Turn. 8hdc.
Cont to inc 1hdc at each end of every row until there are 52hdc.
Next row 3ch to count as first dc, 2dc into first hdc, 1dc into each of next 24hdc, 5ch, skip next 2hdc, 1dc into each of next 24hdc, 3dc into last hdc. Turn.
Next row 3ch, 2dc into first dc, 1dc into each of next 24dc, 5ch, skip next 2dc, 1sc into next 5ch sp, 3ch, sl st into first of the 3ch – picot formed –, 5ch, skip next 2dc, 1dc into each of next 24dc, 3dc into top of turning ch. Turn.
Next row 3ch, 2dc into first dc, 1dc into each of next 24dc, 5ch, skip next 2dc, *1sc into next 5ch sp, work a picot, 5ch*, rep from * to * once more, skip next 2dc, 1dc into each of next 24dc, 3dc into top of turning ch. Turn.
Rep last row working from * to * **twice** in the next row, **3 times** in the foll row, inc 1 time each row until there are 90 5ch sps.
Next row 3ch, 2dc into first dc, 1dc into each of next 24dc, 3ch, skip next 2dc, *1sc into next 5ch sp, 3ch, * rep from * to * to last 5ch sp, 3ch, skip next 2dc, 1dc into each of next 24dc, 3dc into top of turning ch. Fasten off.

Fringe
Using main color cut lengths of yarn 12in (30cm) long and knot, 2 strands at a time, into each row end. Trim ends to same length to neaten fringe.

Tulips (make 12)
Using size C (3.00mm) hook make 2ch.
Base row 2sc into 2nd ch from hook. Turn.

1st row 1ch, 2sc into each sc. Turn. 4sc.
2nd row 1ch, 2sc into first sc, 1sc into each sc to within last sc, 2sc into last sc. Turn.
3rd row As 2nd.
4th – 7th rows 1ch, 1sc into each sc to end. Turn.
8th row *Skip next sc, 4dc all into next sc, skip next sc, sl st into next sc, rep from * to end of row, do not turn but work along side of flower, working 1sc into each row end, 3sc into base of flower and 1sc into each row end along other side, sl st into first dc of 4dc at top. Fasten off.

Pansy petals (make 12)
Using size C (3.00mm) hook make 5ch, sl st into first ch to form a circle.
Next round Into circle work 1ch, 2sc, 2hdc, 2dc, 1tr, 2dc, 2hdc and 2sc, sl st into first ch. Cut off yarn.
Next round Join on contrasting color and work 1sc into each of first 2sc, 1hdc into each of next 2 sts, 2dc into each of next 2 sts, 3tr into next st, 2dc into each of next 2 sts, 1hdc into each of next 2 sts, 1sc into each of last 2 sts, sl st into first st. Fasten off.

Little flowers (make 48)
Using size C (3.00mm) hook make 5ch, sl st into first ch to form a circle.
Next round 1ch, 2sc into circle, sl st into first ch.
Next round *Skip next sc, 5dc all into next sc, skip next sc, sl st into next sc, rep from * twice more. Fasten off.

Leaves (make 18)
Using size C (3.00mm) hook and green make 10ch.
Base row 1sc into 2nd ch from hook, 1sc into each of next 7ch, 3sc into last ch, do not turn but work along other side of ch, working 1sc into next 8ch. Turn.
Next row 1ch, 1sc into first sc, 1hdc into next sc, 1dc into each of next 4sc, 1hdc into each of next 2sc, 1sc into next sc, sl st into point of leaf, 1sc into next sc, 1hdc into each of next 2sc, 1dc into each of next 4sc, 1hdc into next sc, 1sc into last sc, 1sc into base of leaf, sl st into first ch. Fasten off.

Stems
Make appropriate number of ch for length of stem required, 1sc into 2nd ch from hook, 1sc into each ch to end. Fasten off.

To finish
Arrange flowers, leaves and stems on shawl border and sew in place.

Wired flowers

The pick of the bunch — roses and sweet peas for you to crochet.
Use nature's colors for petals and leaves and you'll have a
beautiful bouquet that will never fade.

Materials

Fine mercerized crochet cotton
Approx 1oz (20g) makes 6 leaves
Approx 1oz (20g) makes 3 roses or
2 sprays of sweet peas
No. 7 (1.50mm) steel crochet hook
Florist's wire
Florist's tape
Small amount of absorbent cotton

Sweet peas

Petals (make 10)
Using No. 7 (1.50mm) hook make 5ch, sl st into first ch to form a circle.
1st round 1ch, work 10sc into circle, sl st into first ch.
2nd round 1ch, 1sc into each of next 3sc, 2hdc into each of next 4sc, 1sc into each of last 3sc, sl st into first ch.
3rd round 1ch, 1sc into each of next 3sc, 2hdc into each of next 8hdc, 1sc into each of last 3sc, sl st into first ch.
4th round 1ch, 1sc into each of next 3sc, 2 hdc into each of next 16hdc, 1sc into each of last 3sc, sl st into first ch.
5th round 1ch, 1 sc into each of next 3sc, 2hdc into each of next 32 hdc, 1sc into each of last 3sc, sl st into first ch.
Wire petal by holding wire against the edge of petal and then working a row of sc around the entire edge enclosing the wire at the same time. Twist the 2 ends of wire tog at base of petal.

To finish

Use 2 petals for each flower; crinkle edges of petals, then fold top half of petal down. Place one petal in front of the other and twist wires tog. Tape each stem for approx 3¼ (8cm).
Twist wires tog then tape main stem.

Rose

Small petals (make 2)
Using No. 7 (1.50mm) hook make 5ch.
1st row 1sc into 2nd ch from hook, 1sc into each of next 3ch. Turn.
2nd row 1ch, 2sc into first sc, 2sc into each sc to end. Turn.
3rd row 1ch, 2sc into first sc, 1sc into each of next 6sc, 2sc into last sc. Turn.
4th row 1ch, 2sc into first sc, 1sc into each sc to within last sc, 2sc into last sc. Turn. 1sc.
5th row As 4th. 14sc.
Work 9 rows without shaping.
Next row 1ch, skip first sc, 1sc into next sc, 1hdc into each of next 3sc, 1dc into each of next 4sc, 1hdc into each of next 3sc, 1sc into next sc, sl st into last sc. Fasten off.

Medium petals (make 2)
Using No. 7 (1.50mm) hook make 5ch.
1st - 4th rows As 1st—4th rows of small petals.
5th and 6th rows Rep 4th row twice. Work 10 rows without shaping.
Next row 1ch, skip first sc, 1sc into next sc, 1hdc into next sc, 1dc into each of next 2sc, 1hdc into each of next 2sc, sl st into each of next 2sc, 1hdc into each of next 2sc, 1dc into each of next 2sc, 1hdc into next sc, 1sc into next sc, sl st into last sc. Fasten off.

Large petals (make 3)
Using No. 7 (1.50mm) hook make 5ch.
1st—4th rows As 1st—4th rows of small petals.
5th—8th rows Rep 4th row 4 times. Work 10 rows without shaping.
Next row 1ch, skip first sc, 1sc into next sc, 1hdc into next sc, 1dc into each of next 3sc, 1hdc into each of next 2sc, 1sc into next sc, sl st into each of next 2sc, 1sc into next sc, 1hdc into each of next 2sc, 1dc into each of next 3sc, 1hdc into next sc, 1sc into next sc, sl st into last sc. Fasten off.
Wire petals by holding wire against the edge of petal and then working a row of sc around the center edge enclosing the wire at the same time. Twist the two ends of wire tog at base of petal.

To finish
Wrap one of the small petals tightly around a small piece of absorbent cotton. Take second small petal and wrap it across in front of first petal so that no cotton shows; twist wires tog. Add the 2 medium petals and 3 large petals, molding the flower into shape as you work. Twist all wires tog. Cover wires with florist's tape.

Rose leaves

Top leaf (make 1)
Using No. 7 (1.50mm) hook make 13ch.
1st row 1sc into 2nd ch from hook, 1sc into each of next 10ch, 3sc into last ch, 1sc into each ch along other side. Turn.
2nd row 1ch, 1sc into each of first 2sc, *1hdc into each of next 2sc 1dc into each of next 3sc, 1hdc into each of next 3sc, 1sc into each of next 2sc, 3sc into end sc, 1sc into each of next 2sc, 1hdc into each of next 3sc, 1dc into each of next 3sc, 1hdc into each of next 2sc,* 1sc into each of last 2sc, sl st into first sc of row at base of leaf. Turn.
3rd row 1ch, 1sc into each of first 3sc, rep from * to * of 2nd row, 1sc into each of last 3sc, sl st into first sc of row at base of leaf. Turn.
4th row 1ch, 1sc into each sc, working 3sc at point of leaf, 1sc into each sc to end. Turn.
Next row Working over wire, work as 4th row to base of leaf.

Twist 2 ends of wire tog and work approx 10sc very tightly over wire to form stem of leaf. Fasten off.

Medium leaves (make 2)
Using No. 7 (1.50mm) hook make 12ch.
1st—3rd rows As 1st—3rd rows of top leaf.
Wire as for top leaf working 8sc for stem. Place these 2 leaves in position at base of stem of top leaf and twist wires tog, work approx 20sc over twisted wires.

Small leaves (make 2)
Using No. 7 (1.50mm) hook make 10ch.
1st row 1sc into 2nd ch from hook, 1sc into each of next 7ch, 3sc into end ch, 1sc into each ch along other side. Turn.
2nd row 1ch, 1sc into each of next 3sc, 1hdc into each of next 4sc, 1sc into each of next 2sc, sl st into sc at top of leaf, 1sc into each of next 2sc, 1hdc into each of next 4sc, 1sc into each of next 3sc, sl st into first sc of row. Turn.
3rd row 1ch, 1sc into each sc, working 3sc at point of leaf.
Wire as for top leaf working 4sc for stem. Place 2 small leaves in position and twist all wires tog, work approx 25sc over all wires. Fasten off.
To make a bouquet, tape leaf stems for approx 6in (15cm). Tape stems of roses as appropriate.

Shoestring

Woven rug

Weave yourself a rug from strong webbing and make a tough floor covering for an informal room.

Finished size
58 × 30½in (147 × 78cm).

Materials
19⅝yd (18.1m) of 2¾in (7cm)-wide
   solid webbing
18⅝yd (17.2m) of 2¾in (7cm)-wide
   striped webbing
Matching thread

1 From the solid webbing cut 21 lengths, each 34in (86cm) long.
2 From striped webbing cut 11 lengths, each 61½in (156cm) long.
3 On each length of solid webbing, measure 1¼in (3cm) from one end; mark.
4 Feed the webbing lengths through the sewing machine, one after another, with the long edges flush against each other, and stitch the lengths together at one end, along the marked lines.
5 Lay the joined webbing lengths on the floor, with the long edges together.
6 On each length of striped webbing,

measure 1¼in (3cm) from one end and mark.
7 Take one length of striped webbing and place it under the first length of plain webbing at a right angle to the stitched edge. Align the marked line with the outer edge of the first plain length.
8 Weave the striped length over and under the remaining plain lengths and pin it to the last one. Push the striped length up against the stitching at the side. Pin the webbing together at intervals to hold the strips in place.
9 Take the next striped length and place it over the first plain length, with the mark even with the outer edge, and with the long edge butted up against the first striped length.
10 Weave the striped length under and over each plain length and pin it to the last one. Pin the strips of webbing together at intervals.
11 Continue with each striped length, alternately weaving and butting the

edges together until all of them have been woven.
12 Starting at one corner, with the stitched edge on the right-hand side, remove the pins in turn and push the webbing lengths close together. Re-pin. Keep removing and replacing the pins along the complete length of the rug until all the lengths are woven tightly together.
13 Make sure that the lengths look straight, both widthwise and lengthwise. Baste around all four edges.
14 Stitch around the entire rug, about ½in (1.2cm) from the edge, using a larger-than-average stitch.
15 Trim the overlapping ends all around the rug to ¾in (2cm). Finish the trimmed edges with zig-zag stitch.
16 Turn under the ends for ¾in (2cm), flush with the edge of the rug. Pin, baste and hand-sew the ends in place with herringbone stitch.
17 Press the rug thoroughly with a hot iron over a damp cloth.

Crochet / COURSE 82

*Crochet rag rugs
*How to crochet with fabric strips
*Working colored patterns with rags
*Stitch Wise: more color patterns
*Pattern for a rag rug

Crochet rag rugs

Solving the problem of what to do with fabric remnants led to the creation of two crafts—patchwork and rag rugs. If you do not have the time to spend piecing and then quilting large patchwork items, crocheting a rag rug would be a way of putting a drawer full of fabric scraps or a bag full of old clothes to a good use.

Most types of fabric can be crocheted, but for rugs, fabrics of a medium weight will give the best results. Suit- and dress-weight woolens are especially good, because they will produce a soft, elastic rug. Do not be afraid to mix different types of fabric, so long as they are similar in weight. The most important thing to remember about sorting your scraps into color groups is that it is not the color itself which is important in forming a pattern but the *tone* Divide the remnants into dark-, medium- and light-colored groups, just as you would sort the laundry.

How to crochet with fabric strips

It can take up to 5in (12.5cm) of a $\frac{1}{2}$in (1.3cm)-wide strip to make one single crochet stitch, so the longer the fabric strip is, the better. For this reason it is best to cut round and round in a spiral toward the center of the remnant, producing a long strip with a minimum of seams.

The hook used varies according to the weight of the fabric but you will probably find between a size K (7.00mm) and a size 15 wood (9.00mm) suitable. The instructions here show how to work stripes in single crochet with rag strips.

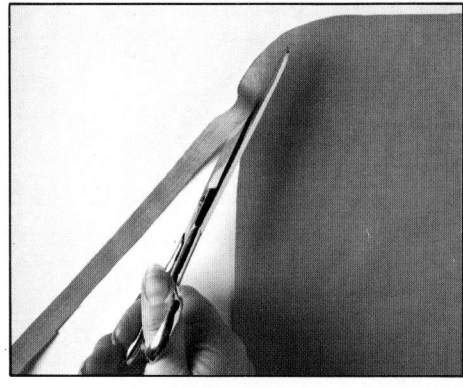

1 To cut the remnant into a long strip, lay it on a flat surface and round off three corners. You can mark the curves using a dinner plate and a pencil. If the piece of fabric is an irregular shape, just round off all edges in the same way.

2 Start cutting the strip $\frac{1}{2}$in (1.3cm) wide at the corner that has not been rounded off. Cut all the way around the piece until you reach the corner where you started. Then round this corner off and go on cutting a continuous strip around the remnant edge.

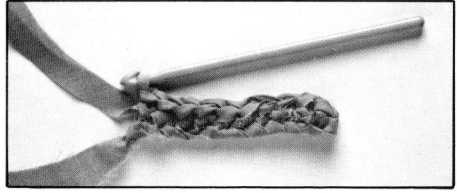

3 Prepare all your strips, keeping the dark-toned ones together and the light-toned ones together. Then take a dark strip and make a foundation chain. Work single crochet across the chain. Turn the work and make 1 chain, then, inserting the hook into the back loop only, work 1 single crochet into each each single crochet to the end.

4 Continue using the dark strip, making a few rows of single crochet, always working into the back loop of the stitch. When you come to the end of a strip, join a new dark strip as follows: first clip the ends of the old and new strips diagonally.

5 Then place the strips end to end so that they overlap by at least 2$\frac{1}{4}$in (6cm). Pull the new strip in by working with this double thickness.

24

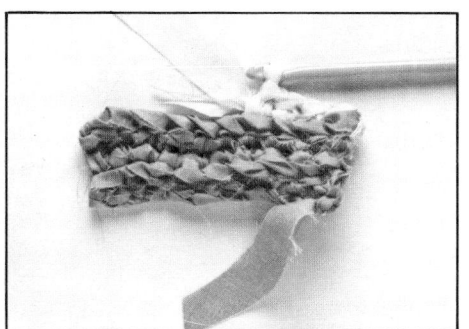

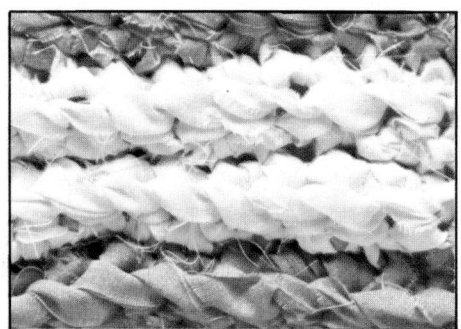

6 When you have made a dark stripe of the required depth, join in a light strip by completing the last single crochet at the end of a row with a light strip, leaving an end of at least 2¼in (6cm).

7 Turn the work and make one turning chain with the light strip. Lay the dark strip and the loose end of the light strip across the top of the previous row. Work the single crochet over these strips for several stitches. Then cut the strip ends and continue across the row with the new light strip.

8 Make light and dark stripes until the rug is the required size. After working the last single crochet, cut the strip and draw it through the loop on the hook. Weave the last loose end back and forth through the last row as you would if you were using yarn.

Working colored patterns with rags

You can work any crochet stitch with fabric strips, but anything taller than a double is awkward to work and would not give the solid crochet fabric essential for a durable rug. One of the crochet techniques best suited to rag rugs is colorwork in single crochet. By using two colors, or tones, in a row you can create endless patterns. But remember that, since the stitches are large, the best results will be achieved with simple bold designs. The pictures here show diagonal stripes being worked, but you could make zig-zags, triangles, circles, checks, etc., in a similar way. Just work your pattern out on graph paper, with each square on the graph paper representing one single crochet stitch.

1 This pattern uses 2 colors—called A (dark) and B (light). Using A make a multiple of 4ch plus one extra. Begin the first row by inserting the hook into the 2nd ch from the hook. Work 4sc in A but do not complete the last sc. When there are still 2 loops on the hook drop A and draw through B.

2 Lay A and the loose end of B across the top of the previous row. Work 4sc in B covering A and the loose end of B; on the 4th single crochet drop B and draw through A when there are still 2 loops on the hook.

3 Work 4 more single crochets in A carrying B across the top of the previous row. Continue across the row in this way making 4 single crochets using the light strip and then 4 single crochets using the dark strip.

4 At the end of the row turn the work and make one turning chain. Work a row of 4 single crochets in A followed by 4 single crochets in B, but this time move the groups of 4 stitches one stitch to the right in order to begin the diagonal slant.

5 On the next (RS) row carry the groups of 4 stitches over one stitch to the left. This will continue the slant in the same direction. In the next row (WS) they are moved one stitch to the right and so on. When you come to the end of a strip, join a new strip of the same tone.

Stitch Wise

Striped medallion

This pattern requires a dark color and a light color (A and B). Either continue working the pattern round and round until it forms a rug of the required size, or make small squares and join them together with a strong sewing thread. Work all single crochets into the back loop of each stitch.
Using A make 4ch, sl st into first ch to form a circle.
1st round 1ch, 11sc into circle, sl st into first ch.
2nd round 1 ch, 1sc into next sc, *3sc into next sc, 1sc into each of next 2sc, rep from * to within last sc, 3sc into next sc, drop A and join in B, sl st into first ch.
3rd round 1ch, 1sc, into each of next 2sc, *3sc into next sc, 1sc into each of next 4sc, rep from * twice more, 3sc into next sc, 1sc into next sc, sl st into first ch.
4th round 1ch, 1sc into each of next 3sc, *3sc into next sc, 1sc into each of next 6sc, rep from * twice more, 3sc into next sc, 1sc into each of next 2sc, drop B and pick up A, sl st into first ch.
Continue in this way adding 2sc to each side in each round and working 2 rounds in A and then 2 rounds in B.

Tricolor chevron

This pattern requires 3 colors (A, B and C).
Using A make a multiple of 14ch plus 3 extra.
1st row Using A work 1sc into 3rd ch from hook, *1sc into each of next 5ch, skip next 3ch, 1sc into each of next 5ch, 3 sc into next ch, rep from * to within last ch, 2 sc into last ch. Turn.
2nd row Using A work 1ch, 1sc into first sc, *1sc into each of next 5sc, skip next 2sc, 1sc into each of next 5sc, 3sc into next sc, rep from * to within turning ch, 2sc into turning ch. Turn.
3rd-6th rows Using B, rep 2nd row 4 times.
7th and 8th rows Using A, rep 2nd row twice.
9th and 10th rows Using C, rep 2nd row 4 times.
11th row As 2nd.
The 2nd to 11th rows form patt and are rep throughout.

Rag rug

Harmonizing printed and solid color fabrics are used for this beautiful, durable rug.

Size
Approx 20 × 33½in (51 × 85cm).

Materials
Approx. 5½yd (5m) of 36in (90cm)-wide fabric in each of 2 colors
Size K (7.00mm) crochet hook

Gauge
10hdc to 4in (10cm) worked on size K (7.00mm) hook.

To make
Cut fabric in ⅜in (1cm)-wide strips following instructions on page 24. Sew the strips together, then wind them into a ball.
Using size K (7.00mm) hook and first color, make 50ch.
Base row 1 hdc into 3rd ch from hook, 1hdc into each ch to end. Turn.
Patt row 2ch to count as first hdc, 1hdc into each st to end. Turn.
Rep the patt row until work measures 3in (7.5cm).
Join on second color and rep the patt row for 3in (7.5cm). Cont in patt working in 3in (7.5cm) stripes of each color until the 6th stripe in first color has been worked. Fasten off.

Border
Using size K (7.00mm) hook join on second color and work a row of sc evenly around outer edge, working 3sc at corners. Fasten off.

Simon Butcher

Crochet / COURSE 83

Color stitch patterns

Crochet has been so successfully developed to produce fine, complex lace fabrics and textures that its potential in multicolor work is often overlooked. Virtually any pattern can be created by working a single crochet fabric in a variety of colors. If using more than one color in a row seems a dauntingly slow process, you can turn to two-color or three-color crochet stitch patterns for decorative color effects. These stitch patterns usually use only one color in a row but the rows overlap to give a colorful effect.

In this course we give some tips for working with more than one color (color stitch patterns were introduced in Volume 11, page 11).

Changing colors in every alternate row

In most two-color stitch patterns the color is changed at the end of every other row so that each color is worked over two rows. In this way you always come back to the position at the edge of the fabric where the last color was dropped. In the instructions here, two-color fan stitch, given in Stitch Wise, is used to illustrate the change of color.

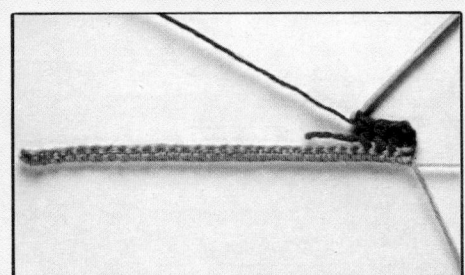

1 When first introducing the second color in a two-color pattern, after drawing the new color through, tighten the first color and drop it at the side of the work. Then lay the new loose end of the second color across the top of the previous row and work all the stitches over it.

2 Work the two rows in the second color and then drop it and pick up the first color taking care not to pull it too tightly up the side of the work.
Tighten the second color slightly, leave it hanging at the edge and work the next two rows in the first color. Change the colors each time in the same way.

Changing in every row

More difficult color patterns may call for the color to be changed in every row. If you are working the pattern in the round, this will present no problems as the rounds all end in the same place. But if you are working the rows back and forth, you will have to carry the color not in use across the row under the stitches being made in the other color. The pattern for fly stitch used here is given in full in Stitch Wise.

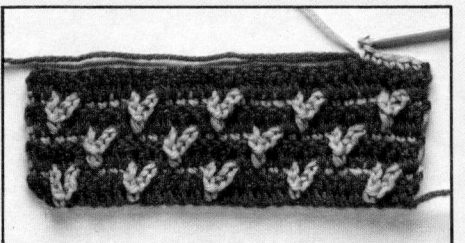

1 When the second color is first drawn through tighten the first color. Then lay the loose ends of the second color along with the first color across the top of the previous row. Work the stitches in the second color over both strands, carrying the first color to the end of the row.

2 At the beginning of the next row draw the first color through again. Tighten the second color and lay it across the top of the previous row. Carry the second color to the end of the row working all of the stitches in the first color over it. The colors are alternated throughout the pattern in this way.

Making colored bobbles

Colors need not always be repeated across a crochet fabric. You may want to insert isolated motifs into a plain crochet background. Working colored bobble motifs employs the technique for introducing colors in the middle of a row in this way. When making multicolor crochet patterns you can use different textures of yarn together as long as they are similar in thickness. Bobbles look very striking if they are worked not only in a different color but also in a different texture of yarn. The step-by-step instructions for the raised bobbles can be found in Volume 5, page 28. Each bobble consists of 5 doubles which protrude from a single crochet background.

These bobbles are especially useful in picture-making, in which they could be used to suggest, for example, fruit on trees or the centers of flowers.

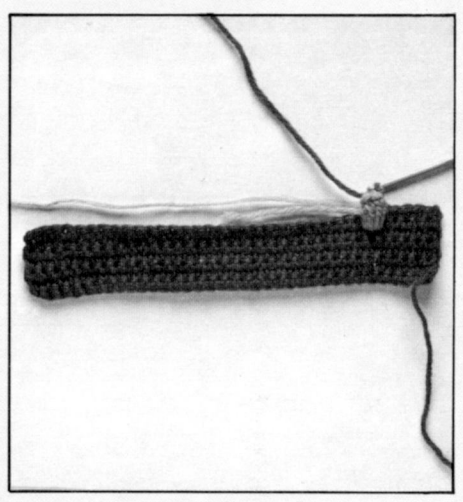

1 First plan your bobble motif on graph paper using colored pencils. Leave at least one stitch and one row between the bobbles. The bobbles are worked only on the right side rows.

2 When you reach the position of the motif draw the new yarn through the two loops of the last single crochet before the bobble. Lay the new loose end and the background yarn across the top of the previous row and work the bobble over both strands.

3 Make 5 doubles into the stitch below the next single crochet, take the hook out of the last loop and insert it through the top of the first double. Draw the last loop through the first double and drop the yarn for bobble to the back of the work. Pick up the background yarn and make one chain.

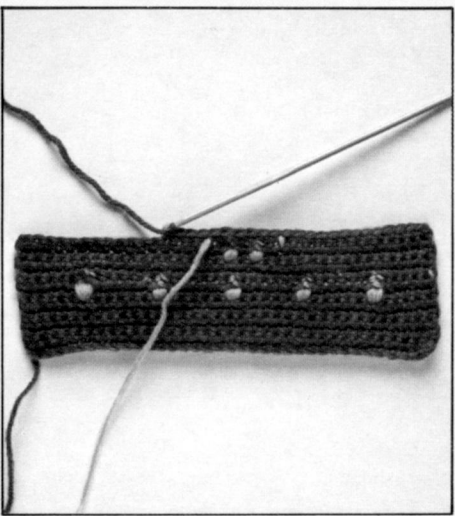

4 Then continue across the row working single crochets. On the next wrong side row work 1 single crochet into each single stitch in the previous row except the extra chain stitch of the bobble. Make bobbles at each position indicated on the chart, introducing new colors when necessary.

5 Where there are 2 or more bobbles in a row carrying the yarn for bobbles along under the intervening stitches, and after the last bobble is completed drop it to the back of the work. So that there is no need for stranding, carry the yarn back to the beginning of the motif under the stitches of the next wrong side row. Only the bobbles will be visible on the right side.

6 Any number of colors can be used to make a bobble motif. There will not be any loose ends at the back of the work as they have all been worked into the main fabric.

Shaping

When using two colors in a pattern, each over two rows, you will find that your main problem is how to carry the yarn not in use to the position where it will be needed after an increase or decrease of several stitches. This difficulty arises when shaping the edge at which the colors are changed. The yarn not in use can be brought up to the new position either by working single crochet or slip stitch along the edge or by carrying it to the new position under the stitches of the working yarn. These methods eliminate the need to darn in ends when the work is finished.

1 If your pattern uses each color over two rows and you are decreasing at the end of the 2nd row of one color, first take the hook out of the last loop, then work slip stitch or single crochet up to the loose loop with the other color. Draw the yarn through the loose loop and continue in pattern from there.

2 When decreasing at the beginning of the first row of a color you can carry the second color to the position where it will next be needed under the stitches of the decrease and then drop it and leave it until it is next required.

3 To increase at the side where the colors are changed, work a length of chains with the yarn to be used in the next row, then work the stitches back over the chains and across the rest of the row. To take the other yarn to the beginning of the extended row when it is next needed work slip stitch or single crochet along the edge of the fabric as explained in step 1.

Stitch Wise

Two-color fan stitch

This pattern uses 2 colors, A and B.
Using A make a multiple of 8ch.
1st row Using A, work 1sc into 2nd ch from hook, 1sc into each ch to end. Turn.
2nd row (RS) Using B, work 3ch, 1dc into 2nd sc in row below, *1dc into next sc, rep from * to end. Turn.
3rd row Using B, work 1 ch, 1sc into each dc to end, 1sc into top of turning ch. Turn.
4th row Using A, work 1ch, 1sc into each of first 3sc, yo and insert hook from front to back between turning ch and first dc 2 rows below, around dc at left and through work from back to front between first and 2nd dc (called working around the st), yo and draw a loop through, yo and draw through 2 loops on hook, yo and insert hook around next sc 3 rows below, yo and draw a loop through,

yo and draw through 2 loops on hook, yo, skip 3 dc after the first dc that was worked around 2 rows below, and insert hook around next dc, yo and draw a loop through, yo and draw through 2 loops on hook, yo and draw through all 4 loops on hook—fan formed—, *skip next sc of previous row, 1sc into each of next 7sc, 1 fan st into 2nd and 3rd rows below in same way as first fan st, rep from * to last 3 sts, 1sc into each of next 3sc. Turn.
5th row Using A, work 1ch, 1sc into each sc to end. Turn.
6th and 7th rows As 2nd and 3rd.
8th row Using A, work 1ch, 1sc into each of first 7sc, *1 fan st, skip 1sc, 1sc into each of next 7sc, rep from * to end. Turn.
9th row As 5th.
The 2nd-9th rows form pattern and are rep throughout.

Fly stitch

This pattern uses 2 colors, A and B.
Using A make a multiple of 6ch plus 2.
1st row (WS) Using A, work 1dc into 5th ch from hook, 1dc into each ch to end. Turn.
2nd row Carry A across the rop of the row below and work all sts over it. Using B, work 1 ch, 1sc into first dc, *1sc, 3ch and 1sc all into base of next dc, 3ch, skip next dc, 1sc into each of next 5dc, rep from * ending last repeat with 1sc.

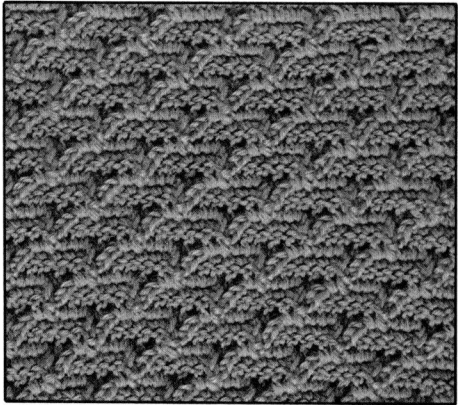

into last dc and 1sc into turning ch. Turn.
3rd row Carry B across the top of row below and work all sts over it. Using A, work 3ch, 1dc into next sc, *1dc into skipped dc, 1dc into each of next 5sc, rep from * to within last 2sc, 1dc into each of last 2sc. Turn.
4th row Carry A across the top of row below and work all sts over it. Using B, work 1 ch, 1 sc into each of first 4dc, *1 sc, 3ch and 1sc all into base of next dc, 3ch, skip next dc, 1sc into each of next 5dc, rep from * to end working last sc into turning ch. Turn.
5th row Carry B across the top of row below and work all sts over it. Using A, work 3ch, 1dc into each of next sc, 1dc into skipped dc, 1dc into each of next 5dc, rep from * to end. Turn.
The 2nd-5th rows form the patt.

Victor Yuan

Cardigan with two-color yoke

We've used soft Shetland yarn to crochet a pretty cardigan to wear with tartan or tweed.

Sizes

To fit 32[34:36]in (83[87:92]cm) bust. Length, 23[24½:26]in (60[63:66]cm). Sleeve seam, 18[18½:19]in (46[47:48]cm).

Note Directions for larger sizes are in brackets []; if there is only one set of figures it applies to all sizes.

Materials

18[20:22]oz (500[550:600]g) of a knitting worsted in main color (A)
2[2:4]oz (50[50:100]g) in contrasting color (B)
Size E (3.50mm) crochet hook
7 buttons

Gauge

18½ sts and 15 rows to 4in (10cm) in main patt.

22 sts and 15 rows to 4in (10cm) in yoke patt.

Back

Using size E (3.50mm) hook and A, make 87[91:95]ch.
Base row 1hdc into 3rd ch from hook, *skip next ch, 2hdc into next ch, rep from * to end. Turn.
Patt row 2 ch to count as first hdc, 1hdc into first hdc, *skip next hdc, 2hdc into next hdc, rep from * to end. Turn.
Rep the patt row until work measures 15[16:17]in (39[41:43]cm).
Shape armholes
Next row Sl st across first 4[7:6]hdc, patt to within last 3[4:5]hdc, turn.
Next row Patt to end. Turn.
Next row Sl st across first 3[4:4]hdc, patt to within last 2[3:3]hdc, turn.
Next row Patt to end. Turn.
Dec one hdc at end of next 4[4:6] rows, by leaving last hdc unworked. 72hdc.
Cont straight until armhole measures 2¼[2¾:3¼]in (6[7:8]cm). Fasten off.

Right front

Using size E (3.50mm) hook and A, make 43[45:47]ch. Work base row and patt row as for back.
Cont in patt until work measures

15[16:17]in (39[41:43]cm).
Shape armhole
Next row Patt to within last 4[4:5]hdc, turn.
Patt 1 row.
Next row Patt to within last 3[4:5]hdc, turn.
Patt 1 row.
Dec one hdc at end of next and foll 2[3:3] alternate rows. 32hdc. Cont straight until armhole measures 2¼[2¾:3¼]in (6[7:8]cm). Fasten off.

Left front

Work as for right front, reversing shaping.

Sleeves

Using size E (3.50mm) hook and A, make 75ch.
Base row 1sc into 2nd ch from hook, 1sc into each ch to end. Turn.
Work 5 rows in sc.
Next row 1sc into each of next 35sc, 4ch, skip next 4sc, 1sc into each sc to end. Turn.
Next row 1sc into each sc and 4sc into 4ch sp. Turn.
Work 1 row in sc. Fold work in half and work 1sc into each sc and corresponding loop of foundation ch to form casing. Turn.

Next row 2 ch to count as first hdc, 1hdc into first sc, *skip next sc, 2hdc into next sc, rep from * to end. Turn.
Cont in patt as for back, until work measures 18[18½:19]in (46[47:48]cm) from top of casing.

Shape top
Next row Sl st across first 5hdc, patt to within last 4hdc, turn.
Next row Patt to end. Turn.
Next row Sl st across first 4hdc, patt to within last 3hdc, turn.
Next row Patt to end. Turn.
Dec one hdc at end of next 4 rows. 56hdc.
Cont straight until work measures 2¼[2¾:3¼]in (6[7:8]cm) from beg of shaping.
Fasten off.

Yoke
Sew sleeves to armholes. With RS facing, using size E (3.50mm) hook and A, work 1sc into each st along each section. 248sc.
Beg patt.
1st row 1ch, 1sc into first sc, skip next 2sc, now leaving last loop of each on hook work 2dc into next st, yo and draw through 3 loops on hook—called cluster or cl—, now work (4ch and 1cl) twice into same place as last cl, skip next 3sc, 1sc into next sc, *skip next 3sc, now work 1cl, (4ch and 1cl) twice all into next sc, skip next 3sc, 1sc into next sc, rep from * to end. 31 sprays formed. Join on B.
2nd row (RS) With B, work 1ch, 1sc into first sc, *working over next 4ch work 3dc into same place as cls were

worked 1 row below, 1sc into top of center cl of spray, working over next 4ch work 3dc into same place as cls were worked 1 row below, 1sc into next sc between sprays, rep from * to end, working 1sc into last sc. Turn.
3rd row With B, work 1ch, 1sc into first sc, *3ch, 1sc into next sc, rep from * to end. Turn.
4th row With A, work 4ch, 1dc into first sc, 1ch, 1sc into next sc, 1ch, *1dc, 3ch and 1dc all into next sc 1 row below, 1ch, 1sc into next sc, 1ch, rep from * to within last sc, 1dc, 1ch and 1dc all into last sc. Turn.
5th row With A, work 1ch, 1sc into first dc, 1cl, (4ch and 1cl) twice all into next sc, *1sc into next 3ch sp, 1sc into next sc at top of spray—(1sc into next 3ch sp, 1cl, 4ch, 1cl, 4ch and 1cl all into next sc) 6 times, rep from * 3 times more, 1sc into next 3ch sp, dec 1 spray, 1sc into next 3ch sp, 1cl, (4ch and 1cl) twice all into next sc, 1sc into last st. Turn. 26 sprays.
6th row As 2nd, working 1sc into top of sc of skipped spray to complete dec.
7th and 8th rows As 3rd and 4th.
9th row With A, work 1ch, 1sc into first dc, (1cl, 4ch, 1cl, 4ch and 1cl all into next sc, 1sc into next 3ch sp) twice, dec 1 spray, *(1sc into next 3ch sp, 1cl, 4ch, 1cl, 4ch and 1cl all into next sc) 4 times, dec 1 spray *, rep from * to * three times, **1sc into next 3ch sp, 1cl, 4ch, 1cl, 4ch and 1cl all into next sc, rep from **twice more, 1sc into top of turning ch. Turn. 21 sprays.
10th row As 6th.

11th and 12th rows As 3rd and 4th.
13th row With A, work 1ch, 1sc into first dc, (1cl, 4ch, 1cl, 4ch and 1cl all into next sc, 1sc into next 3ch sp) twice, dec 1 spray, *(1sc into next 3ch sp, 1cl, 4ch, 1cl, 4ch and 1cl all into next sc) 3 times, dec 1 spray *, rep from * to * 3 times more, **1sc into next 3ch sp, 1cl, 4ch, 1cl, 4ch and 1cl all into next sc, rep from ** once more, 1sc into top of turning ch. Turn. 16 sprays.
14th row As 6th.
15th and 16th rows As 3rd and 4th.
17th row With A, work 1ch, 1sc into first dc, 1cl, 4ch, 1cl, 4ch and 1cl all into next sc, 1sc into next 3ch sp, dec 1 spray, *(1sc into next 3ch sp, 1cl, 4ch, 1cl, 4ch and 1cl all into next sc) twice, dec 1 spray *, rep from * to * 3 times more, ** 1sc into next 3ch sp, 1cl, 4ch, 1cl, 4ch and 1cl all into next sc, rep from ** once more, 1sc into top of turning ch. Turn. 11 sprays.
18th row As 6th.
Cut off B.
Next row 1sc into each st to end. Turn. 89sc.
Work 2 rows in sc.
Dec row *1sc into each of next 7sc, skip next sc, rep from * 9 times more, skip next sc, 1sc into each sc to end. Turn.
Work 2 rows in sc. Fasten off.

Waistband
Join side seams. With RS facing, using size E (3.50mm) hook and A, work 1sc into each loop along foundation ch. 170[178:186]sc.
Next row 1sc into each of next 8[12:12]sc, *skip next sc, 1sc into each of next 16[16:17]sc, rep from * 8 times more, skip next sc, 1sc into each sc to end. Turn. 160[168:176]sc. Work 7 rows in sc. Fasten off.

Button border
With RS facing, using size E (3.50mm) hook and A, work 97[103:109]sc evenly along front edge. Work 5 rows in sc. Fasten off.

Buttonhole border
Work as for button border, but work buttonholes over 3rd and 4th rows as foll:
1st buttonhole row 1sc into each of next 2sc, *skip next 3sc, 3ch, 1sc into each of next 12[13:14]sc, rep from * 5 times more, skip next 3sc, 1sc into each of next 2sc. Turn.
2nd buttonhole row Work 1sc into each sc and ch to end. Turn.

To finish
Press or block, according to yarn used.
Join sleeve seams.
Sew on buttons.
Using six 36in (90cm) lengths of yarn tog, make a twisted cord for each sleeve.
Thread cord through casing and tie.

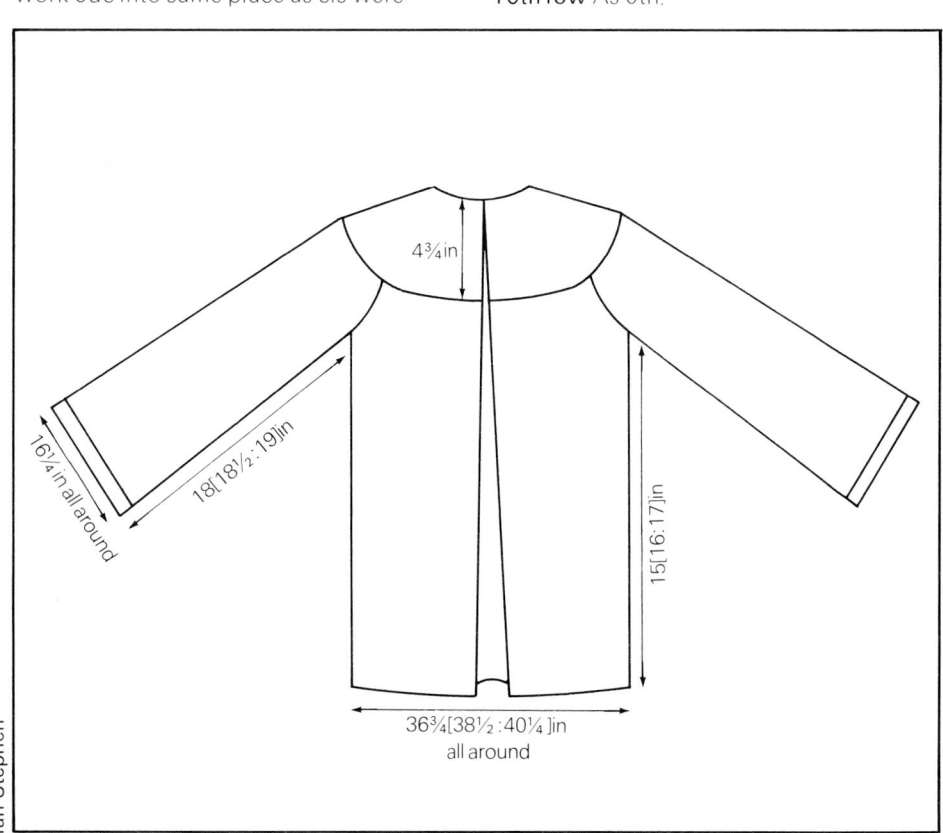

4¾in
16¼in all around
18[18½:19]in
15[16:17]in
36¾[38½:40¼]in all around

*First steps in toy making
*Making a simple shape
  as a basis for a toy
*Trimming to create
  individual toys
*Stitch Wise: small-
  pattern fabrics
*Patterns for knitted toys

First steps in toy making

Knitted toys have a delightful charm with a special appeal for youngsters of all ages!

You definitely don't have to be a knitting expert to turn a simple shape into a charming character—or a series of characters. The toys on pages 36 and 37 are all based on a simple shape—a rectangle gathered at the top and base. When the side seam is joined and the shape is stuffed, the shape becomes a tube.

Once you have completed the simple, basic shape, you can experiment with various knitted limbs, tails, ears, etc. to make an original toy. Finally, add the facial features; these determine the character of the toy.

Choose colors carefully for the toy; there is no need to be true to life, so make them bright and eye-catching for a child. All kinds of odds and ends of trimmings and notions are useful for decorating toys. Scraps of felt are especially useful in making facial features. Keep the finished toy simple, rather than ornate. Provide mere suggestions of detail: the toys shown here use only lengths of spool knitting, knotted fringe and scraps of felt for main trimmings.

Always use wool, or a wool and nylon mixture for the basic shape. The nylon content of a yarn provides strength and prevents it from breaking at gathering points. All synthetic yarns get dirty easily and tend to stretch, especially in larger toys. Most toys need cleaning in time. If the stuffing is washable, wash by hand, gently squeezing out excess water. Dry naturally. Don't worry if a toy that is not washable becomes dirty; simply "dry clean" it with talcum powder.

Making a simple shape as a basis for a toy

1 Choose a very simple shape for your toy, such as the rectangle used for the toys on pages 36 and 37. You can control the size of the toy—which incorporates the head and body in one shape—by making the rectangle smaller or larger as required. Use knitting worsted, No. 3 (3¼mm) needles and stockinette stitch to give a firm fabric. Here the top and lower edges are shaped: the stitches are not bound off, but the yarn is cut and threaded through them.

2 The ends of the rectangle are shaped so that they close together completely and neatly when the toy is finished. Gathered openings are frequently used in simple toy making to give roundness to a flat shape: choose an inconspicuous place for the opening such as a base or under a hat. Pull the rectangle stitches tightly together, then secure with the yarn. Join the side edges with a backstitch seam. Pressing is never necessary when stuffing a shape unless it is made from recycled yarn. A gathering thread has been run through the fabric to mark the position of the neck (above).

3 There is a variety of lightweight fillings you can use to stuff the toy to give it shape. Remember, if you want to wash the toy, the filling must also be washable. You can also make your own stuffing with old, cut-up stockings and pantyhose. Avoid using foam rubber, as it becomes lumpy with age and the colored variety shows through a knitted fabric.

Mike Berend

continued

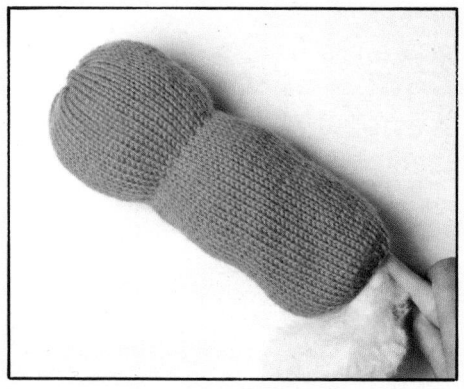 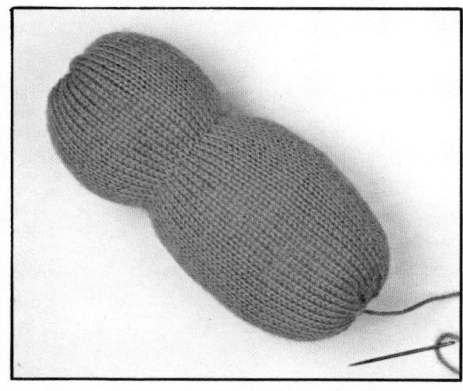 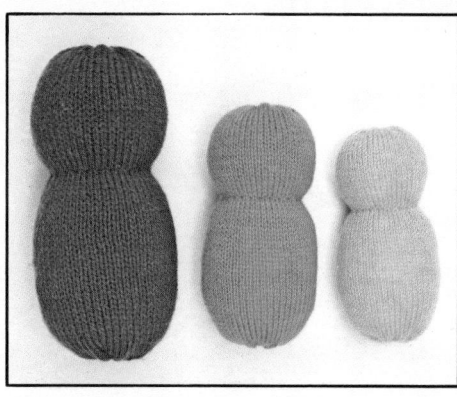

4 Insert the stuffing into the shape a little at a time, pushing it down well with a wooden spoon handle. At the same time, mold the toy into the shape you want. Molding can be controlled by the amount of stuffing in a particular spot: *never* use wire to shape a toy. Always tend to overstuff the shape, as the stuffing settles with time.

5 Close the opening by pulling the stitches together to match the opening at the opposite end. Run a gathering thread through the cast-on loops, then draw the stitches tightly together to close the hole. Also make any neck indentation by pulling and securing the gathering thread inserted there.

6 You can make a family of toys from the same basic shape as the one described and shown here. Scale them in proportion by using various thicknesses of yarn and the appropriate needles. Here "Dad" is knitted in bulky yarn, "Mom" in knitting worsted and "Baby" in sport yarn.

Trimming to create individual toys

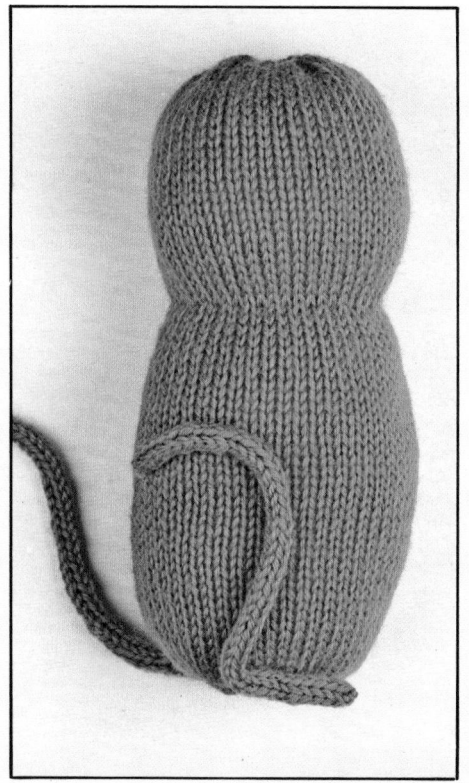  

Simple lengths of spool knitting cord have many uses in trimming toys. Use them to suggest limbs or wings, to outline shapes or purely for decoration. Either sew the cords completely onto the body, as with the cat's legs here, or just attach them in one or two places—like the tail—with the rest hanging free.

Another simple, multi-purpose trimming is knotted fringe. Use it for hands, feet, beard, feathers, fur and anything else that can be represented by the soft little tufts. If necessary, knot the fringe directly onto the knitted background, using a crochet hook to pull the strands through.

Add the facial features last. Be inventive with expressions to give the toy its character and charm. Felt is best, because embroidered features pull slightly and make holes in the fabric. Glue the felt to the background instead of sewing it on; use a clear fabric glue and apply it sparingly.

Stitch Wise

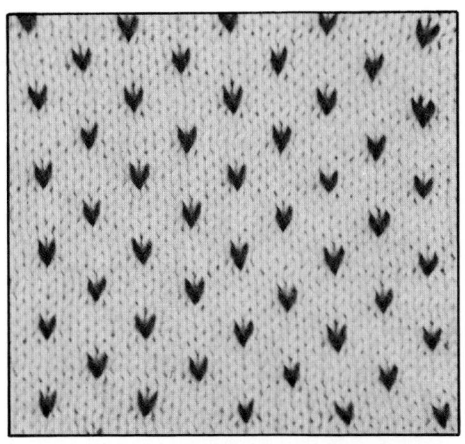

Single dot pattern

Here a single knitted stitch is worked at intervals in a color different from the background to produce a small dot. The yarn for the dot is carried across the back of the work on a pattern row, then carried up the side of the work to the next row where it is needed. This design requires 2 colors coded as A and B. Using A, cast on a multiple of 6 sts plus 5 extra.

1st row Using A, K to end.
2nd row P to end.
3rd row K2 A, *1 B, 5 A, rep from * to last 3 sts, 1 B, 2 A.
4th row As 2nd.
5th row As first.
6th row P5 A, *1 B, 5 A, rep from * to end.
These 6 rows form the pattern.

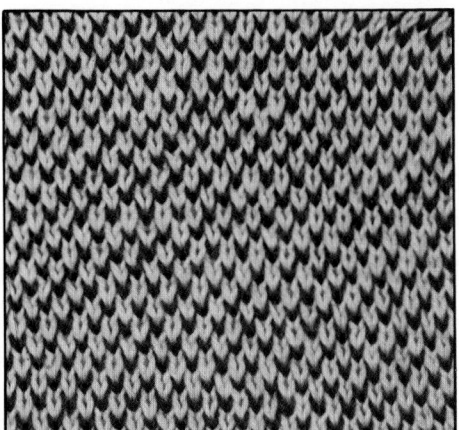

Small checked pattern

The single stitch "dots" of contrasting color in this fabric are so close together that they form a check pattern. The working method involves slip stitch techniques. You must use a pair of double-pointed needles, or knit in rows with a circular needle, to move stitches from one end of row to other where appropriate yarn is waiting.
This design requires 2 colors coded as A and B. Using A, cast on an uneven number of sts.

1st row (WS) Using A, P to end.
2nd row Using B, K1, *keeping yarn at back, sl 1, K1, rep from * to end.
3rd row Sl all sts to other end of needle, using A, K to end.
4th row Using B, P2, *keeping yarn at front, sl 1, P1, rep from * to last st, P1, then sl all sts to other end of needle.
These 4 rows form the pattern and are repeated throughout.

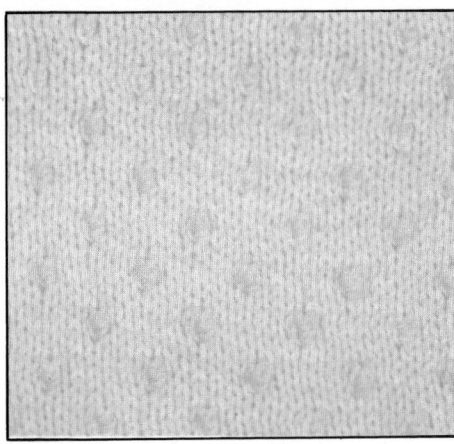

Knotted dot pattern

This pattern is worked in one color, with knotted stitches forming a slightly-textured pattern on stockinette stitch.
Cast on a multiple of 6 sts plus 1 extra.
1st row (WS) P to end.
2nd row K to end.
3rd row As first.
4th row K3, *insert right-hand needle under horizontal loop lying between first and 2nd sts on left-hand needle, wind yarn around needle and draw through a loop, then insert right-hand needle between same sts but above horizontal loop and draw through another loop, bring yarn to front and P first st on left-hand needle, use left-hand needle to lift first loop over 2nd and purled st, and off needle, then lift 2nd loop over purled st and off—called "make a knot," K5, rep from * ending with K3.
5th - 7th rows As first—3rd.
8th row K6, *make a knot, K5, rep from * ending with K6.
These 8 rows form the pattern.

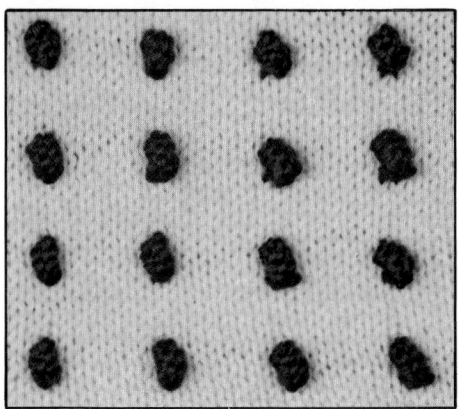

Colored knot pattern

In this pattern on a stockinette stitch background, knots are worked on a single stitch in a contrasting color. The yarn for the knots is carried across the back of the row, but must be cut off and finished at the edges after each pattern row.
This design requires 2 colors coded as A and B. Using A, cast on a multiple of 7 sts plus 2 extra.

1st row Using A, K to end.
2nd row P to end.
Rep last 2 rows twice more.

7th row Using A, K4, *using B, cast on 5 new sts out of next loop on left-hand needle, K6 sts (5 new sts in B and original st in A), using left-hand needle lift 2nd, 3rd, 4th, 5th and 6th sts on right-hand needle over original st—called "make a knot"—, using A, K6, rep from * to last 5 sts, using B, make a knot, using A, K4.
8th row P to end.
These 8 rows form the pattern and are repeated throughout.

Robert Enever

Knitted toys

These soft stuffed toys will give lots of pleasure and appeal to tiny hands. They are fun to make — you can create characters with their own special personalities to take their places among a child's favorite toys.

Sizes
All toys are based on a knitted tube about 8¾in (22cm) long and 10in (25cm) in circumference when finished and stuffed.

Materials
    Sport yarn
    Bird *2oz (50g) in blue*
    Pieces of navy yarn
    Scraps of blue and navy felt
    Frog *2oz (50g) in green*
    Scraps of dark green, pale green and black felt
    Lion *2oz (50g) in honey*
    Pieces of gold yarn
    Scraps of honey, green and black felt
    Black embroidery thread
    White thread
    Gnome *1oz (25g) in each of dark green, red and pale pink*
    Pieces of white and gray yarn
    Scraps of dark green, light green, white and red felt
    Bell for hat
    Soldier *1oz (25g) in each of royal blue, red, pale pink and black*
    Scraps of black and red felt
    Gold sequins and rickrack for trimming
    Indian squaw *1oz (25g) each in medium brown, sand, pale peach and dark brown*
    Pieces of red and orange yarn
    Scraps of dark brown, medium brown and tan felt
    1 pair No. 3 (3¼mm) needles
    Knitting spool
    Stuffing

Gauge
24 sts and 36 rows to 4in (10cm) in stockinette st on No. 3 (3¼mm) needles.

Basic shape
Using No. 3 (3¼mm) needles and appropriate color cast on 27 sts for base.
Next row *K1, pick up loop lying between cast-on sts and K tbl—called make 1 or M1—, rep from * to last 2 sts, K2. 52 sts. Beg with a P row, work 68 rows stockinette st.
Next row *P2 tog, rep from * to end. 26 sts. Cut off yarn leaving a long end. Thread yarn through rem sts and gather very tightly to close top of head.

37

To finish

With all shapes except lion, run a gathering thread through 40th row from base to shape neck at a later stage. Join side seam. Insert stuffing through base opening. Fasten by running gathering thread along cast-on loops and gathering tightly. Pull gathering thread to shape neck.

Bird

Make basic shape with reverse side of the stockinette stitch on the outside of the fabric.

Make lengths of spool knitting in navy — one 8in (20cm) to form wing shapes at sides, one 11in (28cm) for feet and one 10¼in (26cm) for comb on top of head. Make eyes and beak in felt, from patterns. Trim wing tips with short lengths of blue and navy knotted fringe.

Frog

Make lengths of spool knitting in green — two 8in (20cm) for back legs and two 6¾in (17cm) for front legs. Trim ends of legs with knotted fringe.
Make facial features in felt from patterns.

Lion

Cut circle of honey-colored felt about 3½in (9cm) in diameter and sew to one end of tube. Work facial features following pattern. Make lengths of spool knitting in honey — one 10¼in (26cm) to frame face, one 4¾in (12cm) for tail and one 9in (23cm) to sew on side of tube to represent back legs. Trim cord framing face with honey and gold knotted fringe. Trim end of tail with honey knotted fringe.

Gnome

Work basic shape in colors as foll: 16 rows dark green, 24 rows red and 30 rows pale pink.
Hat Using No. 3 (3¼mm) needles and dark green, cast on 54 sts. Work 12 rows stockinette st. Change to red. Work 4 rows. Dec one st at beg of next 12 rows. 42 sts. Dec one st at each end of next 18 rows. 6 sts. Cut off yarn, thread through rem sts and fasten off. Join side seam. Allow cast-on edge to roll up on RS of hat. Sew bell to hat. Sew hat on head,

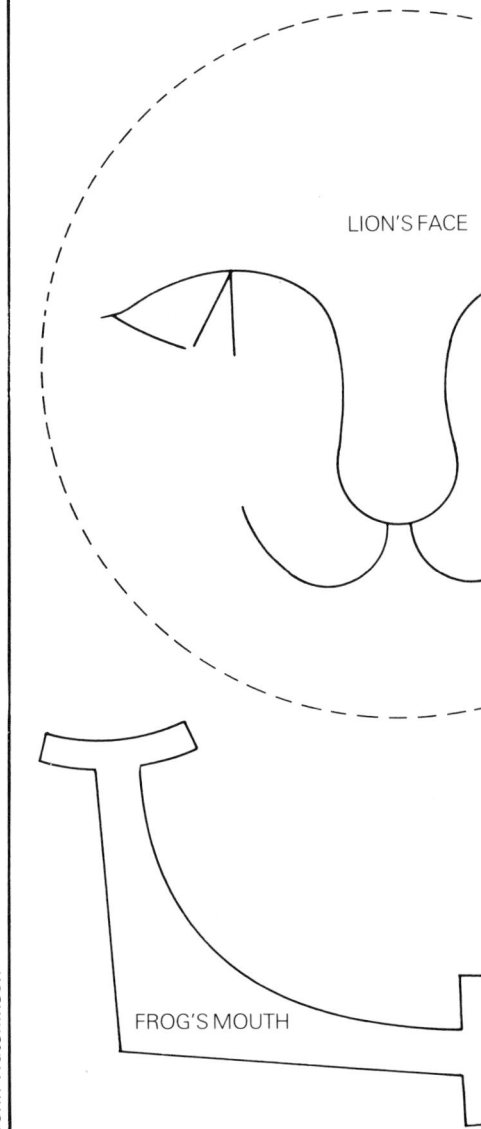

LION'S FACE

FROG'S MOUTH

then embroider straight stitches around face and back of head with gray yarn to make hair. Make facial features from felt as shown. Make beard with knotted fringe.

Soldier

Work basic shape as foll: 16 rows royal blue, 24 rows red, 12 rows pale pink, then 18 rows reverse stockinette st in black. Make facial features from felt; trim uniform with rickrack and sequins.

Indian squaw

Work basic shape in colors as foll: 16 rows medium brown, 24 rows sand, 12 rows pale peach and 18 rows dark brown. Make 9in (23cm) lengths of spool knitting in red, orange, medium brown and red. Sew around face and head to form headdress; trim with knotted fringe in orange, red, dark brown, medium brown and pale peach. Trim lower edge of dress with sand knotted fringe; embroider orange cross stitches above fringe for decoration. Make facial features in felt as shown.

BIRD'S EYES

BIRD'S BEAK

fold

OG'S EYES

INNER EYE

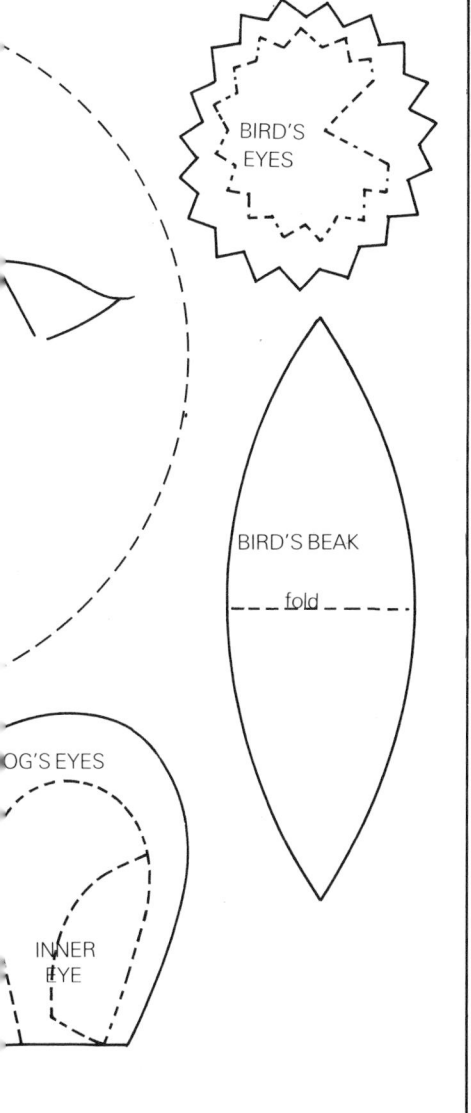

Robert Enever

*Rag and ribbon knitting
*Knitting with left-over lengths of yarn
*Pattern for a woman's rag jacket

Rag and ribbon knitting

This type of knitting is an excellent way of using up scraps of fabric such as those left over from dressmaking or cut-up, old and worn out garments.

The various materials must all be about the same weight. You may have to buy some extra lengths of fabric if you do not have enough scraps in a particular color; remnants are ideal for this purpose; check the remnant counter for bargains.

Knitting with ribbons rather than rags produces a more luxurious-looking fabric. Buying lengths of ribbon for knitting is very expensive; here you can see how to make them from inexpensive lining material.

Preparing the fabric for knitting is quite simple. There are a number of ways of joining the strips; two of the best methods are outlined below to help you get started on this interesting technique.

Rag knitting

1 Lightweight cotton is one of the most suitable fabrics. Patterns on a fabric show up as flecks of color when knitted up. This harmonizing selection of solid and printed fabrics is ideal.

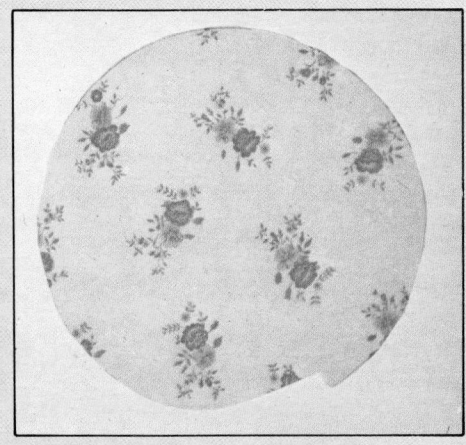

2 Cut fabric into circles as large as possible; draw around a template such as a plate. Make a ½ in (1 cm) slit into circle and trim away fabric for a few inches along edge of circle.

3 Then, following the outline of the circle by eye, cut a ½ in (1 cm)-wide strip in a continuous spiral, ending almost at the center of the circle. Cut off the center of circle as the strip becomes too twisted.

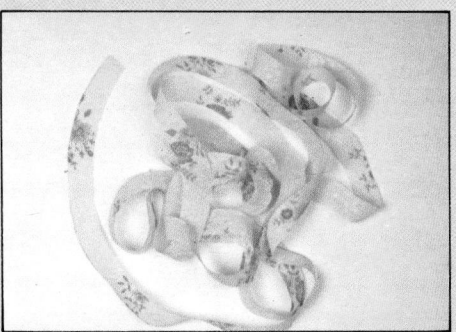

4 The strips of fabric are cut in a spiral to give them a bias effect. Strips cut on the bias are less likely to ravel, but it is very wasteful, and unnecessary, to cut fabric on the true bias. These bias strips have some elasticity; the wavy edge and inclination to coil disappear when the strip is knitted.

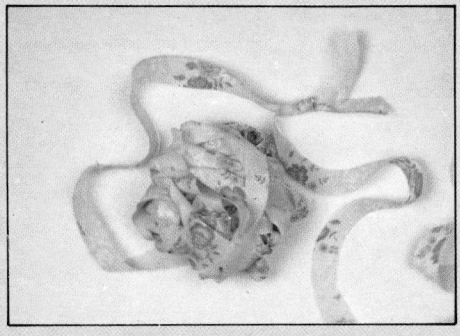

5 You must join the separate strips together to form a long length of "thread" for knitting. The easiest way to do this is simply to knot the strips together (although they can be sewn). Check that the knots are secure, then wind the strips into a ball to prevent them from tangling.

6 The knitted rag fabric must not be too solid, so choose a pair of large needles to work—between Nos. 10 and 10½ (6½ and 7mm). Cast on in the usual way: the strip may seem too wide to form a "thread," but it automatically folds in half as you are working.

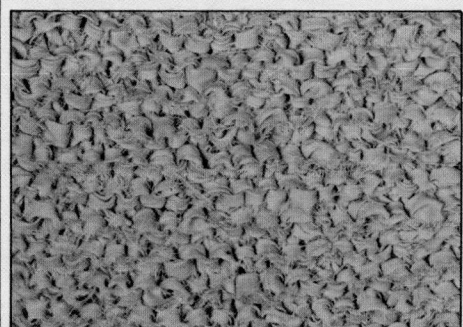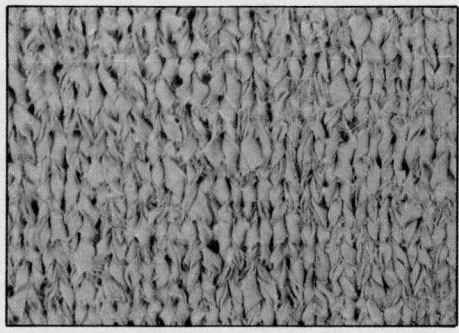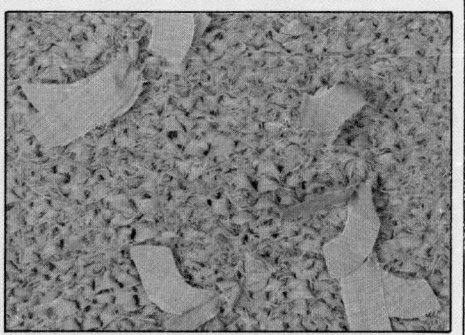

7 Simple stitch patterns are the most suitable for rag knitting. Most work is done in garter stitch, which has a highly textured appearance and produces an elastic fabric. Push the knots through to the wrong side of the work.

8 When rags are worked in stockinette stitch, the right side has a smooth appearance like ordinary knitting. Although the strips are bias cut, they tend to fray slightly in time. The wispiness of the fraying adds to the charm of the fabric.

9 This is the reverse side of the stockinette stitch with its more sculptured ridges. The knots are a feature of this side of the work. Trim the ends of the knotted strips close to the knitted fabric if you do not want them to protrude.

Ribbon knitting

1 Either buy lining material or use the lining of an old garment. Cut the fabric into ½in (1cm) strips across the width of the fabric. Fold the strips in half, then stitch the ends of adjacent strips together, working in a continuous line with a short gap between each strip.

2 Now cut the stitching between each strip to make one continuous length of ribbon. To prevent the strips from becoming tangled, cut only about 20 strips at a time. Wind the long strip into a ball after each cutting session.

3 This is the finished effect when the "ribbons" are knitted in garter stitch. The fabric has an unusual silky sheen, while the wispy ends where the lining material has frayed slightly give it a brushed appearance.

Knitting with left-over lengths of yarn

This is a novel way of using up even the smallest scrap of yarn to make a bright, solid fabric suitable for rugs, pillow covers, blankets and outdoor garments. First check that all the yarns are a similar weight, or use two thin yarns together to make a thicker one.
Now, all you need to know is how to tie a simple knot, crochet a length of chains (the very simplest form of crochet) and knit in a basic stitch.

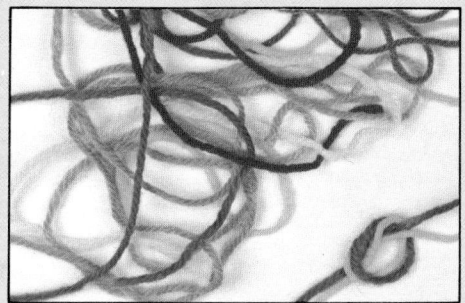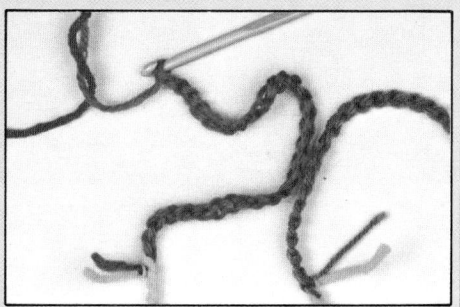

1 Collect together any left-over pieces of yarn, any length and color. The design is much more fun if the yarns differ considerably in length. Simply knot 2 colors together about 1in (2.5cm) from the ends. The knotted ends are left and can become a feature of the design.

2 Choose a crochet hook suitable for the type of yarn you are using—sizes C, E and F (3.00, 3.50 and 4.00mm) for knitting worsted—and work a length of simple chains. See "The basis of crochet" in Volume 1 pages 8 and 9 if you are unable to crochet, or get a friend to show you.

continued

Mike Berend

41

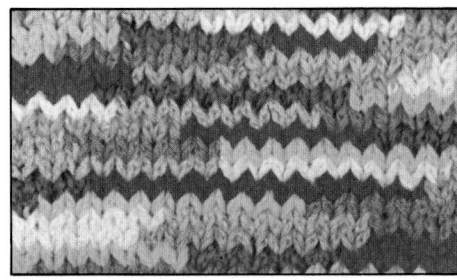

3 When you have used up all the yarn, transfer the loop on the crochet hook onto a safety pin. You can extend the lengths as required. Now use the length of chains as your yarn and work in stockinette stitch on large needles to prevent the fabric from being too rough.

4 Here you can see the smooth side of the stockinette stitch fabric; all the knots have been pushed through to the wrong side. The various lengths of yarn make totally random colored patterns—sometimes blocks or stripes, or a mixture of both.

5 The reverse side of the stockinette stitch is even more interesting, with the colors much more broken up and the tufts of knots adding another dimension.

Rag jacket

Clean out your fabric scraps and remnants to knit this classic jacket. The knotted ends and reverse stockinette stitch give an interesting textured look.

Sizes
To fit 32-34[36-38]in (83-87[92-97] cm) bust.
Length, 21[22¼]in (53.5[56.5]cm).
Sleeve seam, 15[15½]in (38[39]cm).
Note Directions for larger size are in brackets []; if there is only one set of figures it applies to both sizes.

Materials
Approx 11yd (10m) of 36in (90cm)-wide fabric—we have used 4 contrasting colors
1oz (25g) of a knitting worsted
1 pair each of Nos. 6 and 13 (4½ and 9mm) knitting needles
2 buttons; matching thread

Gauge
10 sts to 4in (10cm) in reverse stockinette st. Cut fabric in ½in (1cm)-wide strips; knot the strips tog as required.

Back
Using No. 13 (9mm) needles and fabric, cast on 54[58] sts. K 5 rows. Beg with a P row, cont in reverse stockinette st until work measures 13[13½]in (33[34.5]cm).
Shape armholes
Bind off 3 sts at beg of next 2 rows, then dec one st at beg of next 4[6] rows. 44[46] sts. Cont straight until work measures 17½[18½]in (44.5[47]cm). Now inc one st at each end of next and every foll 4th row until there are 52[54] sts. Cont straight until work measures 21[22¼]in (53.5[56.5]cm).
Shape shoulders and neck
Next row P 17[18], bind off center 18[20] sts, P to end.
Work on last set of 17[18] sts. Bind off 9 sts at beg of next row. Work 1 row. Bind off.
With WS facing rejoin fabric to rem sts, K to end of row. Bind off 9 sts at beg of next row. Work 1 row. Bind off.

Left front
Using No. 13 (9mm) needles and fabric, cast on 29[30] sts.
K 5 rows. Beg with a P row, cont in reverse stockinette st until work measures 13[13½]in (33[34.5]cm); end with K row.

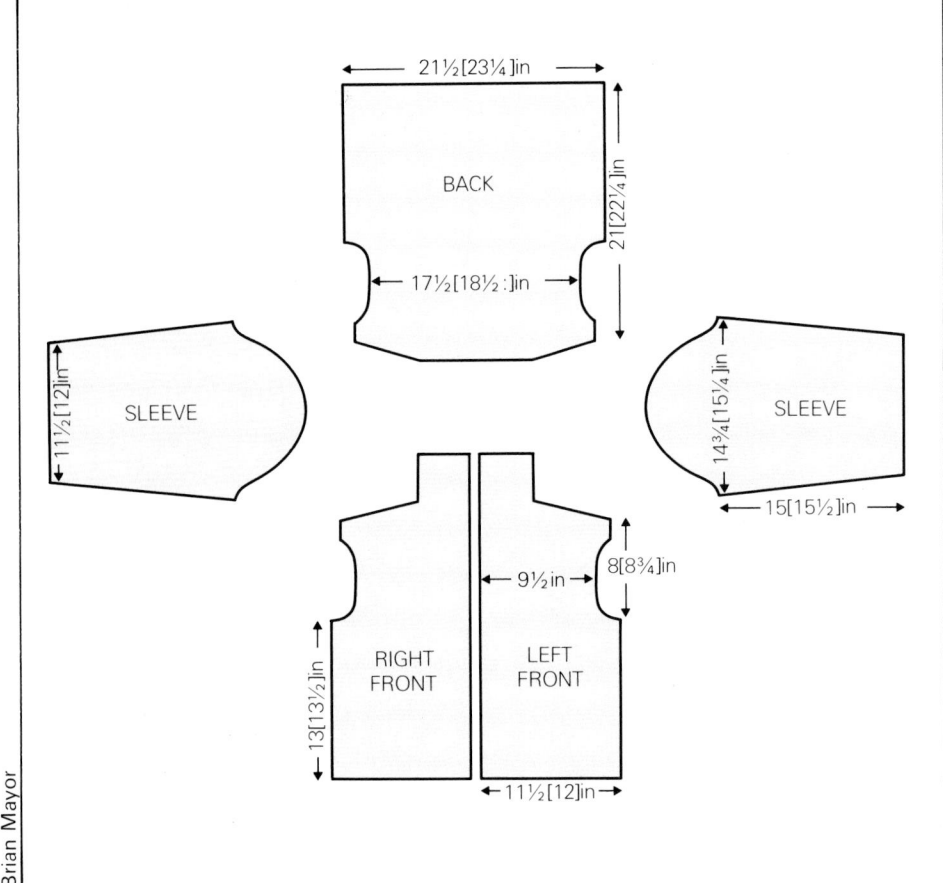

21½[23¼]in

BACK

21[22¼]in

17½[18½ :]in

SLEEVE

11½[12]in

SLEEVE

14¾[15¼]in

15[15½]in

9½in

8[8¾]in

RIGHT FRONT

LEFT FRONT

13[13½]in

11½[12]in

Brian Mayor

Rod Delroy/Designed by Sandy Black

Shape armhole
Bind off 3 sts at beg of next row, then dec one st at beg of next 2[3] alternate rows. 24 sts. Cont straight until work measures 17½[18½]in (44.5[47]cm); end at armhole edge. Now inc one st at armhole edge on next and every foll 4th row until there are 28[29] sts. Cont straight until work measures same as back to shoulder shaping; end at armhole edge.
Shape shoulder
Bind off 9 sts at beg of next row and 8[9] sts at beg of foll alternate row. Cont on rem 11 sts until the collar fits around neck to center back. Bind off.
Right front
Work as for left front, reversing shaping and working buttonholes 4[4¼]in (10[11]cm) and 6[6¼]in (15[16]cm) from beg as foll:

1st buttonhole row P3, bind off 2, P to end.
2nd buttonhole row K to end, casting on 2 sts over those bound off on previous row.

Sleeves
Using No. 13 (9mm) needles and fabric, cast on 29[30] sts. K 5 rows. Beg with a P row, cont in reverse stockinette st inc one st at each end of every foll 11th row until there are 37[38] sts. Cont straight until work measures 15[15½]in (38[39]cm); end with a K row.
Shape top
Bind off 2 sts at beg of next 2 rows. Dec one st at each end of next 5 alternate rows, then at each end of every row 6[7] times.
Bind off.

Bindings
Outer edge Using No. 6 (4½mm) needles and knitting worsted, cast on 14 sts. Cont in stockinette st for 96[100]in (244[255]cm). Bind off.
Cuffs (alike) Using No. 6 (4½mm) needles and knitting worsted, cast on 14 sts. Cont in stockinette st for 11½[12]in (29[30]cm).
Bind off.

To finish
Using matching thread, join shoulder seams. Fold point at shoulder to WS and slip stitch in place to form shoulder pads. Set in sleeves, then join side and sleeve seams. Join center back seam of collar, then sew collar to neck edge. Sew bindings to RS of fabric, double to WS and slip stitch in place. Sew on buttons.

*Knitted corners
*Garter stitch corners
*Stockinette stitch corners
*Patterns for tea and coffee
  cozies

Knitted corners

Knitted corners are closely linked with bands and borders, since they are often the finishing trim for a fabric that tends to curl, such as stockinette stitch. There are four basic ways of making bands incorporating corners: working in one with the main fabric, picking up stitches along finished edges and increasing out at the corners, working the border entirely separately by starting at the outer edge and decreasing toward the inner edge, and making a turned corner that is worked on a few stitches across the width of the fabric.

The most common method is to make corners in garter stitch (or some other reversible stitch) or stockinette stitch; the choice depends on the item being made.

Garter stitch corners

Simple garter stitch corner

 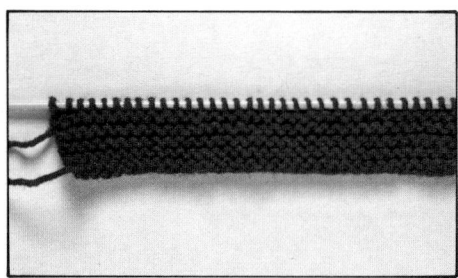 

1 Here the border is in garter stitch to contrast with the main stockinette stitch fabric. This is a convenient border to use and doubles as a corner: it is worked in one with the main fabric and requires no sewing on at a later point. The horizontal upper and lower borders must be the same width as those at the sides.

2 Using the correct size of needles for the main fabric, cast on the stitches for the entire lower edge, including the borders. If you want a 5-stitch border at the sides, then you must work double that number of rows (i.e. 10) to form the border at the lower edge. Here there are 5 ridges on the right side of the work.

3 Beginning with a purl row, continue in stockinette stitch, working the required number of stitches in garter stitch at the ends of the rows. If the number of side stitches equals the number of ridges in the lower edge, they will be the same width. The corner is automatically formed while working the border.

Mitered garter stitch corner

 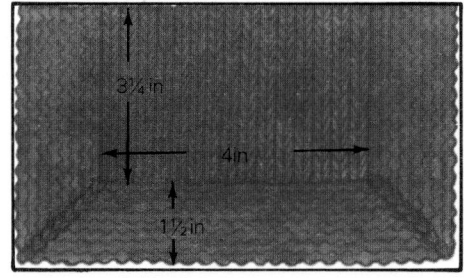 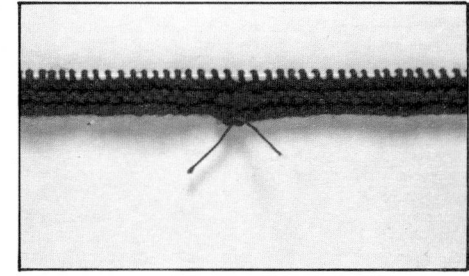

1 This is a separate border with a mitered corner. The corner is worked over 5 stitches and has a central stitch that forms a chain effect. The border is worked from the outer edge inward—with the bound-off edge being sewn onto the main fabric. Unless you are following written instructions, you must make some careful calculations before starting to knit.

2 First measure all the edges on which the border is to be sewn to calculate the number of stitches to bind off. Count the number of garter stitch ridges that you want in the width and add 2 stitches for each ridge for decreasing at each corner; also add 5 extra working stitches for each corner to give the total number of cast-on stitches.

3 Mark the center stitch of each corner with colored thread. On the right side of the work, knit to 2 stitches before the marked stitch then work corners as follows: "K2 tog, K1, K2 tog tbl." On wrong-side rows knit all the stitches except the center corner stitches, which are purled. Here you can see the chain effect.

Mitered openwork garter stitch corner

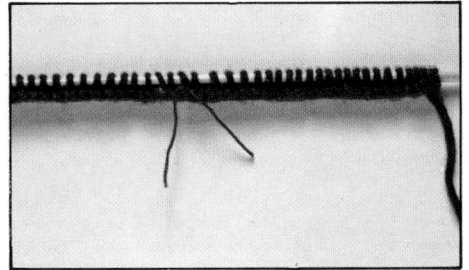

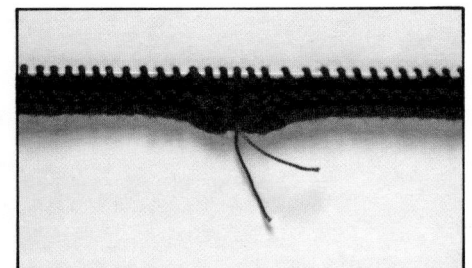

1 This is a more decorative version of the mitered corner. Again the corner is worked over 5 stitches with the center stitch producing a chain effect. Here the "chain" is emphasized by a line of openwork holes at each side.

2 Following step 2 of "Mitered garter stitch corner," calculate and cast on the required number of stitches for the outer edge. Mark the center stitch of each corner with colored thread. On the right side, knit to 3 stitches before the marked stitch, then work corner as follows: "K3 tog, yo, K1, yo, K3 tog tbl."

3 On wrong side rows knit all the stitches except the center corner stitches, which are purled. The "yo" on right-side rows makes a stitch (counter-balanced by working 3 stitches together to decrease for corner); the "made" stitches form a line of holes.

Stockinette stitch corners

Mitered stockinette stitch corner

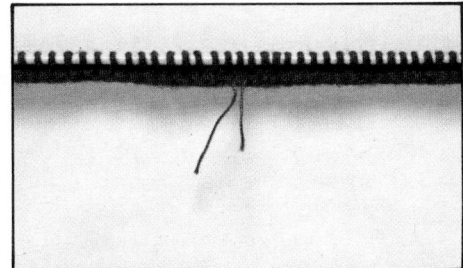

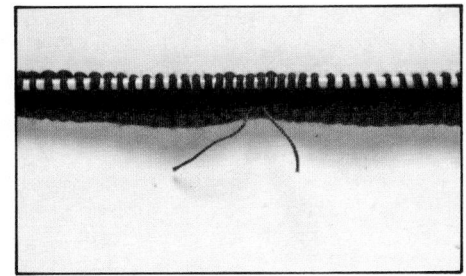

1 This corner is worked either as a separate border or by picking up stitches along the selvages of the fabric and working from the inside outward. The corner is formed by making invisible increases at each side of a central "axis" of 3 stitches.

2 Cast on enough stitches to fit along the edges to be bordered. **1st row** *K to within 2 sts of corner, pick up loop lying between needles and K tbl—called make 1 (M1)—, K3, M1, rep from * to end. **2nd row** P to end.

3 Repeat these 2 rows until the border is the required depth. Note that on subsequent increase rows you must work 2 more stitches each time before making a stitch. When the work is bound off, the angle forms at each side of the 3 corner stitches.

Turned stockinette stitch corner

1 To make this corner you cast on the number of stitches required for the width of the border. Work in stockinette stitch to fit along the length of each side, then use "turning rows" to angle the corner from the inner edge to the outer point.

2 To start turning the corner, purl until only the last stitch remains on left-hand needle. Slip the last stitch, then take yarn to back of work and return last stitch to left-hand needle.

3 Turn the work around so that the single stitch is now on the needle in your right hand. Take the yarn across the front of the slipped stitch and around to the back between the needles. Knit to the end of the row. *continued*

Fred Mancini

4 Repeat steps 2 and 3, leaving one more stitch unworked on left-hand needle each time until the last stitch has been knitted on a right-side row.

5 You have now built up to the outer point and must start working from there inward—again using "turning rows." **Next row** P2, turn. **Next row** K2.

6 Continue in this way, working one more stitch on next and every following alternate row until you have the original number of stitches on one needle on a wrong side row. Work in stockinette stitch to the next corner.

Tea and coffee cozies

Combine your knitting and sewing skills to brighten up your table and kitchen with these colorful quilted tea and coffee cozies in warm shades of red and brown. They'll keep your drinks piping hot.

Sizes
13¼ × 10¾in (35 × 27.5cm).

Note Both cozies are made from the same pattern with different edges left open.

Materials
Knitting-worsted weight yarn
Tea cozy 2oz (40g) in cream
2oz (40g) in brown
2oz (40g) in red

Coffee cozy 2oz (40g) in cream
2oz (40g) in brown
2oz (40g) in rust
1 pair No. 5 (4mm) knitting needles
Knitting spool
14in (35cm) of medium-weight batting
14in (35cm) of thin muslin
12in (30cm) of cotton fabric for lining
Sewing thread for quilting and finishing

Gauge
24 sts and 32 rows to 4in (10cm) in stockinette st on No. 5 (4mm) needles.

Tea cozy

Shape 1 Using red, cast on 12 sts. Work 2in (5cm) stockinette st. Bind off.
Shape 2 Using brown, cast on 6 sts. Work 2in (5cm) stockinette st; end with a K row.
Turn corner
1st row P to last st, sl 1 purlwise, yarn to back, pass sl st back to left-hand needle, turn.
2nd row Yarn to back around st that was slipped, K to end.
3rd row P to last 2 sts, sl 1 purlwise, yarn to back, pass sl st back to left-hand needle, turn.
4th row As 2nd.
Cont in this way, working one st less each time, until the row "Yarn to back around

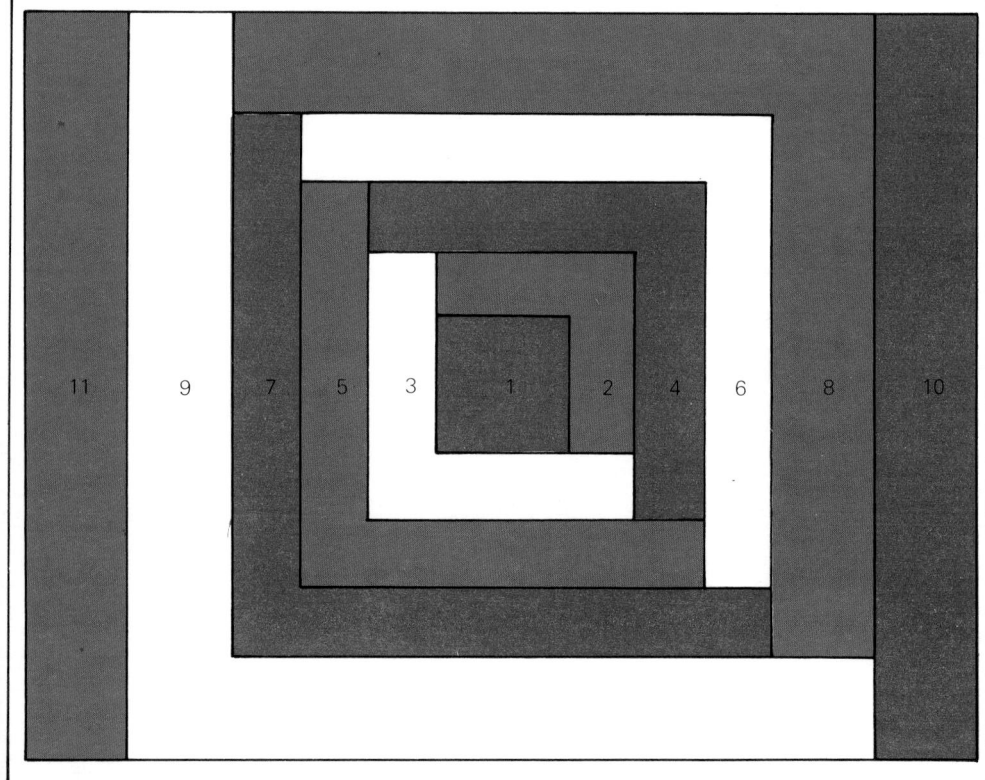

11	9	7	5	3	1	2	4	6	8	10

John Hutchinson

st, K1'' has been worked.

Next row P2, turn.

Next row K2.

Next row P3, turn.

Cont in this way until all sts are worked.
Work 2in (5cm) straight. Bind off.

Shape 3 Using cream, cast on 6 sts. Work 3in (7.5cm) stockinette st, turn corner, then work another 3in (7.5cm). Bind off.

Shape 4 Using red, cast on 6 sts. Work 4in (10cm) stockinette st, turn corner, then work another 4in (10cm). Bind off.

Shape 5 Using brown, cast on 6 sts. Work 5in (12.5cm) stockinette st, turn corner, then work another 5in (12.5cm). Bind off.

Shape 6 Using cream, cast on 6 sts. Work 6in (15cm) stockinette st, turn corner, then work another 6in (15cm). Bind off.

Shape 7 Using red, cast on 6 sts. Work 7in (17.5cm) stockinette st, turn corner, then work another 7in (17.5cm). Bind off.

Shape 8 Using brown, cast on 9 sts. Work 8in (20cm) stockinette st, turn corner, then work another 8in (20cm). Bind off.

Shape 9 Using cream, cast on 9 sts. Work $9\frac{1}{4}$in (23.5cm) stockinette st, turn corner, then work another $9\frac{1}{4}$in (23.5cm). Bind off.

Shape 10 Using red, cast on 9 sts. Work $10\frac{3}{4}$in (27.5cm) stockinette st. Bind off.

Shape 11 Using brown, cast on 9 sts. Work $10\frac{3}{4}$in (27.5cm) stockinette st. Bind off.

Press or block each shape according to yarn used.

Working from the diagram, join shapes in numerical order.

First pin sides to be joined to fit, then sew close to edge with a neat backstitch seam.

To join shapes

Press or block finished rectangular fabric as before.

Make another piece of rectangular fabric in the same way.

To finish

Join knitted sections, using a back stitch seam, following the chart on page 46.

Cut two pieces of batting and two pieces of muslin so that they are $\frac{3}{4}$in (2cm) larger all around than the knitted patchwork sections.

Lay knitting on top of batting and batting on top of muslin. Pin knitting to batting and muslin, easing it into a neat rectangular shape. Baste knitting to batting, following seamlines.

Quilt the knitting by machine stitching through all three layers, following the seamlines.

Continue stitching all around outer edge. Repeat on other patchwork piece.

Trim away excess batting and muslin close to line of stitching. With RS tog and edges matching, pin the two quilted sections tog, leaving one long edge open. Join the two sections by hand, using a back stitch seam, working close to the line

John Hutchinson

of machine stitching.

Measure the outer cover accurately. Cut two pieces of cotton fabric $\frac{1}{2}$in (1cm) larger all around than the finished outer cover. Pin, baste and stitch the two pieces tog, leaving one long edge open, taking $\frac{1}{2}$in (1cm)-wide seams. With RS inside, clip across corners, press seam allowances back and turn up $\frac{1}{2}$in (1cm) all around lower edge.

Slip lining inside outer cover, WS tog. Slip stitch lining to outer cover all around lower edge, close to line of machine stitching, rolling edge of outer cover to inside as you stitch.

Press.

Make $33\frac{1}{2}$in (85cm) of spool knitting and

sew in place around seamline, following instructions in Volume 16, page 50.

Coffee cozy

Work as instructed for tea cozy, but changing colors as foll: shapes 1, 4, 7 and 10 in brown, shapes 2, 5, 8 and 11 in cream and shapes 3, 6 and 9 in rust.

To finish

Finish as for tea cozy, following chart above and leaving one short edge open when making outer cover lining. Make 32in (92cm) of spool knitting and sew in place around seamline, following instructions in Volume 16, page 50.

Shoestring

Bear badges

These amusing badges will brighten up a child's jacket or overalls. And because they're so simple, a child could sew the badges together by himself.

Vince Loden

Finished size
About $2\frac{3}{4} \times 2\frac{3}{4}$in (7×7cm).

Materials for each badge
Scraps of felt in main color, a contrasting color (cheeks and ears), black and red or pink
Embroidery thread in two main colors and white
8in (20cm) of $\frac{1}{4}$in (6mm)-wide ribbon
Matching thread
Small safety pin
Small amount of stuffing
Pinking shears
Tracing paper

1 Trace the main bear face and features.
2 Cut out two main face pieces from the main color felt, using pinking shears.
3 Cut out two inner ears and one cheek piece in the main contrasting felt, using pinking shears.
4 From black felt cut out two eyes and one nose. From pink or red felt cut out one tongue.
5 Place the tongue on one face piece, following pattern for position. Place cheeks over the tongue and the nose over cheeks and tongue. Pin and baste them in position. Back stitch around the edge of cheeks and down the center of the nose in matching embroidery thread to hold all three features in place.
6 Position the eyes on the face. Hold the eyes in place with a French knot in white embroidery thread.
7 Work four straight stitches above each eye in contrasting thread, for eyebrows.
8 Position the inner ears on the face. Pin and baste them in place. Back stitch around each inner ear in matching
embroidery thread to hold them in place.
9 Tie the ribbon into a neat bow. Cut the raw ends into V shapes to finish them. Hand sew the bow in place under the tongue.
10 On one side of the other face piece place the safety pin horizontally, in the center, about $\frac{3}{4}$in (2cm) down from the top edge, and sew it in place.
11 Place the bear faces together with wrong sides facing. Pin and baste around the edge. Work running stitch in matching embroidery thread around the edge of the face, leaving a small opening for inserting the stuffing.
12 Stuff the bear lightly. Close the opening with running stitches in matching embroidery thread. Work back around the badge using matching embroidery thread, filling in the gaps between the first running stitches.

Knitting/COURSE 82

Ladder and elongated stitch techniques

A ladder in knitting is produced by dropping a stitch. Ladders form vertical decoration, usually by being repeated across a fabric to give a lacy, openwork effect.

A ladder may be decorated to imitate drawn thread work. Short ladders are often used as repeating decorative motifs. A repeat of ladder motifs, such as the butterfly ones used on the cardigans on page 53, give interesting texture to a fabric. The horizontal equivalent of a dropped stitch is formed by lengthening stitches, so that the drawn thread effect is produced between rows instead of between stitches. Again, you can either create an allover pattern with elongated stitches, or use them to add detail.

Fred Mancini

Making a ladder

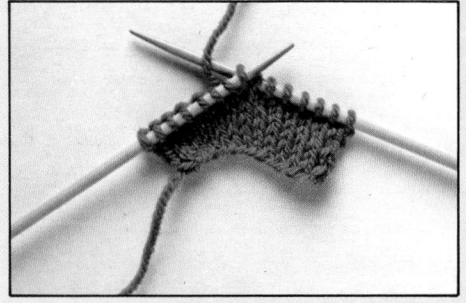
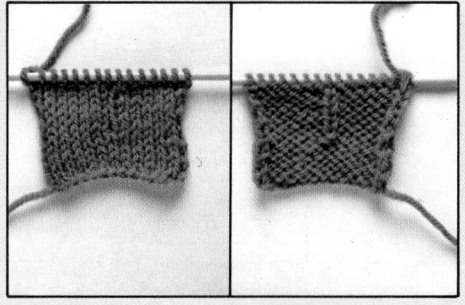
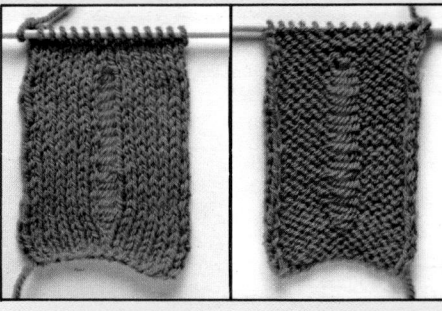

1 Work a base for the ladder to control, or stop, it at that point. The base is an invisible increase made by picking up the horizontal loop lying between stitches and working into the back of it.

2 Pinpoint the position of the "made" stitch by working it in a stitch contrasting with the background. On RS of this stockinette stitch fabric you can barely see it, but it is visible on WS.

3 Work to the desired depth of the ladder. Drop the extra stitch either in binding off or when the ladder is finished. The ladder is easier to see on the wrong side of this fabric.

Making a decorated ladder

1 To make a wide gap in the fabric as a basis for decoration, you must work a double ladder. Again you require a base for the ladder: here it is 2 bound-off stitches at the lower position of the ladder.

2 On following row—here it is reverse side of a stockinette stitch fabric—pick up a loop from each of bound-off stitches and knit them so that they contrast with reverse stockinette stitch. Work until ladder is desired depth.

3 Work to position of contrasting stitches. Drop next 2 stitches from left-hand needle. Replace 2 stitches by inserting left-hand needle from front to back under last rung; knit into front and back of picked-up loop.

50

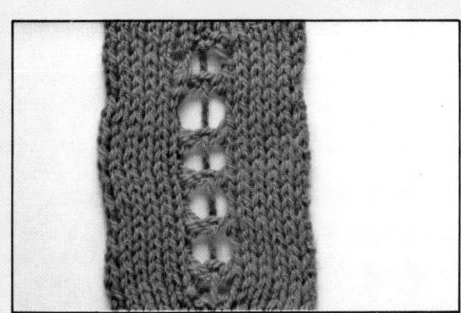

4 To decorate the ladder, thread a tapestry needle with matching yarn and secure it at the center of the base of bound-off stitches. Count 4 bars up and insert the needle from the front of the work and through to the back after the 4th bar, then through to the front again between the 2nd and 3rd bars.

5 Now twist the needle by re-inserting it from front to back and under the 1st bar and out to the front again in the original space after the 4th bar. The twisting action of the needle and yarn between pairs of rungs makes a decorative braided effect.

6 Repeat at the motif by counting another 4 bars up each time and working another twist. The finished, decorated ladder has a pretty, lacy appearance.

Lengthening a stitch

1 The stitches are lengthened across a complete row of this stockinette stitch fabric. Insert right-hand needle into first stitch as if to knit it, but wind yarn twice around needle point. Knit stitch in usual way so that it forms 2 loops on right-hand needle. Work each stitch in row in same way.

2 On the following row, purl each stitch in the usual way, dropping the extra loop from the left-hand needle after working each stitch. When the row is completed pull the fabric sharply to even out the stitches.

3 Repeat these elongated rows at intervals throughout the fabric. The stitches may vary in length depending on the number of times the yarn is wound around the needle; here it is twice, 3 times and 4 times from bottom to top.

Making an elongated cross stitch

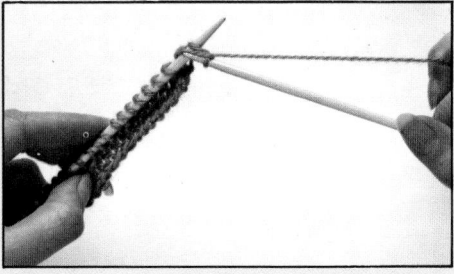

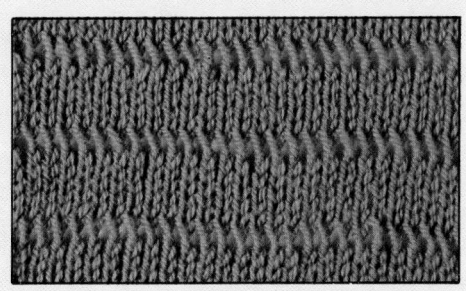

1 This is a way of winding the yarn around the needle to make a firm, elongated cross stitch. Insert right-hand needle into stitch; wind yarn under and over right-hand needle in usual way, then under and over left-hand needle and finally under and around right-hand needle again.

2 Slightly open the needles and draw a single loop through the first space on the right below the needles. When the loop is on the right-hand needle allow the original stitch and extra yarn around needle to fall from the left-hand needle.

3 Single rows of these elongated crossed stitches can be used as decoration across any solid fabric. You can also make fancy fabrics in the same way; see "Special crossed garter stitch" in Stitch Wise, page 52.

Stitch Wise

Cable and ladder pattern

In this pattern a combination of classic cables separated by ladders produces a ribbed effect.
Cast on a multiple of 6 stitches plus 2 extra.
1st row (RS) K1, pick up loop lying between needles and K tbl—called make 1 (M1)—, *K6, M1, rep from * to last st, K1.
2nd row P1, K1, *P6, K1, rep from * to last st, P1.
3rd row K1, P1, *sl next 3 sts onto cable

needle and hold at front of work, K3, then K3 sts from cable needle—called C6F—, P1, rep from * to last st, K1.
4th row As 2nd.
5th row K1, P1, *K6, P1, rep from * to last st, K1.
6th row As 2nd.
7th row As 5th.
8th row As 2nd.
Rep 3rd—8th rows for the required depth. Bind off, dropping the extra sts made in first row to form ladders.

Ladder dot pattern

Here short ladder motifs are arranged to give allover dot pattern.
Cast on a multiple of 10 stitches plus 4 extra.
1st row (RS) K2, pick up loop lying between needles and K tbl—called make 1 (M1)—, *K10, M1, rep from * to last 2 sts, K2.
2nd row P to end.

3rd row K to end.
4th row P to end.
5th row K2, drop next st to form ladder, *K5, M1, K5, drop 1, rep from * to last 2 sts, K2.
6th - 8th rows As 2nd—4th rows.
9th row K2, M1, *K5, drop 1, K5, M1, rep from * to last 2 sts, K2.
Rep 2nd—9th rows for the required depth.

Special crossed garter stitch

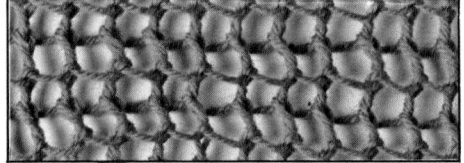

This allover fabric using elongated crossed stitches is traditional for veils and shawls worked in fine yarns on large needles such as No. 11 (8mm).
Note that you must pull the stitches into shape at the end of each row; hold the

needle firmly while doing this.
Cast on any number of stitches.
Work elongated crossed stitch (see page 51) on each stitch in every row to produce the fabric shown in the photograph.

Double elongated stitch insertion

Here 2 rows of crossed stitches are bordered by garter stitch (as a contrast to the main stockinette stitch fabric) to make a fancy insertion. You could repeat this insertion at intervals to make an allover pattern of decorative horizontal stripes.

Cast on any number of stitches. Work the required number of rows in stockinette stitch, ending with a knit row. Knit 4 rows, so ending with a RS row. Work 2 rows of elongated cross stitches, then knit another 6 rows. Beg with a purl row, cont in stockinette stitch.

Mother and daughter cardigans

We used a soft yarn in pastel colors for a pretty cardigan in a wide range of sizes, knitted in simple seed stitch with bands of ladder stitch.

Sizes
To fit 24[27:31:34:37:40]in (62 [70:78:86:94:102]cm) chest/bust.
Length, 18[19½:21:21½:24¼:25:25¼]in (46[50:55:61:63:64]cm).
Sleeve seam, 12[13¼:14½:16¼:16¼:16¼] in (31[34:37:41:41:41]cm).
Note Directions for larger sizes are in

brackets []: if there is only one set of figures it applies to all sizes.

Materials
9[9:11:12:12:13]oz 240[240:280: 320:320:360]g) of a sport-weight mohair-type yarn
1 pair each Nos. 3 and 5 (3¼ and 4mm) knitting needles
4[4:4:5:5:5] buttons

Gauge
22 sts and 32 rows to 4in (10cm) in stockinette st worked on No. 5 (4mm) needles.

Back
Using No. 3 (3¼mm) needles cast on 75[85:95:105:115:125] sts.
1st row P1, *K1, P1, rep from * to end.
2nd low K1, *P1, K1, rep from * to end.
Rep these 2 rows for 1½[1½:1½:

2:2:2]in (4[4:4:5:5:5]cm; end with a 2nd row and inc one st in center of last row. 76[86:96:106:116:126] sts.
Change to No. 5 (4mm) needles. Work 10[12:14:16:16:16] rows seed st.
Work patt band as foll:
1st row (RS) K to end.
2nd row P to end.
3rd - 7th rows Beg with a P row, work 5 rows reverse stockinette st.
8th row K5, *drop next st down 5 rows, insert needle into dropped st and under the 5 loops and K them all tog, K4, rep from * to last st, K1.
9th row K to end.
10th row P to end.
Rep last 20[22:24:26:26:26] rows 4 times more.
Shape armholes
Cont in seed st throughout, bind off 3[4:5:6:7:8] sts at beg of next 2 rows.
Dec one st at each end of next and every

Victor Yuan

foll 3rd row until 34[38:42:46:50:54] sts rem; end with a WS row.

Shape shoulders
Bind off 4[4:5:5:6:6] sts at beg of next 2 rows. Bind off rem 26[30:32:36:38:42] sts.

Left front
Using No. 3 (3¼mm) needles cast on 45[51:55:63:67:73] sts. Rib 1½[1½:1½: 2:2:2]in (4[4:4:5:5:5]cm) as for back; end with a 2nd row and inc one st in center of last row on first, 3rd and 5th sizes. 46[51:56:63:68:73] sts. Change to No. 5 (4mm) needles.
Next row Working in seed st, patt 36[41:46:51:56:61], turn and leave rem 10[10:10:12:12:12] sts on holder. Cont in patt to match back to armholes; end with a WS row.

Shape armhole and front edge
Bind off 3[4:5:6:7:8] sts at beg of next row. Work 1 row. Dec one st at front edge on next and every foll 4th row 11[13:14: 16:17:19] times in all, **at the same time** dec one st at armhole edge on next and every 3rd row until 4[4:5:5:6:6] sts rem; end with a WS row. Bind off.

Right front
Using No. 3 (3¼mm) needles cast on 45[51:55:63:67:73] sts. Rib ¾[¾:¾: 1:1:1]in (2[2:2:2.5:2.5:2.5]cm) as for back; end with a WS row.
Next row (buttonhole row) Rib 4[4:4:5:5:5], bind off 2, rib to end.
Next row Rib to end, casting on 2 sts over those bound off in previous row. Cont in ribbing until work measures same as left front ribbing; end with a 2nd row and inc one st in last row on first, 3rd and 5th sizes.
Next row Rib 10[10:10:12:12:12] and leave these sts on a holder, change to No. 5 (4mm) needles and work in seed st to end. Complete to match left front, reversing all shaping.

Sleeves
Using No. 3 (3¼mm) needles cast on

31[35:39:43:47:51] sts. Work ribbing as for back; end with a first row.
Next row K1, then K twice into each st to end. 61[69:77:85:93:101] sts. Change to No. 5 (4mm) needles. Work in patt as for back, rep the 20[22:24: 26:26:26] rows 5 times in all (note that the row where you drop the sts starts with K5[4:3:2:1:5].

Shape top
Working in seed st throughout, bind off 3[4:5:6:7:8] sts at beg of next 2 rows. Dec one st at each end of next and every alternate row until 3 sts rem; end with a WS row. Bind off.

To finish
Do not press. Join shoulder seams.

Left front band With RS facing and using No. 3 (3¼mm) needles, rejoin yarn to inner edge of sts on holder, inc in first st, rib to end. Cont in ribbing until band, slightly stretched, fits up front edge to center back neck. Bind off. Sew band in position and mark position of buttons—first in center of waistband and last about ¾in (2cm) below beg of front shaping with 2[2:2:3:3:3] more evenly spaced between.

Right front band Work to match left front band, making buttonholes as before to correspond with position of buttons. Sew band in place. Set in sleeves. Join side and sleeve seams. Press seams. Sew on buttons.

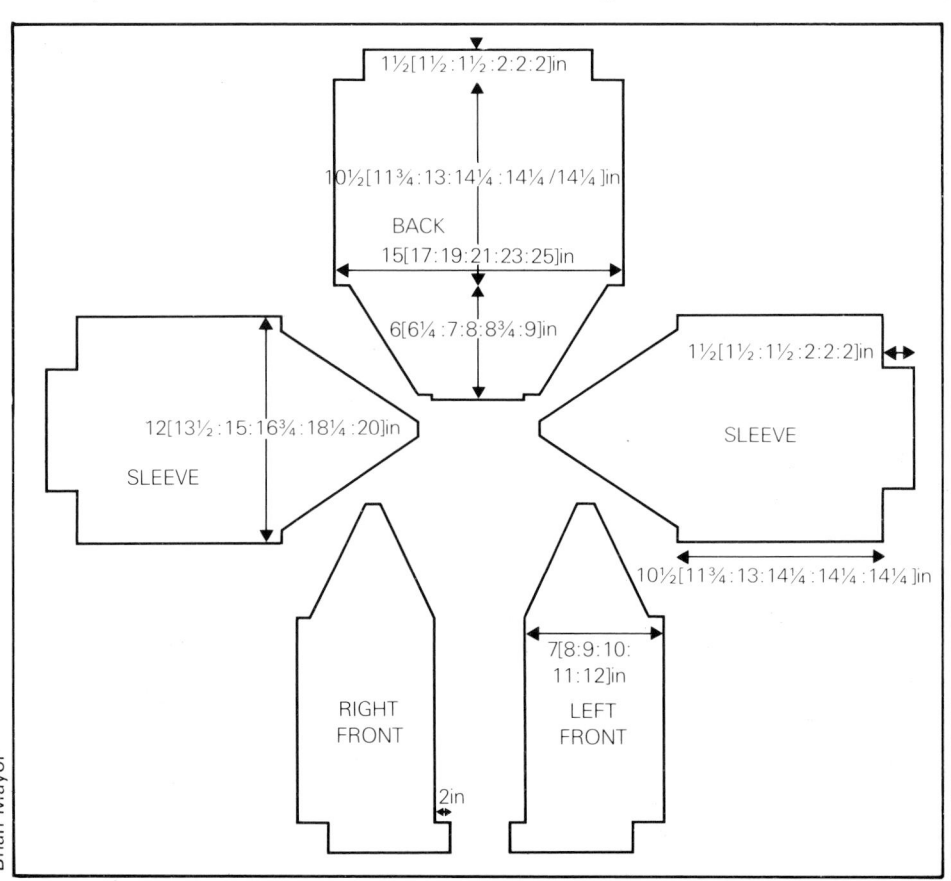

Brian Mayor

Sewing / COURSE 79

*Safari pocket
*Detachable epaulette
*Pattern for a safari shirt:
adapting the pattern;
directions for making

Safari pocket

These pockets take their name from the safari jackets worn by big-game hunters in Africa. The original pockets were capacious and the box pleat gave even more room for bulky items. The flap which buttoned over the pocket ensured that the pocket contents did not fall out even when the wearer was moving quickly. Fashion shirts, such as the safari shirt on page 57, incorporate safari pockets not only for functional reasons but also because they look good.

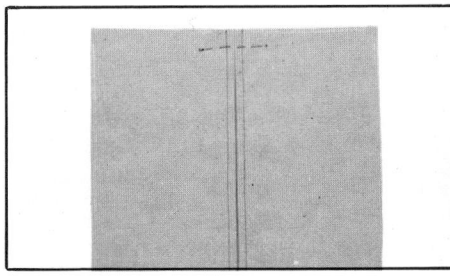

1 Mark the pocket pleat foldlines with basting. Fold and pin the pleat in place, matching the pleat lines. Press pleat folds and topstitch $\frac{1}{4}$in (5mm) in from folded edges through double thickness only. Remove basting. Press the pleat flat and baste across top and bottom to hold.

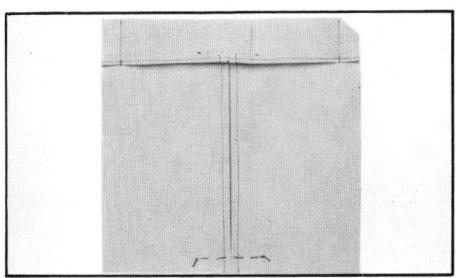

2 Finish the top edge of the pocket by turning in $\frac{1}{4}$in (5mm) and machine stitching. Press. Fold the top edge allowance down on the foldline, right sides together, and baste and stitch the short ends. Trim seams and clip corners.

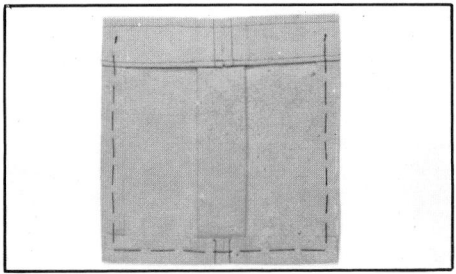

3 Turn right side out and baste along the top edge. Press. From the right side, top-stitch $\frac{1}{4}$in (5mm) in from top edge of pocket. Remove all basting and press. Turn under the seam allowance along the side and bottom edges of pocket and baste. Press flat.

4 Baste pocket to garment in the position indicated on the pattern and topstitch in place $\frac{1}{4}$in (5mm) from the side and bottom edges. Remove basting and press.

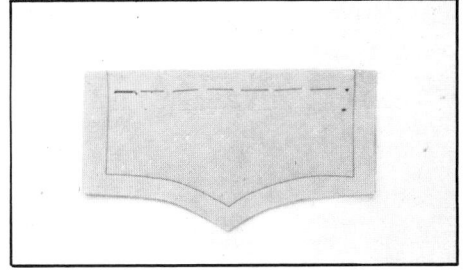

5 Baste interfacing to the wrong side of one flap piece. With right sides together, baste and stitch the two flap pieces together, leaving the top edge open.

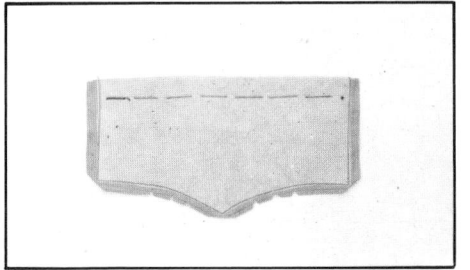

6 Trim the interfacing close to the stitching. Trim the other seam allowances and cut diagonally across the corners. Clip any curves so that edges will lie flat when turned right side out.

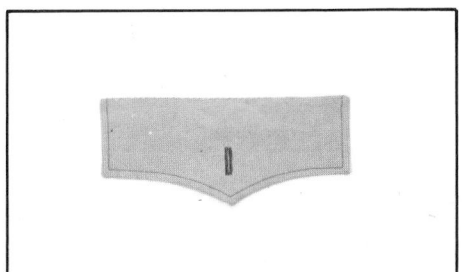

7 Turn flap right side out and baste around stitched edges. Press. Turn under seam allowances at opening and slip stitch together. Topstitch $\frac{1}{4}$in (5mm) in from side and bottom edges. Remove basting and press. Make buttonhole.

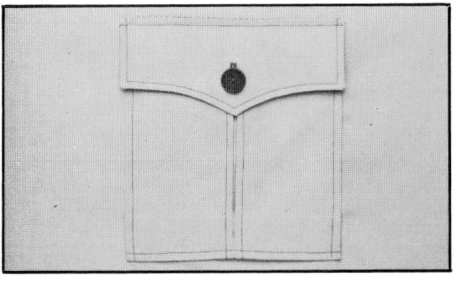

8 Baste the flap $\frac{1}{2}$in (1.3cm) above pocket and topstitch in place, stitching $\frac{1}{4}$in (5mm) in from the top edge of the flap. Press. Sew button to pocket directly under the buttonhole.

Simon Butcher

Detachable epaulette

Epaulettes have traditionally been used on military garments to hold gloves or caps neatly out of the way when not being worn. They can be used for the same purpose on the safari shirt shown opposite, or they can be used for decoration only. These epaulettes are detachable, which simplifies the washing and ironing of the shirt.

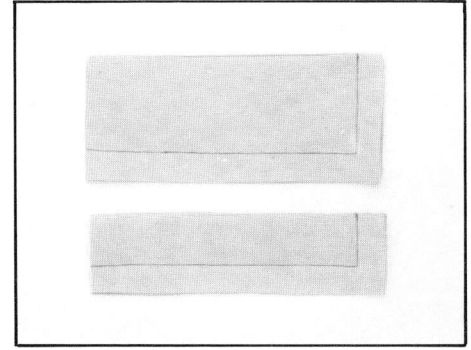

1 If the epaulette and strap need interfacing, baste this to the wrong side of one piece of the epaulette and one piece of the strap. With right sides together, baste and stitch the epaulette and strap pieces together, leaving open the end that will have the button or buttonhole.

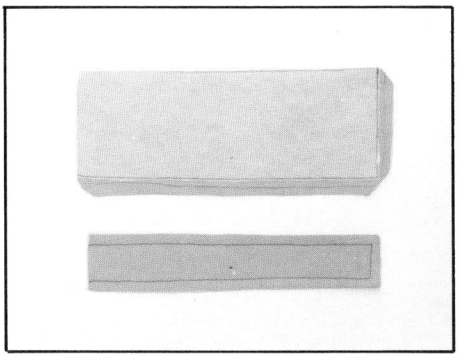

2 Trim interfacing close to stitching, trim seams and clip corners. Turn the sections right side out and baste around the stitched edge. Press. Topstitch $\frac{1}{4}$in (5mm) in from the stitched edges of the epaulette strap. Remove basting and press.

3 Turn in the seam allowance at the open end of the epaulette and press. Slip the raw ends of the strap into the open end of the epaulette and baste in place. Slip stitch the edges together to close the opening and secure the strap. Topstitch $\frac{1}{4}$in (5mm) in from three edges of epaulette as shown.

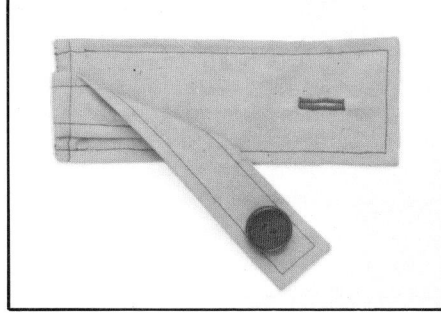

4 Fold the strap back over the epaulette and topstitch $\frac{1}{4}$in (5mm) from the edge as shown, stitching through all thicknesses. Remove basting and press. Make a buttonhole in the epaulette and sew a button to the strap directly opposite the buttonhole.

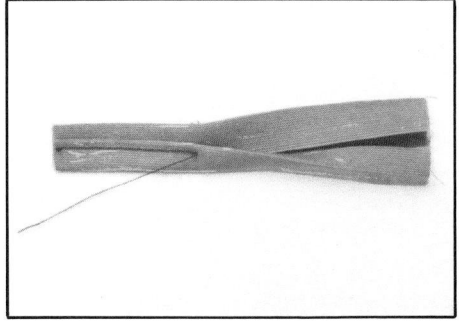

5 To make the carrier, cut a rectangle to the finished width of the epaulette plus $\frac{3}{4}$in (2cm) seam allowance and $1\frac{1}{4}$in (3cm) wide. This will give a finished width of $\frac{3}{8}$in (1cm).
Fold down $\frac{3}{8}$in (1cm) on one long edge and press flat. Turn in $\frac{1}{4}$in (5mm) on the other long edge and then overlap this to the center of the carrier. Baste and stitch along the center through all thicknesses.

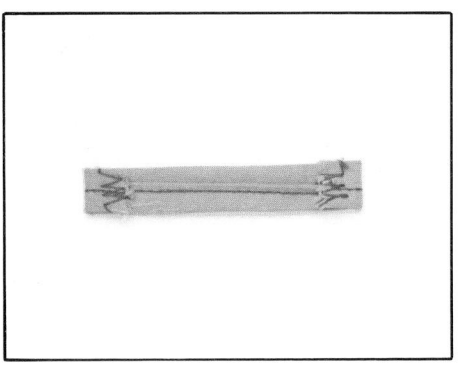

6 Remove basting, press and finish the raw edges at each end. Turn under $\frac{3}{8}$in (1cm) at each end to the wrong side and press flat.

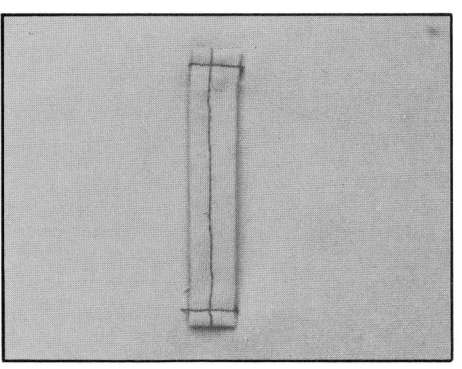

7 Position the carrier on the garment and baste and stitch it in place, stitching across each end through all thicknesses. On the safari shirt the carrier is positioned directly over the shoulder seam at the armhole.

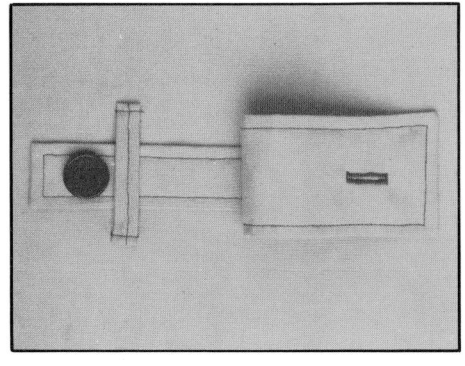

8 Slip the epaulette strap through the carrier and button the epaulette onto it as shown. At the opposite end sew one half of a snap to the underside of the strap and the other half to the shoulder seam. Use clear snaps if possible.

Safari shirt

Hunting is fair game when wearing this safari shirt over shorts or pants.

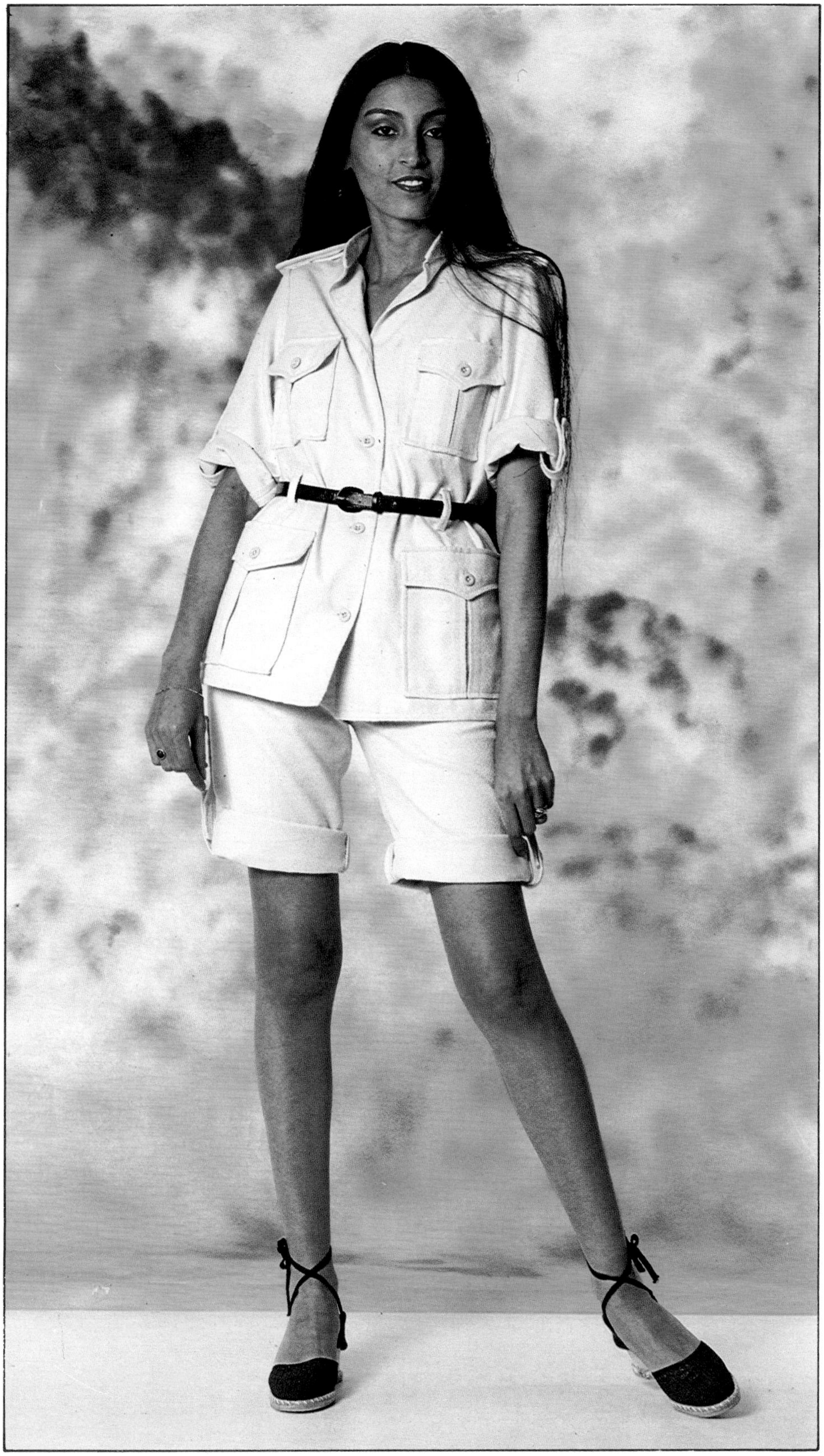

Adapting the pattern

Measurements

The pattern for the safari shirt is adapted from the basic shirt taken from the Stitch by Stitch Pattern Pack, available in sizes 10 to 20 (8 to 18 in ready-made clothes).

Materials

3 sheets of tracing paper 36 × 40in (90 × 100cm)
Flexible curve
Yardstick, right triangle

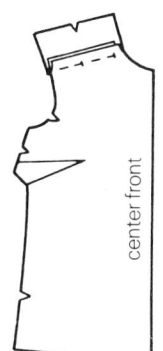 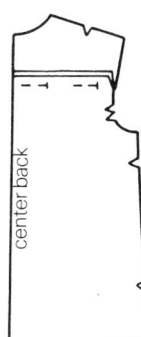

1 Pin the front yoke to the shirt front and the back yoke to the shirt back, overlapping $\frac{5}{8}$in (1.5cm) seam allowances so that the seamlines are aligned. Trace both complete pattern pieces, leaving extra paper at the center front edge.

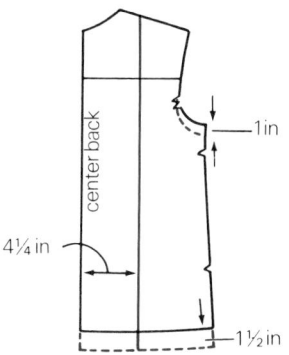

2 To make the back pattern, lengthen back by $1\frac{1}{2}$in (4cm) at lower edge. Lower the armhole by 1in (2.5cm) and, using a flexible curve, re-draw the armhole curve, tapering into the original cutting line at the notches. For the pleat position draw a vertical line from the shoulder to lower edge, $4\frac{1}{4}$in (10.5cm) in from center back edge and parallel to it.

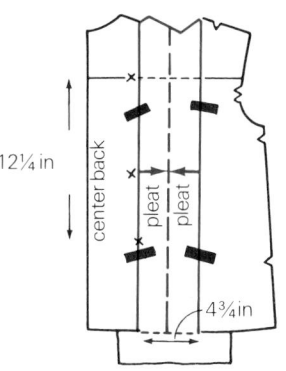

3 Slash along this line and spread the pattern $4\frac{3}{4}$in (12cm). Insert and tape paper behind the slash. Use the yoke line as a guide to keep the pattern square. Draw in the center line of the pleat.

John Hutchinson

4 To shape the top edge of the pleat allowance, fold the pleat in place and cut along the shoulder cutting line. Open out the pattern to see the shaping. The pleat is stitched down to the back yoke line, then left open 12¼in (31cm) for a size 10, adding an extra ¼in (5mm) to this measurement for each larger size. From here it is stitched to the lower edge.

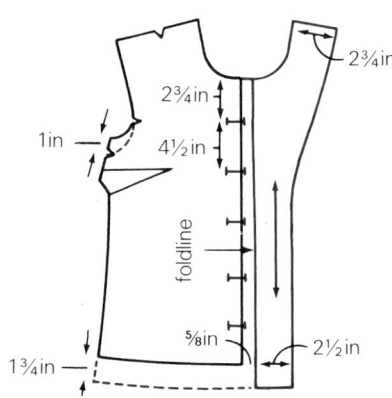

5 To make the front pattern, lengthen the basic pattern and lower the armhole, using the same measurements and directions given for the back.
6 For button stand, add ⅝in (1.5cm) to center front edge. Mark this as the foldline. Add a further 2½in (6.5cm) for front facing from hem to bust dart level.
7 Fold the facing back along the foldline and trace the neck edge and shoulder cutting line to 2¾in (7cm). Using a flexible curve, draw the upper part of the facing, curving the line from the shoulder to meet the lower facing line.
8 Mark the grain line parallel to the center front. Mark the buttonhole positions along the center front, the first 2¾in (7cm) below the neck edge and the other five at 4½in (11.5cm) intervals. The buttonholes are placed horizontally, ⅝in (1.5cm) in front facing foldline.

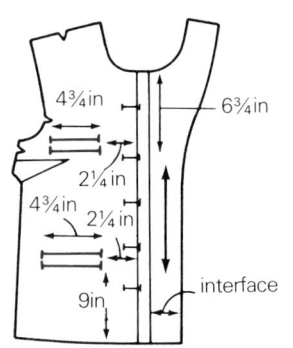

9 For the breast pocket position, measure down center front from neck edge 6¾in (17cm) and in from center front 2¼in (6cm) and mark. Measure a further 4¾in (12cm) and mark.
10 Mark the pocket flap position ½in (1.3cm) above pocket line. For the hip pocket line, measure up from lower edge 9in (23cm) and in 2¼in (6cm) from center front and mark. Measure a further 6¼in

(16cm) and mark. The pocket is positioned between these two points. Mark the pocket flap line ½in (1.3cm) above hip pocket line.

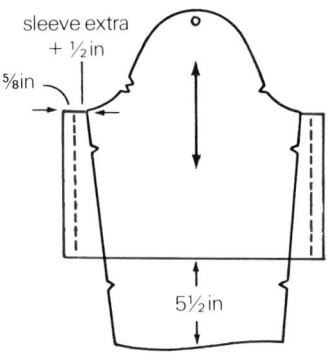

11 To make the sleeve pattern, trace the basic sleeve, enlarging the sleeve cap to fit the enlarged armhole: measure the front and back armhole seamlines, then measure around the sleeve cap seamline. The difference in these measurements is divided between each side of sleeve cap.
12 Add this amount, plus ½in (1cm) ease allowance, to the underarm edge and mark. For example, if front and back armhole seamlines measure 21¼in (54cm) and sleeve cap seamline measures 19½in (50cm), difference is 1¾in (4cm). Therefore 1¼in (3cm) (¾in [2cm] plus ½in [1cm] ease) will be added to each side of sleeve at armhole. Draw a horizontal line across pattern 5½in (14cm) up from original cutting line at lower edge. This includes a ¾in (2cm) hem allowance for new length. Add ¾in (1.5cm) to underarm edges.

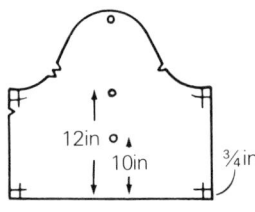

13 Mark the position for the lower sleeve strap (the one with the buttonholes which will be attached to the wrong side of the sleeve) 10in (25cm) up from the lower edge of the sleeve in line with the top of the sleeve cap.
14 Mark the position for the upper sleeve strap (the one with the buttons which is to be attached to the right side of the sleeve), 12in (30cm) from the lower edge of the sleeve in line with the top of the sleeve cap as before.

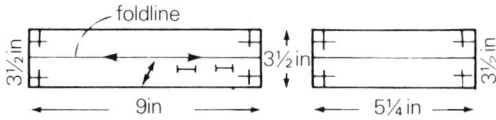

15 For the lower sleeve strap pattern, draw a rectangle 9 × 3½in (23×9cm).

These measurements include a ⅝in (1.5cm) seam allowance on all edges. The finished width of the strap will be 1in (2.5cm). Mark the grainline and the foldline along the center. Mark the buttonhole positions in the center of one half of strap, 1¼in (3cm) in from outer edge. The strap will be interfaced to the foldline. For the upper sleeve strap pattern draw a rectangle 5¼ × 3½in (13 × 9cm) and mark as for upper strap, omitting buttonholes.

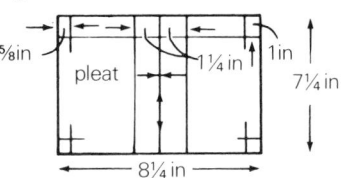

16 To make the breast pocket pattern, draw a rectangle 8¼ × 7¼in (21×18cm). These measurements include a ⅝in (1.5cm) allowance on side and bottom edges and 1in (2.5cm) at top edge. Mark center pleat line in the center of the rectangle and a pleat foldline 1¼in (3cm) each side of center (grain line).

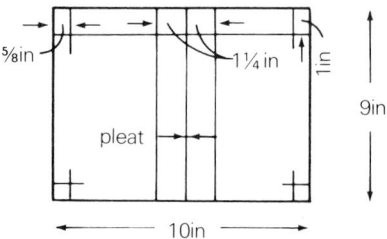

17 To make the hip pocket pattern, draw a rectangle 10×9in (25×23cm). These measurements include seam allowance as for the breast pocket. Mark the pleat lines as before.

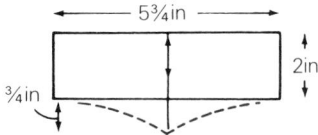

18 To make the breast pocket flap pattern, draw a rectangle 5¾ × 2in (15×5cm). Draw a line through the center of the rectangle and extend it by ¾in (2cm). Using a flexible curve, draw the outer curved edge as shown.

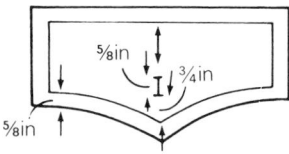

19 Mark the buttonhole in center ¾in (2cm) up from the point. The buttonhole is ⅝in (1.5cm) long. Add a ⅝in (1.5cm) seam allowance to all edges. The central line is the straight grain.
20 To make the hip pocket flap pattern,

Cutting layout for 36in-wide fabric with or without nap

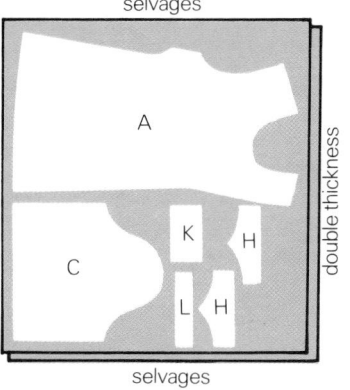

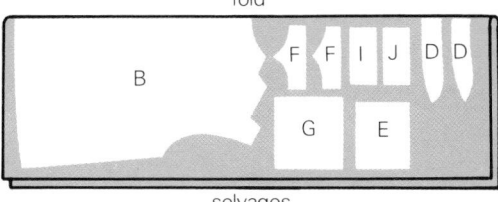

36in-wide interfacing

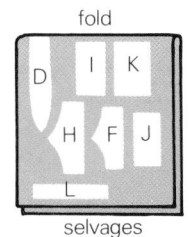

45in-wide fabric with or without nap

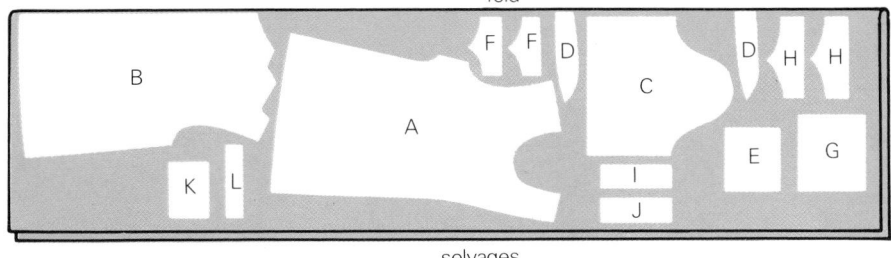

draw a rectangle 7½ × 2in (19 × 5cm). Complete flap as directed for the breast pocket flap pattern.

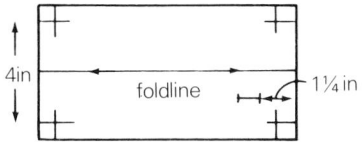

4in — foldline — 1¼ in

21 To make the epaulette pattern, measure the finished length of the shoulder seam from neck seamline to armhole seamline. Draw a rectangle to this length by 4in (10cm) wide. Add ⅝in (1.5cm) seam allowances to all edges. Mark grainline and foldline along center of rectangle. Mark a ⅝in (1.5cm) buttonhole in center of one half of the rectangle, 1¼in (3cm) in from the short end.

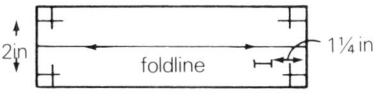

2in — foldline — 1¼ in

22 For the epaulette strap pattern, draw a rectangle 2in (5cm) wide by same length as the epaulette and add ⅝in (1.5cm) seam allowance to all edges. Mark the grain line and the buttonhole position.
23 For the collar pattern, use the basic stand collar from the Pattern Pack.

Directions for making

Materials
36in (90cm)-wide fabric with or without nap:
Sizes 10-14: 3½yd (3.1m)
Sizes 16-20: 3⅝yd (3.3m)
45in (115cm)-wide fabric with or without nap:
Size 10: 2¾yd (2.5m)
Size 12: 2⅞yd (2.6m)
Sizes 14, 16: 3yd (2.7m)
Sizes 18, 20: 3⅛yd (2.8m)

36in (90cm)-wide interfacing: for all sizes:
⅝yd (.5m)
Matching thread, 14 buttons ½in (1.3cm) in diameter

Suggested fabrics
Sailcloth, denim, linen, twill, duck.

Key to adapted pieces
A	Shirt front	Cut 2
B	Shirt back	Cut 1 on fold
C	Sleeve	Cut 2
D	Stand collar	Cut 2
E	Top pocket	Cut 2
F	Top pocket flap	Cut 4
G	Hip pocket	Cut 2
H	Hip pocket flap	Cut 4

I	Top sleeve strap	Cut 2
J	Lower sleeve strap	Cut 2
K	Epaulette	Cut 2
L	Epaulette strap	Cut 2

Interfacing: Use pieces: **D** Cut 1, **F & H** Cut 2 of each, **I & J** Cut 2 of each to half width only. **K & L** Cut 1 of each to half width only.

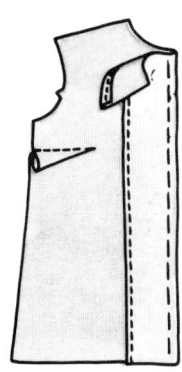

1 Finish the outer edge of the front facings by turning under ¼in (5mm) and machine stitching. Turn the facings to the inside along the foldline and baste in place. Fold, baste and stitch the side bust darts. Press downward. If using interfacing on front edges, allow extra yardage and baste these to wrong side of front facings before applying facings.

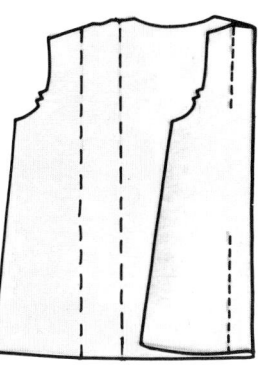

2 With right sides together, fold the back pleat lines together and, on the wrong side, baste along the fold lines from the shoulder edge for 4in (10cm) and again from the waistline to the lower edge.

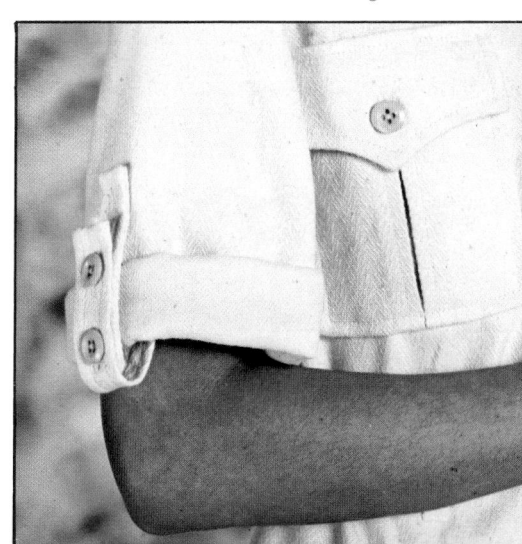

John Hutchinson

Terry Evans

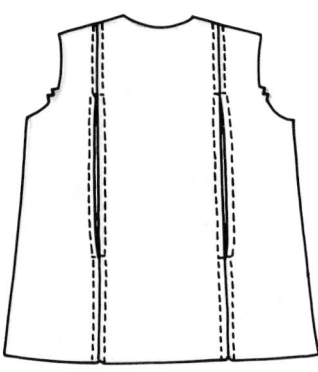

3 Fold the pleats into place and baste along the upper and lower folded edges of the pleats to hold. Press. Double top-stitch the seams of the pleats (see Volume 16, page 73), stitching $\frac{1}{4}$in (5mm) from seamlines on each side as far as the basting. Fasten threads on wrong side.

4 Begin the topstitching again at the end of the previous stitching, but this time stitching through the upper folded edges of the pleats only. Press.

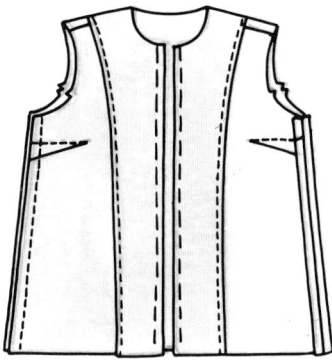

5 With right sides together, baste and stitch the shoulder and side seams. Finish and press seams.

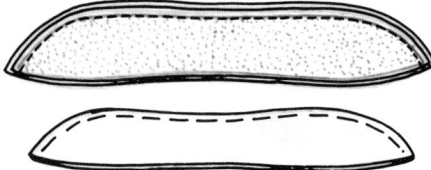

6 Baste the interfacing to the wrong side of one collar stand piece. With right sides together, baste and stitch the two collar pieces together, leaving the neck edge open. Trim the interfacing close to the stitching and trim and clip the other seam allowance. Turn collar right side out and baste around stitched edge. Press.

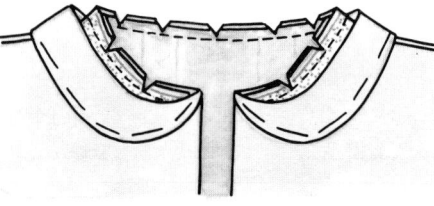

7 Baste the interfaced edge of the collar to the neck edge, matching center fronts,

shoulders and center backs. Stitch the entire seam. Grade and clip the seams. Cut across corners. Press seam allowance upward.

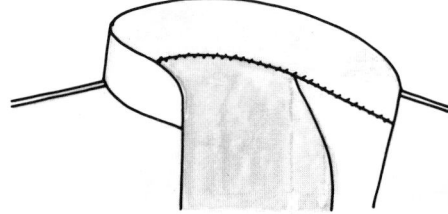

8 On the inside, turn under the seam allowance of the free edge of the collar and slip stitch to the stitching line. Press carefully from the right side.

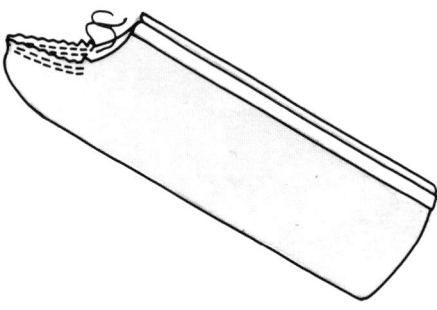

9 Prepare the sleeve cap for easing. With right sides together, baste and stitch the underarm seam. Trim the seam and press it open.

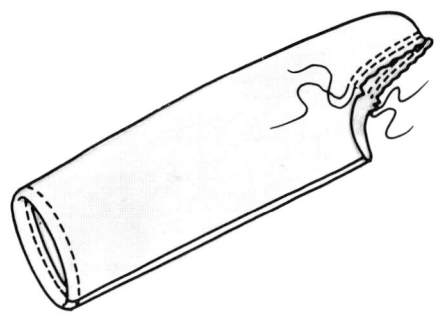

10 Turn up a $\frac{3}{8}$in (1cm) double hem (total of $\frac{3}{4}$in [2cm] hem allowed), pin and baste. Machine stitch all around close to inner fold. Remove basting and press. Repeat with second sleeve.

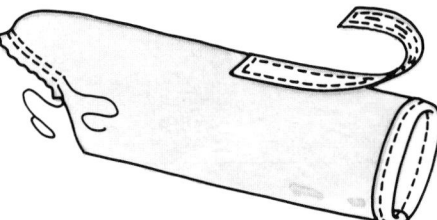

11 Make and apply sleeve straps as for the leg straps of the Bermuda shorts, (see Volume 17, page 83), applying the strap with the buttonholes to the wrong side of the sleeve, and the strap with the buttons to the right side of the sleeve, in the positions indicated on the pattern.

12 Roll up the sleeve hem and sew buttons to the strap beneath the button-holes. These hold the hem in place when the straps are fastened

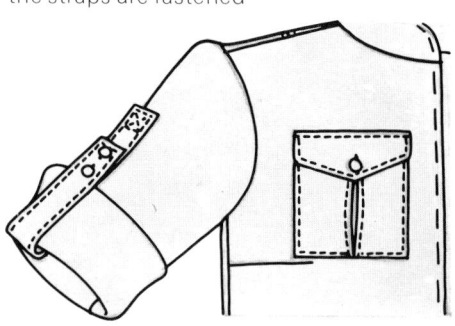

13 Set sleeve into armholes. Finish seam allowances together and press toward the sleeve. Finish the hem edge of the shirt by turning under $\frac{1}{4}$in (5mm) and a further $\frac{1}{2}$in (1.3cm) and machine stitching. Press. Make the four pockets and flaps as shown on page 55 and stitch to the shirt fronts in the positions marked.

14 Make two detachable epaulettes with carriers as shown on page 56 and apply to each shoulder line, positioning the carrier on the shoulder seam.

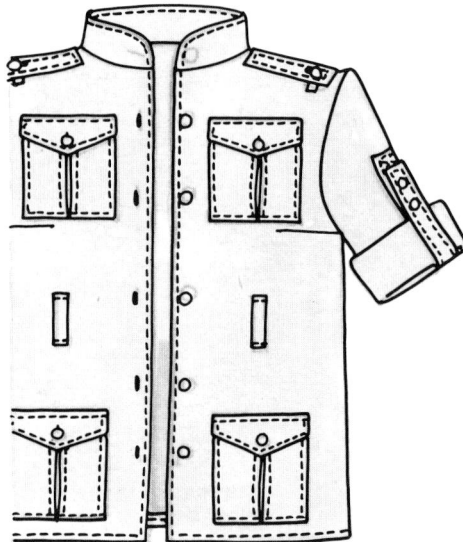

15 Make four belt carriers (finished width of $\frac{3}{8}$in [1cm]) to take a ready-made belt. Sew one at each back pleat and one to each front between center front and the side seam on the waistline as shown.

16 Topstitch $\frac{1}{4}$in (5mm) in from outer edge of the collar and front edges. Make the buttonholes down the center front edge in the positions marked. Sew buttons to the left front directly beneath the buttonholes; slide ready-made belt through carriers at waistline.

Terry Evans

Sewing / COURSE 80

*Conspicuous facings
*Button tab fastenings
*Pattern for a side slit dress:
 adapting the pattern;
 directions for making

Conspicuous facings

These facings are turned to the right side of the garment for a decorative effect. They can be made in a color contrasting with the main fabric, or in plaids or other patterns. If both neck and armhole edges of a garment are to be faced, the facings are applied after the shoulder and side seams have been stitched, and if the neck facings are designed to overlap the arm-hole facings, the latter are applied first. Facings can be made to any width within the area of the garment to be faced, but generally a conspicuous facing is made no narrower than $1\frac{1}{4}$in (3cm). When facing a neck edge and armhole edge, you must reverse shoulder seams under the facing to prevent the raw edges of the seam allowance from showing. If inter-facing is to be used, it is applied to the facing before completion. The facings of the dresses on page 64 have $\frac{5}{8}$in (1.5cm) seam allowances all around.

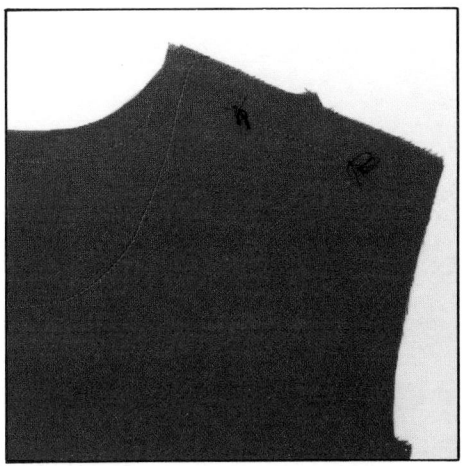

1 Measure the width of the facing at the shoulder and side seam on the garment and mark a point $\frac{3}{8}$in (1cm) inside this measurement (toward the edges). On the wrong side, baste and stitch the shoulder seams from mark to mark; baste and stitch the side seams as far as the mark. Fasten threads securely at each end of the seam.

2 Clip the seam allowance almost to the stitching at the marked points. Press seams open.

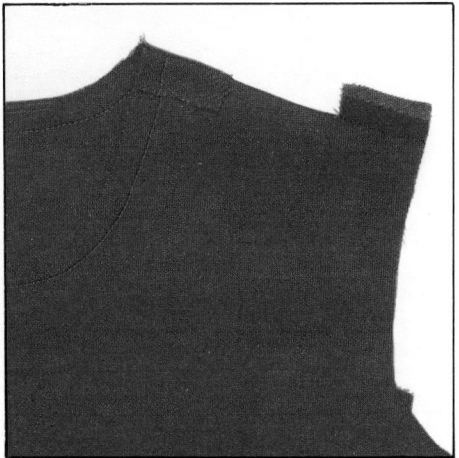

3 Turn the bodice right side out and stitch the remainder of the shoulder and side seams. Press seams open.

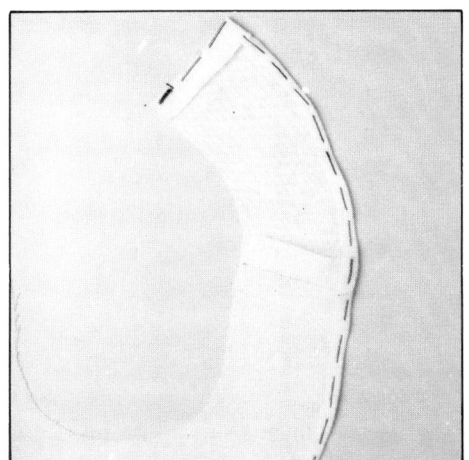

4 With right sides together, baste and stitch the neck facings together at the shoulder seams, and the armhole facings together at the shoulder and underarm seams. Press seams open. Turn under the seam allowance around the outer edge of the facings and baste. Press flat. Do not finish the outer edges at this stage.

5 With **right** side of facings to **wrong** side of garment and center fronts, center backs and shoulder and side seams matching, baste facing to neck and armhole edges. Stitch entire seam. Grade and clip seam allowances.

continued

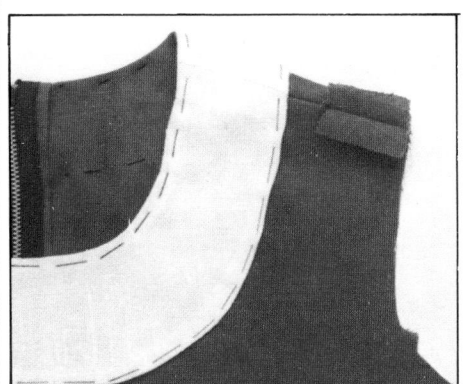

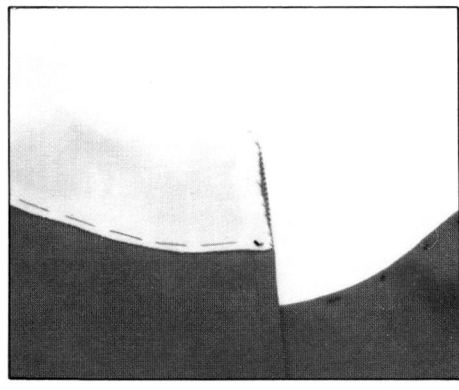

6 Turn the facings to the **right** side and baste close to the stitched seam.

7 If the facing divides at the center back of the garment, turn in the raw edges at the center back and slip stitch them in place.

8 Machine stitch the facings all around $\frac{1}{8}$in (3mm) from the outer edge or slip stitch them to hold them in place. Remove basting stitches and press.

Button tab fastenings

These fastenings are practical as well as pretty. They are very strong[1] and can be used on seam, faced or bound openings. They are easily removed for pressing and can be used for a variety of purposes on clothes and accessories.

As the buttonholes are made in the seamline of the tab, contrasting fabrics can be used for each side, as on the dresses on page 64.

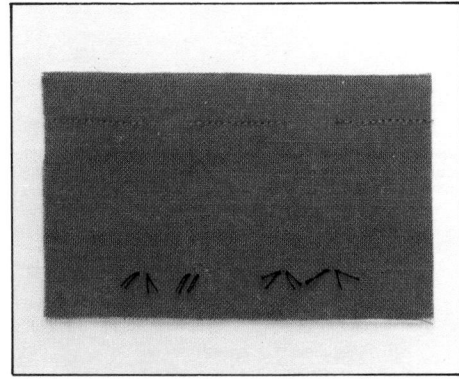

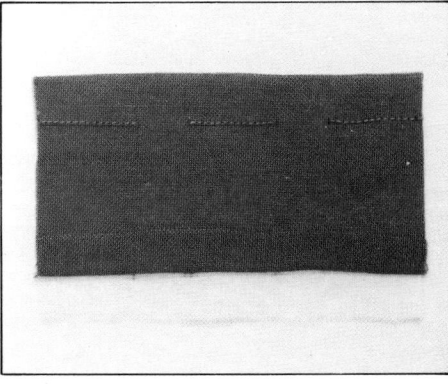

1 Mark the position of the buttonholes and with right sides together, baste and stitch the two tab pieces together along one seam, leaving the seam unstitched at the buttonhole positions. Fasten the thread ends securely. Press seam open.

2 With right sides together, baste and stitch the two tab pieces together along the other seam, leaving open the button-hole positions. Secure the ends and press the seam open.

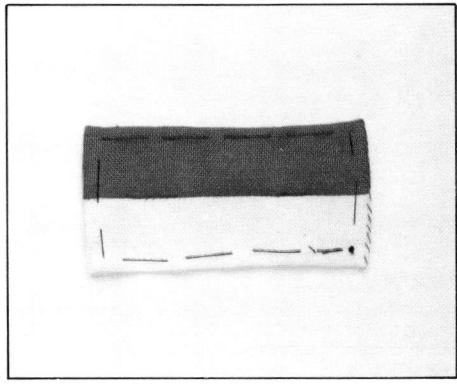

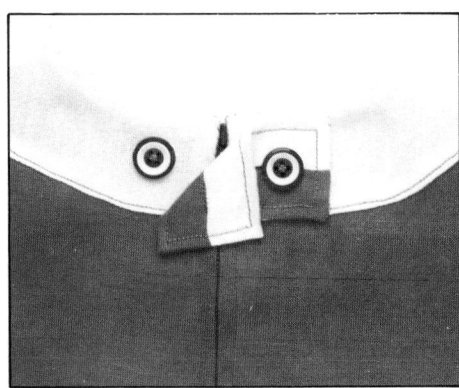

3 Fold the tab so that one seam lies directly over the other. Baste and stitch across one end. Trim seam and cut across corners.

4 Turn tab right side out. Turn in the seam allowance at the open end and slip stitch the edges together. Baste around all edges and press. Slip stitch the two edges of each buttonhole together or machine stitch around each $\frac{1}{8}$in (3mm) from the edge through all thicknesses.

5 Topstitch around the tab, stitching $\frac{1}{4}$in (5mm) in from the edges. Remove basting and press. Position the tab and mark each of the button positions directly underneath the center of the buttonholes. Sew buttons to garment and attach tab.

Side slit dress

Clean lines and sharp colors make this dress stand out in a crowd. The side slit and button tabs provide detail on the skirt.

Adapting the pattern

Measurements
The dress is made by adapting the basic T-shirt pattern from the Stitch by Stitch Pattern Pack, available in sizes 10 to 20, corresponding to sizes 8 to 18 in ready-made clothes.

Materials
2 sheets of tracing paper 36×40in
(90×100cm)
Flexible curve, yardstick

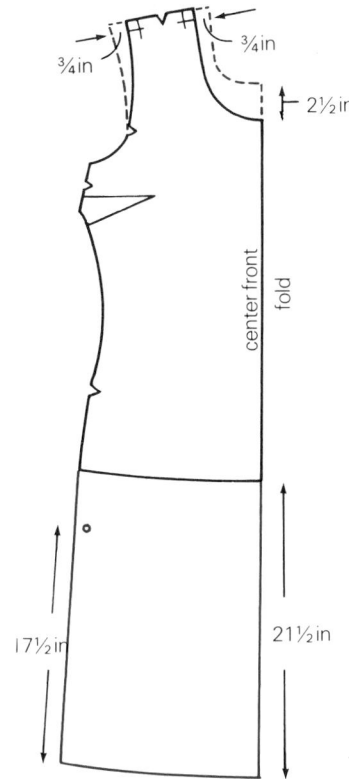

1 For the front pattern, trace the T-shirt front, leaving extra paper at the bottom.
2 To lengthen the pattern, extend the center front line and side cutting line by 21½in (55cm) (or desired length). This measurement includes a ⅝in (1.5cm) hem allowance. The width across the lower edge should measure 12in (30cm) for a size 10; 12½in (31.5cm) for 12; 13in (33cm) for 14; 13½in (34.5cm) for 16; 14in (36cm) for 18; 14½in (37.5cm) for 20. For side slit, measure up side seam 17½in (44cm) from lower edge.
3 To raise the neckline, measure up the center front from the neck cutting line

2½in (6,5cm) and mark. To widen shoulder line, measure out from the neck cutting line ¾in (2cm) and mark. Using a flexible curve, draw the new neck curve from the mark at the shoulder to the mark at center front. Mark seam allowance.
4 At the shoulder seamline, measure out from the armhole cutting line ¾in (2cm) and, using a flexible curve, re-draw the new armhole cutting line, tapering into the original cutting line at the notch. Mark the seam allowance.

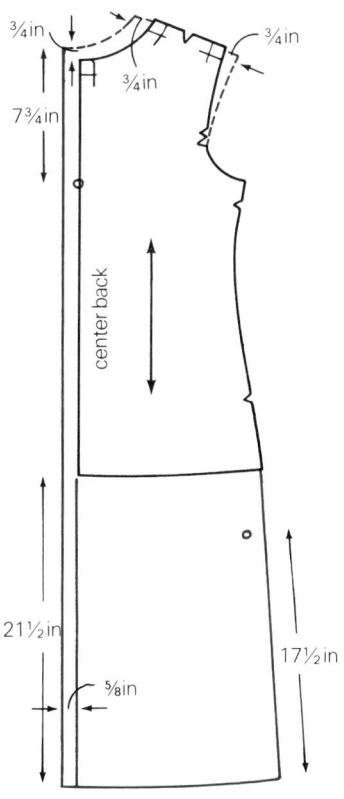

5 For the back pattern, trace the T-shirt back pattern, leaving extra paper at the lower edge for lengthening. Lengthen the pattern using the same measurements and directions as given for the front. The width across the lower edge should be the same as the measurements given for the lower edge of the front pattern. Mark the length of the side slit 17½in (44cm) up from the lower edge. (Note that the side slit will be on the left side only.)
6 To raise the neckline, measure up the center back ¾in (2cm) from neck cutting line and mark. To widen the shoulder line, measure out from the neck cutting line ¾in (2cm) and mark. Using a flexible curve, draw the new back neck cutting line. Mark the seam allowance.
7 Widen the shoulder at the armhole edges as for the front, using the same measurements. Mark the seamlines.
8 Add ⅝in (1.5cm) seam allowance to center back edge. Mark the grain line parallel to the center back. At the center back, mark the bottom of the zipper position 7¾in (19.5cm) below the neck cutting line.

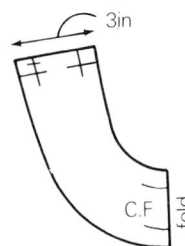
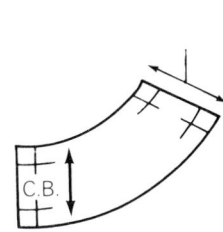

9 For the front and back neck facings, lay tracing paper over the new front and back neck edges. Trace the front and back neck cutting lines and a short distance along the center front, center back and shoulder cutting lines.
10 Measure in from the neck cutting lines 3in (7.5cm) and mark at intervals around the neck edges. Connect these marks to form the outer edge of each facing. The finished width of the facings will be 1¾in (4,5cm). (A ⅝in [1.5cm] seam allowance is included.) Mark center front on a fold and grain lines parallel to center front and center back.

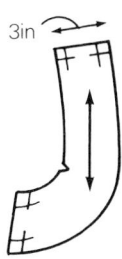
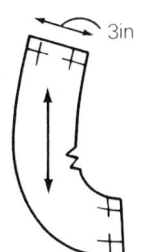

11 For the front and back armhole facings, cut the two pattern pieces, using the same measurements and directions as given for the neck facings. Before removing the tracings, mark the grain lines parallel to the center front and the center back edges.

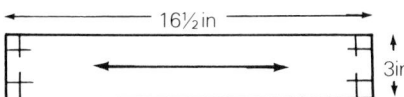

12 For side slit facings, draw a rectangle 16½in (42cm) long by 3in (7.5cm) wide. These measurements include a ⅝in (1.5cm) seam allowance on all edges. Mark the grain lines parallel to long edges.

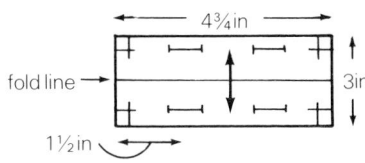

13 For the tab pattern, draw a rectangle 4¾×3in (12×7.5cm). These measurements include ⅝in (1.5cm) seam allowances on all edges. Mark the foldline across the center of the rectangle and mark the seamlines. On the top and bottom seamlines, mark the two buttonhole positions, the center of each being 1½in (4cm) in from side edge.

Rod Delroy

45in-wide fabric with or without nap

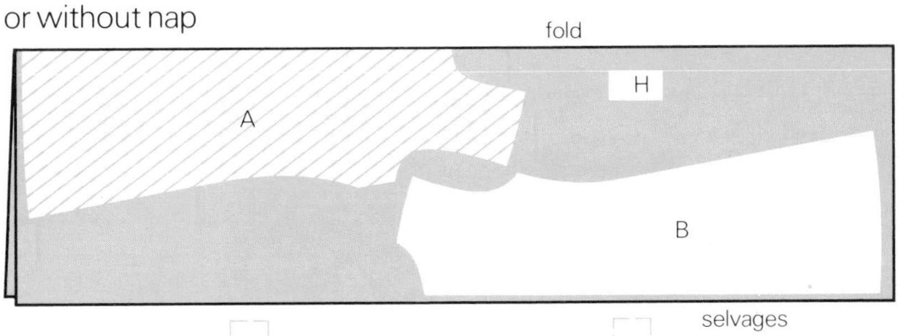

fold

A

H

B

selvages

45in-wide fabric with or without nap (contrasting colors)

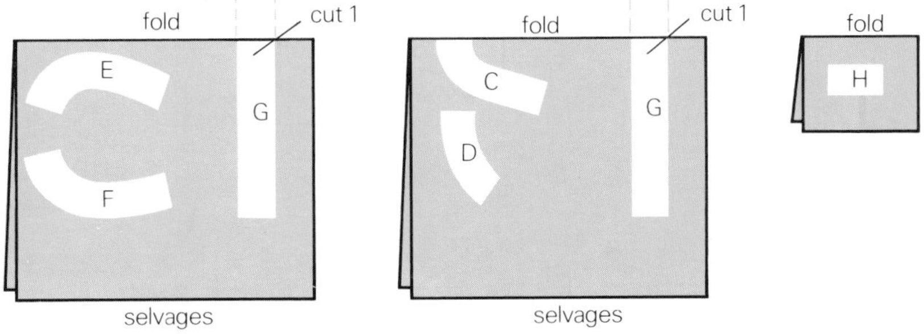

fold   cut 1

E

G

F

selvages

fold   cut 1

C

D

G

selvages

fold

H

Brian Mayor

Interfacing—36in-wide fabric

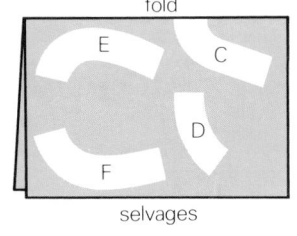

fold

E   C

D

F

selvages

Key to adapted pattern pieces

A Dress front   Cut 1 on fold, main color

B Dress back   Cut 2, main color

C Front neck facing   Cut 1 on fold, contrast X

D Back neck facing   Cut 2, contrast X

E Front armhole facing   Cut 2, contrast Y

F Back armhole facing   Cut 2, contrast Y

G Side slit facing   Cut 1 of X and Y

H Tab   Cut 4, 2 main, 2 of Z (or X and Y)

Interfacing: Use pieces **C** Cut 1 on fold, **D** Cut 2, **E** Cut 2, **F** Cut 2.

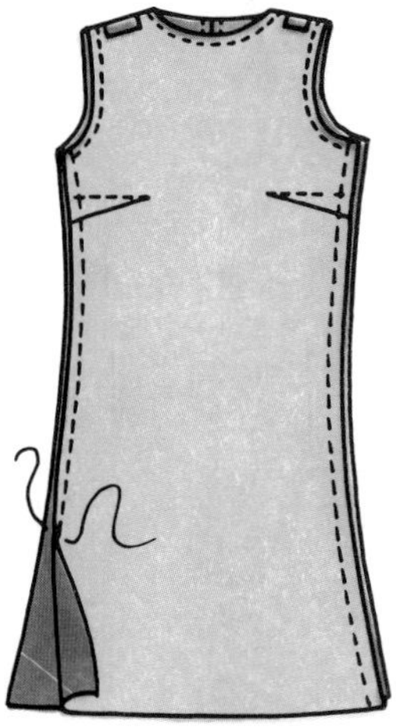

Directions for making

Suggested fabrics

Cotton or synthetic knits, poplin, ciré, satin, crepe.

Materials

Dress

45in (115cm)-wide fabric with or without nap:

    Size 10: $2\frac{7}{8}$yd (2.6m)

    Size 12: $3\frac{1}{8}$yd (2.8m)

    Size 14: $3\frac{3}{8}$yd (3m)

    Size 16: $3\frac{1}{2}$yd (3.1m)

    Sizes 18, 20: $3\frac{3}{4}$yd (3.4m)

Contrasting facings and tabs

45in (115cm)-wide fabric with or without nap:

    For all sizes: $\frac{1}{2}$yd (.4m) of colors X, Y, $\frac{1}{8}$yd (.1m) of color Z (optional)

36in (90cm)-wide interfacing: For all sizes: $\frac{3}{4}$yd (.7m)

Matching thread

7in (18cm) zipper

Four $\frac{1}{2}$in (1.3cm) buttons

Hook and eye

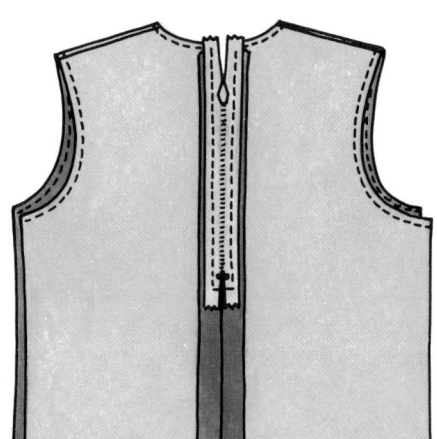

1 Stay-stitch neck and armhole edges. With right sides together, baste and stitch the center back seam to the bottom of zipper opening. Press seam open. Insert zipper into center back opening, placing zipper 1in (2.5cm) down from the top edge.

2 Fold, baste and stitch front bust darts. Press darts downward. With wrong sides together, baste and stitch shoulder seams as shown on page 61. Press seams open.

3 With right sides together, baste and stitch side seams, leaving left side seam open for the slit. Reverse seams at armhole edges as shown on page 61.

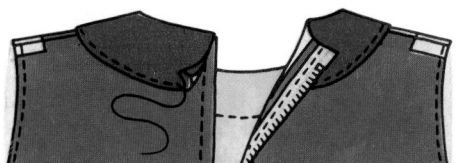

4 Trim away the seam allowance all around the outer edge of the neck interfacing and baste interfacing to the wrong side of neck and armhole facings. Make and apply facings to the neck and armhole edges as shown on page 61. Complete the center back of the neck facing by turning in raw edges and slip stitching down as shown on page 62.

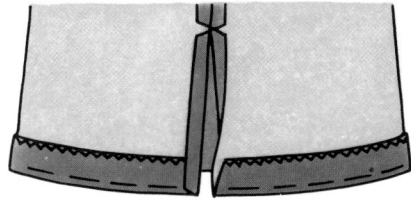

5 Turn up the hem allowance and complete the hem, using the most suitable method for the fabric being used. Press. Clip side seam above slit.

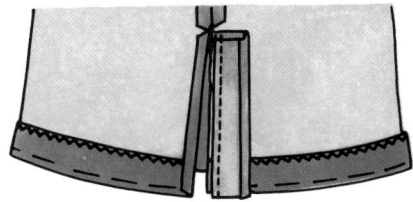

6 With right side of facing to wrong side of the fabric, baste and stitch facings to

both sides of the slit, taking a $\frac{5}{8}$in (1.5cm) allowance. The lower edge of the facing overlaps the hemmed edge by $\frac{5}{8}$in (1.5cm); this is turned under later.

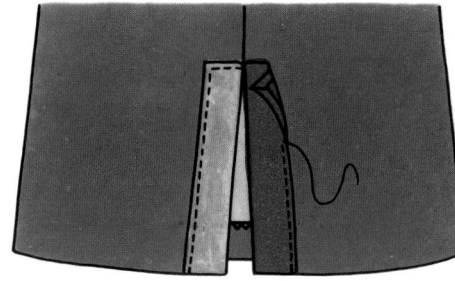

7 Press seam allowance toward facings and turn facings to the right side. Turn under the seam allowance at the top and bottom edges of the facing and press. Baste along stitched edge and baste the facings flat to garment. Stitch the facings in place by machine or by hand as shown on page 62. Remove basting. Press gently from the right side, using a press cloth to avoid marking.

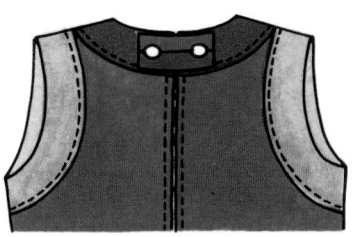

8 Sew hook and eye to the inside of the center back opening at the top edge. Make two tabs as shown on page 62. Pin one tab at the top of the center back seam and mark the two button positions at each end.

9 Pin the second tab to the top of the slit and mark for buttons. Sew buttons in place and fasten.

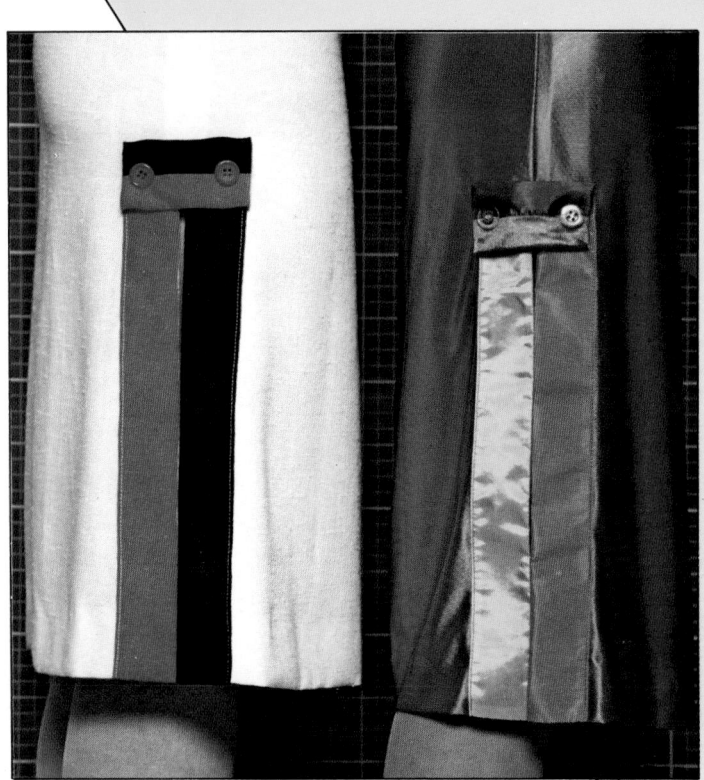

*Methods of shirring
*Pattern for a jacket and
 jumpsuit:
 adapting the pattern;
 directions for making

Methods of shirring

Shirring with elastic is an excellent method of controlling fullness and can be used as a design detail on cuffs, yokes, waistlines, ruffles and larger areas such as bodices and sleeves, or the hip area of skirts and pants, as on the jumpsuit on page 69.

Fabrics such as voile, crepe or soft satin are better for shirring than hard, firm fabrics. The crosswise grain is more easily shirred than the lengthwise grain. A useful tool for keeping the rows of shirring evenly spaced is a quilting guide; for closely spaced rows, use the edge of the presser foot.

Shirring with elastic in the bobbin

Shirring with elastic in the bobbin is a quick method and produces strong, even stitches. It is useful for closely spaced rows—$\frac{1}{4}$in-$\frac{1}{2}$in (5mm-1.3cm) apart, as on the jumpsuit on page 69. Wind the shirring elastic on the bobbin by hand without stretching it. Use ordinary thread on the top—polyester is preferable, since it does not break as easily as cotton thread. Set the tension at normal and the stitch length to 15 stitches to every 2in (5cm) (use longer stitches for tighter shirring). Always test the fullness on a scrap of fabric and, if the shirring is not tight enough, rewind the bobbin. To tighten shirring after stitching, secure the elastic threads at one side and pull the threads at the other end until the piece is gathered evenly to the required length. Fasten ends securely.

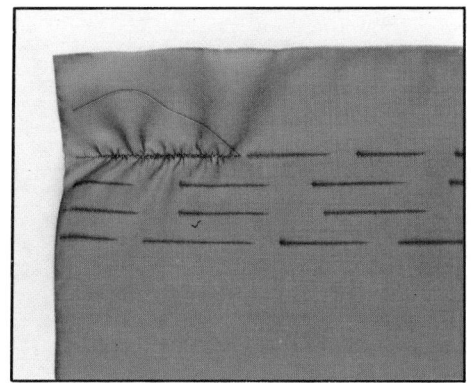

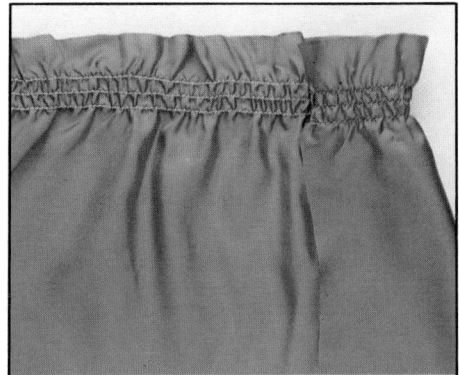

1 Press the fabric and, if necessary, mark the lines on the right side of the fabric. Working from the right side, stitch along each marked row. If the rows are $\frac{1}{4}$in (5mm) apart, use the edge of the presser foot as a guide.

2 When stitching the second and all following rows, stretch the fabric to the original width on the previous row so that the shirring will be even. At the end of the shirring, tie the elastic and threads firmly together or stitch down to hold.

Shirring with couched cording elastic

This method is useful for an individual row of gathering such as at a wrist or waistline, because it is strong. Extra gathers can be made by pulling the ends of the elastic to the size required. Shirring elastic or special cording elastic can be used (the latter will give a firmer, stronger effect).

Secure one end of the elastic with catch-stitching or with a safety pin.

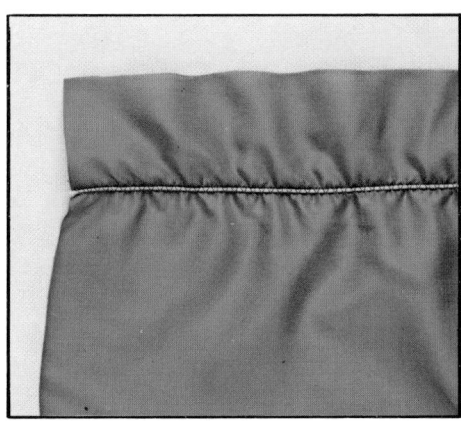

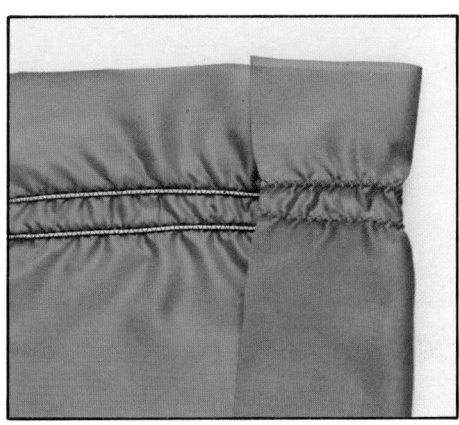

1 Secure one end of the elastic and lay it in place on the wrong side of the fabric. Holding the elastic in place and stretching it gently as you work, zig-zag over it to hold it down. Do not stitch through the elastic; this would make it impossible to adjust the gathers.

2 When stitching the next and all following rows, stretch the elastic of the previous rows, so that the fabric lies flat. A useful method is to cut the elastic for all the rows to the finished length before stitching. When shirring is complete, tie off ends or stitch down.

Simon Butcher

Shirring using $\frac{1}{4}$ in (5mm) elastic

This is the strongest of all the methods of shirring and is best used over one or two rows only—for example, at cuffs, on sleeves or on the ankles of pants.

Cut the flat $\frac{1}{4}$ in (5mm)-wide elastic to the finished length plus about an inch (a few centimeters) extra and stitch it to the wrong side of the fabric, stretching it to fit the width. If the elastic is for a waistline, divide it in half and pin one half to the front and one to the back of the garment. Work the shirring on each piece separately before completing the garment. The elastic is stitched in before any seams are joined.

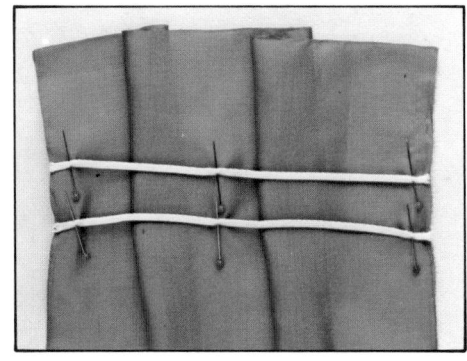

1 Mark the center of each length of elastic and the center of the piece to be shirred. Pin the elastic to the wrong side of the fabric, matching these points. Pin the sides and other points if gathering a long length of fabric.

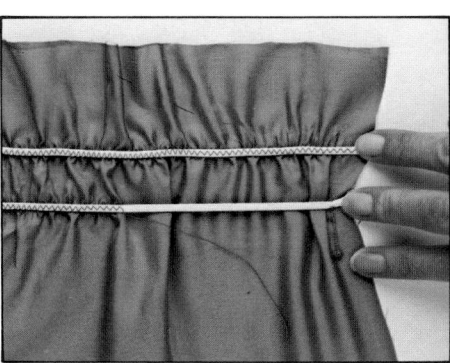

2 Begin zig-zag stitching at the center of the elastic (it should be wide enough almost to cross the elastic), stretching the elastic to fit the fabric piece as it is being stitched. Keep the fabric flat at all times. The elastic ends will be sewn into the seams.

Jacket and jumpsuit

This glamorous outfit is made in a silky fabric.

Adapting the pattern

Measurements
The jacket and jumpsuit are made by adapting the basic dress, jacket and pants from the Stitch by Stitch Pattern Pack, available in sizes 10 to 20, corresponding to sizes 8 to 18 in ready-made clothes.

Materials
4 sheets of tracing paper 36×40in (90×100cm)
Flexible curve; triangle; yardstick

Jacket

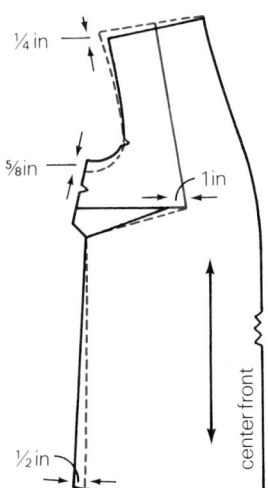

1 For the jacket front, trace the jacket front pattern. Raise and widen the shoulder by $\frac{1}{4}$ in (5mm) at armhole edge. Taper the new lines into the original shoulder cutting line at the neck edge and armhole cutting line at the notch.
2 Lower armhole by $\frac{5}{8}$ in (1.5cm) at side seam. Re-draw armhole, using a flexible curve, to join this point to notch.
3 Straighten the side seams by measuring in $\frac{1}{2}$ in (1.3cm) from side cutting line at lower edge. Draw the new cutting line, tapering into the original line at dart line.
4 The bust dart allowance is transferred to the shoulder line: extend top dart line by 1in (2.5cm) and draw lower dart line to meet this point; draw a line from here to halfway along the shoulder.

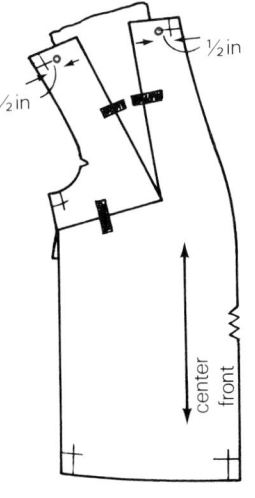

5 Slash along this line to the dart point.

Close the side bust dart by folding so the dart lines match, and tape in place. This will open the pattern at the shoulder. Insert paper behind the slash and tape it in place.

Mark the gathering positions on the shoulder line $\frac{1}{2}$ in (1.3cm) in from the armhole and neck seamlines.

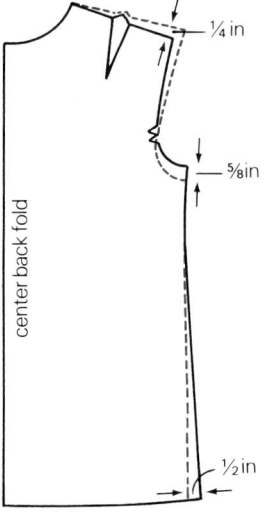

John Hutchinson

6 For the jacket back, trace the jacket back pattern. Raise and widen the shoulder line, lower the armhole at the side seam and straighten the side seam, using the same measurements and directions as given for the jacket front.
Note The front and back neck facings are unchanged.

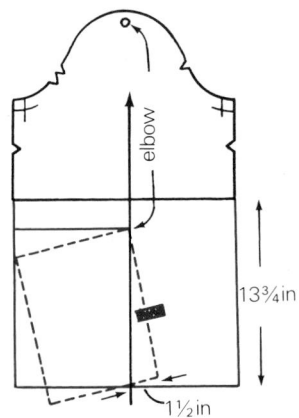

7 For the sleeve pattern, trace the basic sleeve, leaving extra paper at the lower edge to lengthen. Extend side cutting lines down by 13¾in (35cm) for a size 10, adding an extra ¼in (5mm) to this measurement for each larger size. This includes a 2in (5cm) hem allowance. Connect the two side edges for new hem edge. Extend the grain line.

8 Measure from the center point of your shoulder (at the top of the arm) down to the elbow point (bending the arm slightly), and mark this length on grain line, starting from sleeve cap.

9 Slash to the grain line at this point and slash the grain line from the lower edge to the elbow point, but do not cut through it. Overlap this section of the pattern to the front by 1½in (4cm) as shown to open underarm seam.

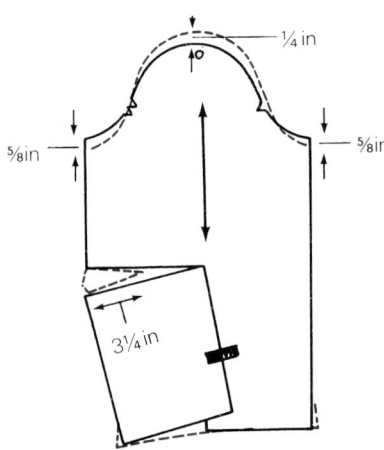

10 Mark a point in the center of the elbow opening 3¼in (8.5cm) from underarm cutting line. Join this point to each side of the opening on the underarm cutting line for the elbow dart. Fold the dart into place and cut along the cutting line to shape the end of the dart as shown.

11 Smooth out the lower edge of the sleeve and shape the side edges of the hem allowance by folding this in place and cutting along the side edges. Open out to see the shaping.

12 Raise sleeve cap by ¼in (5mm) and lower underarm curves by ⅝in (1.5cm) to fit the enlarged armhole. Re-draw the underarm curves and sleeve cap.

13 Before cutting out the sleeve, check that the measurement around the sleeve cap seamline is ¾in (2cm) larger than measurement of front and back jacket armholes. The extra ¾in (2cm) is for ease allowance. Adjust if necessary.

Jumpsuit

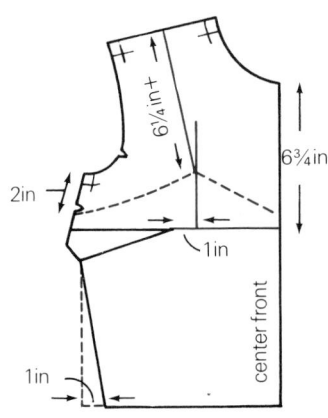

1 For the front bodice, mark the waistline on the basic dress pattern, and trace the top part to the waistline, omitting the waist dart. Extend the top bust dart line to center front and mark a point 1in (2.5cm) along this line from dart point. Draw a vertical line up at this point.

2 From the middle of the shoulder line draw a line to meet the vertical line, making it 6¼in (16cm) long for a size 10, adding an extra ¼in (5mm) for each larger size.

3 Measure down the center front line from neck cutting line 6¾in (17cm) for a size 10 and mark, adding an extra ¼in (5mm) to this measurement for each larger size.

4 At the armhole, measure down the side seam from armhole cutting line 2in (5cm) and mark. Draw the new armhole and neckline, connecting side, bust and front at the marks as shown. The line from side seam to bust should be curved.

5 Make the waistline larger by adding 1in (2.5cm) to side seam edge, tapering the new cutting line into the original cutting line at the lower dart line.

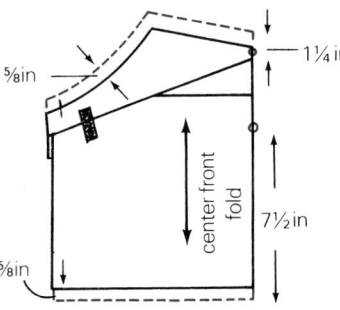

6 Slash along the horizontal line from center front to dart point. Close the side bust dart and tape in place. This will open the pattern at the center front edge. Insert and tape paper behind the slash.

Straighten the center front edge over the bustline so that this can be placed on a fold.

7 Add ⅝in (1.5cm) seam allowance to armhole, neck and waistline edges. Mark the grain line parallel to the center front and mark center front on a fold. For the gathering positions, measure up the center front seamline from the lower edge 7½in (19cm) and mark. Add ¼in (5mm) to this measurement for each larger size. Measure down the center front seamline from the neck cutting line 1¼in (3cm) and mark. The section between the marks is gathered up to about 2¼in (5.5cm).

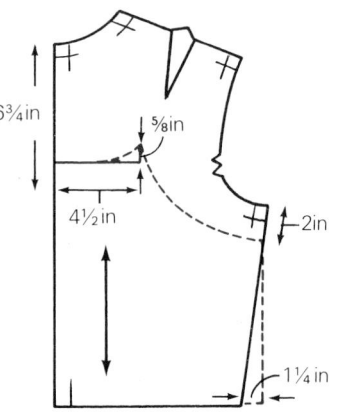

8 For the back bodice pattern, mark the waistline to correspond with the front pattern on the basic dress back. Trace the top part of the dress, omitting the waist dart.

9 For the new neck and armhole shaping, measure down the center back from the back neck cutting line 6¾in (17cm) for a size 10, adding an extra ¼in (5mm) to this measurement for each larger size. Draw a line at this point in from the center back at right angles to the grain line. The line should measure 4½in (11cm) for a size 10 add ⅜in [1cm] extra for each larger size). At the end of this line, draw a line upward for ⅝in (1.5cm).

10 Lower the armhole at the side seam as directed for the front. Using a flexible curve, draw the new neck and armhole edges, curving the lines as shown. Make the waistline larger by adding 1¼in (3cm) to side seam edge, tapering into the original cutting line at the armhole.

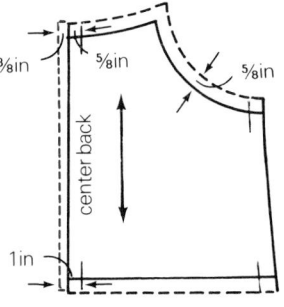

11 Add ⅝in (1.5cm) seam allowance to new neck and armhole edge and waistline

edge; add an extra $\frac{3}{8}$in (1cm) along center back edge (1in [2.5cm] seam allowance).

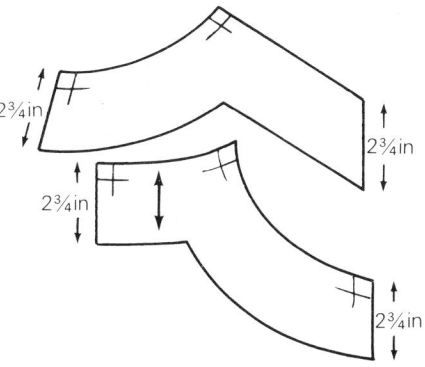

12 For the front and back neck facings, lay tracing paper over the front and back neck and armhole edges. Trace the neck and armhole cutting lines, the center front and center back edges and side seam cutting lines to a depth of $2\frac{3}{4}$in (7cm). Draw the outer edges of the facings, keeping the facings an even depth of $2\frac{3}{4}$in (7cm) all around. Mark seam allowances and grain lines parallel to center back and center front as shown. Mark that center front is on a fold.

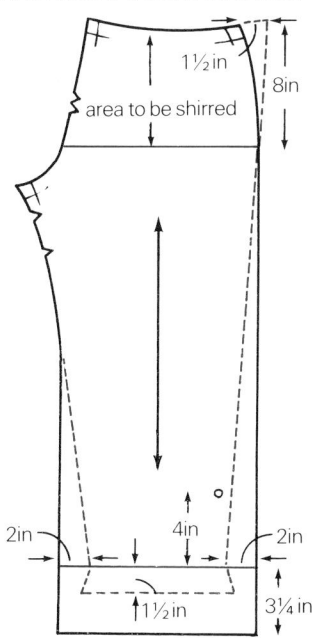

13 Trace the pants back pattern, omitting the waist dart. Mark the hip line 8in (20.5cm) below waist cutting line. At the waist seamline measure out from the side cutting line $1\frac{1}{2}$in (4cm) and draw the new cutting line from this point, tapering into the original cutting line at the hipline.

14 At the lower edge, measure up the inside and outside leg edges $3\frac{1}{4}$in (8.5cm) and draw a line across the pattern. Measure in 2in (5cm) along this line from inside and outside leg cutting lines and mark these points. Re-draw the inside leg cutting line from the mark at the lower edge, tapering into the original line at hip.

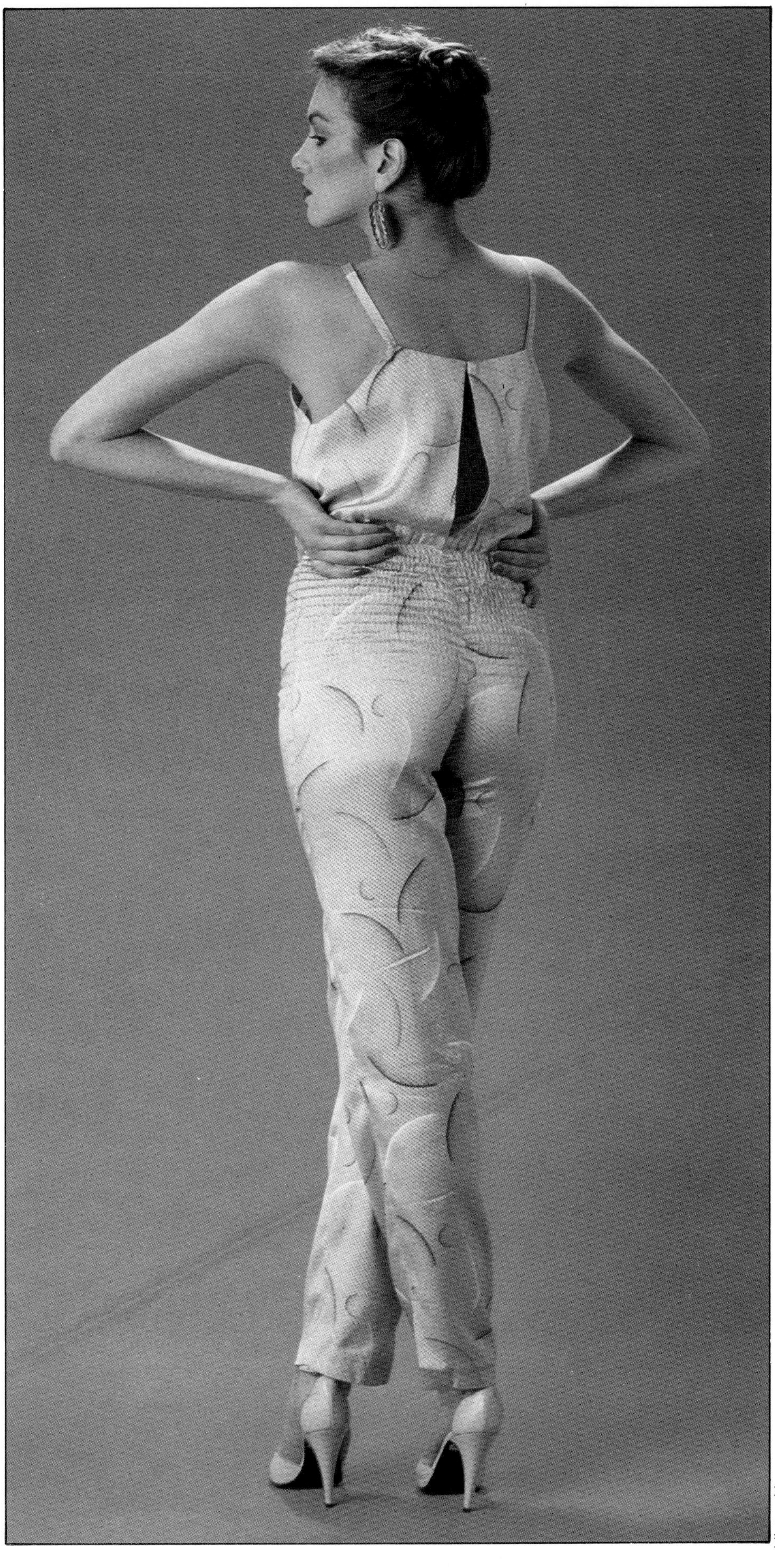

John Hutchinson

Victor Yuan

15 Add 1½in (4cm) hem allowance to lower edge. To shape the side edges of the hem allowance, fold the hem up along the hemline and trace the side edges. Open out the hem allowance to see the shaping. Cut around the pattern along the new lines. Mark a point 4in (10cm) from hem on the side for slit.

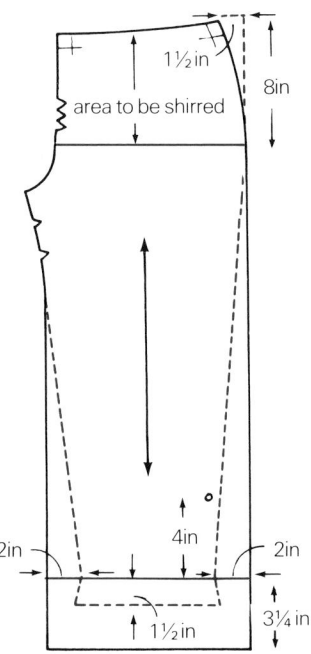

16 For the pants front pattern, trace the basic pants front, omitting the waist dart. Mark the hipline 8in (20.5cm) below the waist cutting line. At the waist seamline, measure out from side seam cutting line 1½in (4cm) and draw the cutting line down, tapering into the original cutting line at the hip. Continue to alter the pattern piece using the same measurements and directions as given for the back.

17 For bodice straps cut two strips 2 × 29½in (5 × 75cm) on straight grain. Finished width is ⅜in (1cm) (⅝in [1.5cm] seam allowances included).

Directions for making

Suggested fabrics

Polyester, rayon or silk crepe, lightweight synthetic or cotton knits, satin or slub-weave rayon.

Materials

45in (115cm)-wide fabric with or without nap:
Sizes 10, 12: 5¾yd (5.2m)
Sizes 14, 16: 6yd (5.4m)
Sizes 18, 20: 6¼yd (5.6m)
36in (90cm)-wide interfacing: for all sizes 1⅛yd (1m). (If interfacing jumpsuit facings, allow extra fabric)
Matching thread; shirring elastic
2 hooks and eyes
Bias binding (optional)
5½yd (5m) seam binding
Batting for shoulder pads; flexible curve; pattern paper

Key to adapted pattern pieces

A	Jacket back	Cut 1 on fold
B	Jacket front	Cut 2
C	Sleeve	Cut 2
D	Front facing (jacket)	Cut 2
E	Back neck facing (jacket)	Cut 1 on fold
F	Bodice front	Cut 1 on fold
G	Bodice back	Cut 2
H	Front facing	Cut 1 on fold
I	Back facing	Cut 2
J	Pants back	Cut 2
K	Pants front	Cut 2

Interfacing: Use pieces **D** Cut 2, **E** Cut 1 on fold, **H** and **I** (optional), cut as for facings of bodice. See Volume 3, page 70 for jacket interfacing layout.

Cutting layout for 45in-wide fabric with or without nap: all sizes

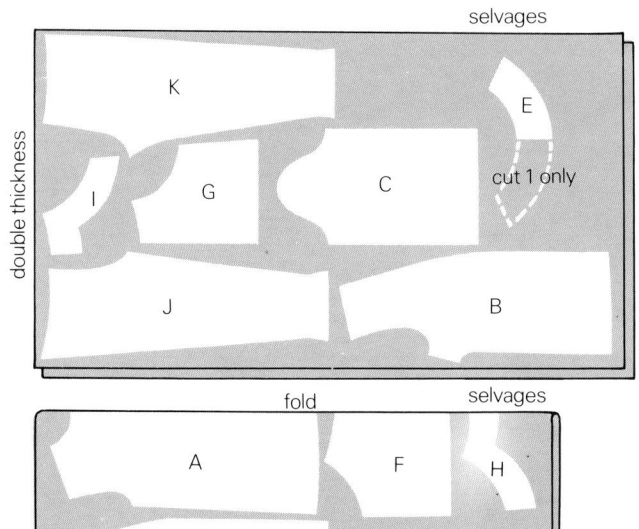

Jacket

1 Stay-stitch the front and back neck edges of the jacket and front and back jacket facings. Run two rows of gathering stitches along each front shoulder between marks indicated on the pattern.

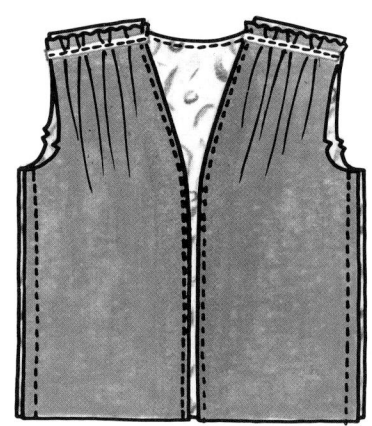

2 With right sides together, pin the fronts to the back at the shoulder seams, pulling up the gathers until the shoulder edges are the same. Cut a length of seam binding for each shoulder edge and baste this to the gathered front shoulder edges.

3 Stitch the shoulder seams, stitching along the center of the tape. Finish seam allowances and press seams open. With right sides together, baste and stitch the side seams. Finish the seams and press them open.

4 Baste interfacing to wrong sides of facings. With right sides together, baste and stitch the front and back neck facings together at the shoulders. Press seams open. Finish the outer edges of the facings. Press. Apply the facings to the neck edges as directed in Volume 4, page 55.

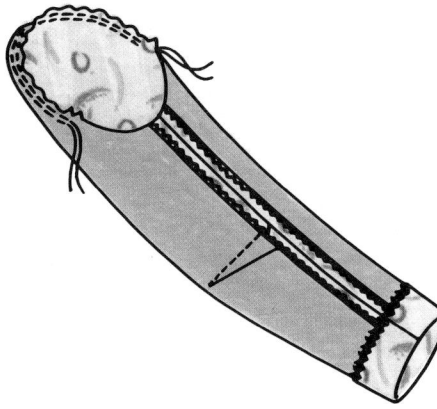

5 Prepare the sleeve caps for easing, fold, baste and stitch the elbow darts. Press darts downward. Baste and stitch the underarm seams of sleeves, with right sides together. Finish and press seams open. Turn up and complete hems, using a suitable method.

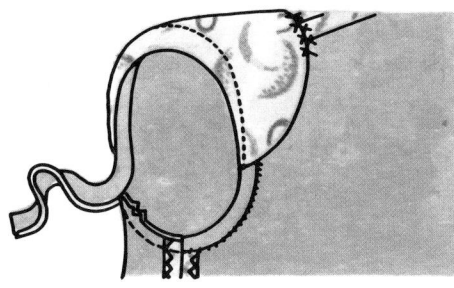

6 Pin, baste and stitch the sleeves into the armholes with sleeves lying on top. Press the seam allowances toward the sleeves and clip the curved edges. Trim the seam allowances and finish with zig-zag stitch or bias binding.

7 Make two shoulder pads as directed in Volume 9, page 60. From scraps of the main fabric, cut two pieces 1 in (2.5cm) larger all around than each pad. Fold edges under and catch-stitch the fabric to the pads all around so that the right side of the pad is completely covered by fabric. Insert the pads into the shoulders of the jacket as shown in Volume 9, page 61, with the fabric-covered part outward.

8 Try the jacket on and mark the hem. Open out the front facings and hem all around, using a method suitable for the fabric.

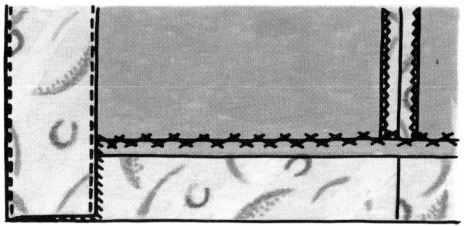

9 Turn the front facings back to the wrong side and slip stitch to the hem edge.
Note When complete, the jacket can be fastened at the front edges with a decorative brooch or pin.

Jumpsuit

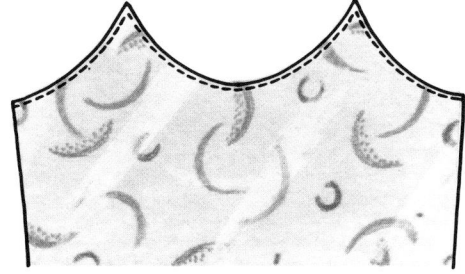

1 Stay-stitch the front and back neck and armhole edges of the bodice and facing.

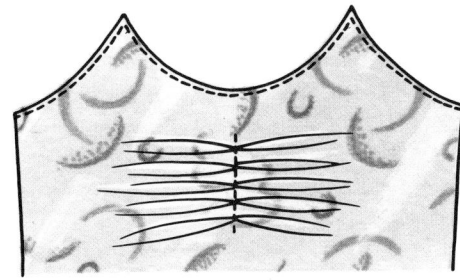

2 Working from the right side, gather the center front between the marks on the pattern, using shirring elastic in the bobbin as shown on page 67, or run two rows of gathering threads, using a smaller stitch than normal, and pull up to $2\frac{1}{4}$ in (5.5cm). Secure all thread ends firmly on the wrong side.

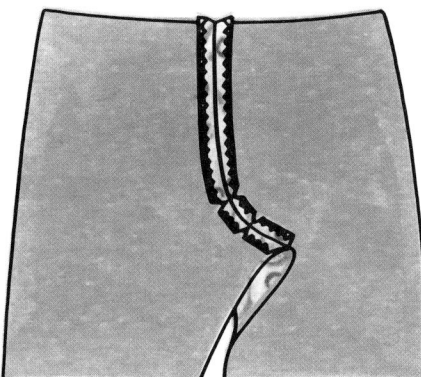

3 With right sides together, pin, baste and stitch the front crotch seam. Clip curves and press seam open. Finish seams with zig-zag stitch.

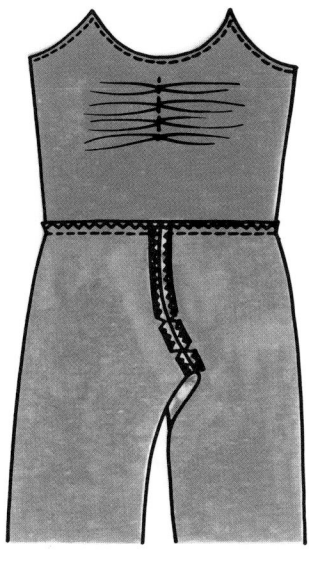

4 With right sides together and center fronts matching, pin, baste and stitch the waistline of the bodice front to the pants fronts. Finish the seam allowances together and press them upward.

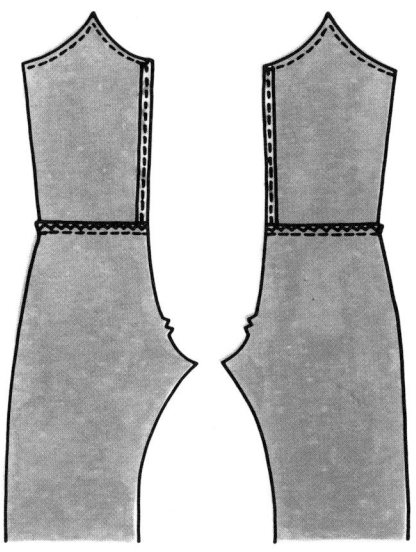

Terry Evans

5 Turn $\frac{3}{8}$ in (1cm) to wrong side of the center backs of the bodices and baste. With right sides together, pin, baste and stitch bodice backs to pants backs, matching center backs and side edges. Finish seam allowances together and press them upward.

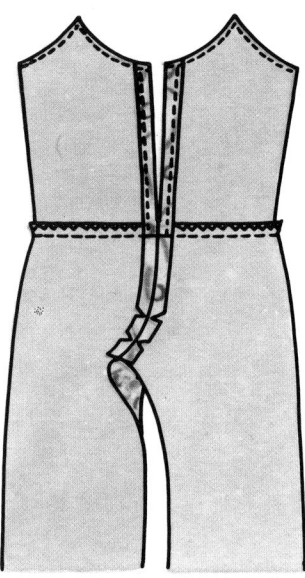

6 With right sides together, pin, baste and stitch back crotch seam; secure thread ends carefully at waistline. Clip curves and press seam open. Finish with zig-zag stitch. Press center back bodice seam allowances down $\frac{5}{8}$in (1.5cm) on each side.

7 With right sides together, pin, baste and stitch side seams from armholes to pants hems just above marks indicated on pattern. Press seams open and finish. Finish slit openings by slip stitching down edges.

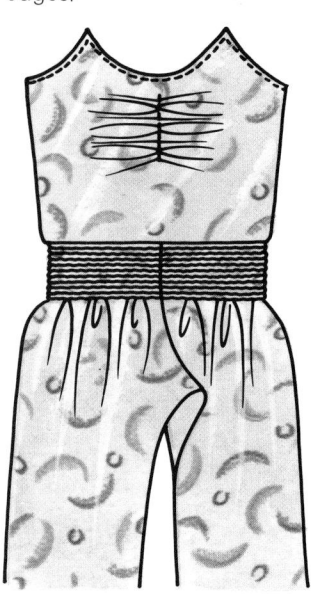

8 Using a suitable method (see page 2139), complete the shirring of the marked area from waistline to hips in rows approximately $\frac{1}{2}$in (1.5cm) apart. Work from whichever side of the fabric is appropriate for the shirring method being used. Keep the lines parallel and start and end at the center back. Secure all thread and elastic ends. For extra strength, the elastic ends can be caught into the rows of stitching on each side of the center back seam.

9 With right sides together, pin, baste and stitch the inner leg seam all around from crotch to leg hems. Reinforce with seam binding if necessary over crotch area. Press seam open, clip curves and finish raw edges.

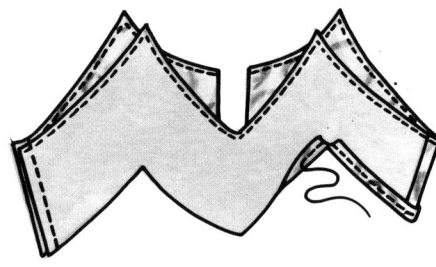

10 With right sides together, pin, baste and stitch front and back facings together at side seams. Press seams open, and turn in $\frac{1}{4}$in (5mm) all around outer edge of facing. Stitch close to edge or finish with zig-zag stitch. If turning in edges, clip inner and outer corners so that the facing lies flat.

11 With right sides together, baste and stitch seams of shoulder straps, reinforcing with seam binding if necessary, as shown. Trim seam to $\frac{1}{4}$in (5mm); turn right side out. Finished width of strap is $\frac{3}{8}$in (1cm).

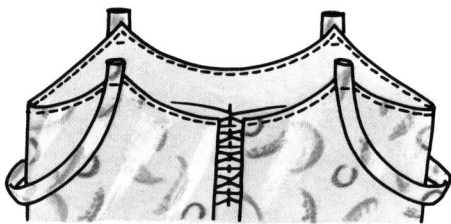

12 Baste each strap to the right side of the front and back bodices as shown. Try on jumpsuit and adjust strap length if necessary.

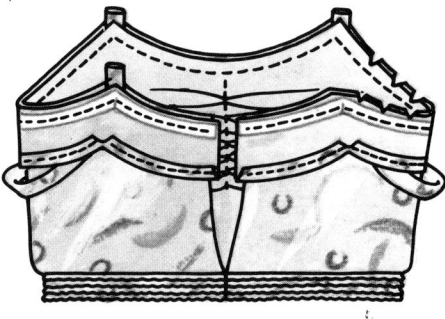

13 With right sides together and center fronts, center backs and side seams matching, baste the facing to the top edge of the bodice, using seam binding (if fabric is very flimsy, interface the facings). Stitch facings in place, securing straps

in the stitching.

14 Trim seams, clip curves and corners. Press seam allowance toward facing and understitch, stitching as far as possible into the corners.

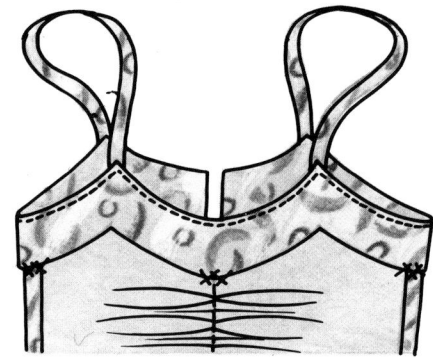

15 Turn the facings to the inside and baste around stitched edges. Catch-stitch the facings to the center front and side seams. Press. Turn in facings at center back and slip stitch to center back seam allowance. Slip stitch seam allowances to back bodices or machine-stitch close to the edges through all thicknesses. Remove the basting.

16 Try on the jumpsuit and mark the bottom hems. Hem the pants using a method suitable for the fabric. At the top edge of the center back opening, sew a hook and eye. Sew a hook and eye to the center back waistline immediately above the shirring. If you prefer, a zipper can be inserted at the center back from neck to waistline.

Sewing / COURSE 82

Applying rickrack to a hem edge

This method will finish and decorate a hem edge in one step and is useful as a quick edging. If the fabric is very lightweight, the hem can be turned under twice before the rickrack is applied, and will therefore be stronger. On thicker fabrics turn the hem under only once. The rickrack should be wide enough to cover the raw edges on the wrong side and then extend out past the edge of the hem for decoration.

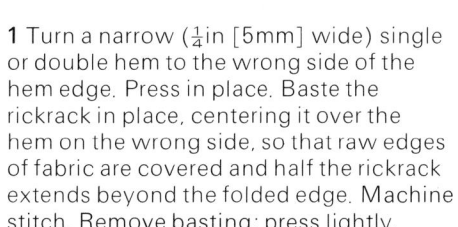

1 Turn a narrow ($\frac{1}{4}$in [5mm] wide) single or double hem to the wrong side of the hem edge. Press in place. Baste the rickrack in place, centering it over the hem on the wrong side, so that raw edges of fabric are covered and half the rickrack extends beyond the folded edge. Machine stitch. Remove basting; press lightly.

2 Where the rickrack needs to be joined, cut extra length and turn in the raw ends, then slip stitch folded edges together before the final machine-stitching.

Inserting rickrack in a faced edge

This is a pretty way to finish an edge, which also gives body and strength to the seamline. It is possible to omit interfacing the edge when using this method. The rickrack should be cut to the measurement of the edge to be decorated, plus an inch or so (a few centimeters) extra for seam allowance. If applying to a curved edge or one with corners, allow extra for easing or mitering.

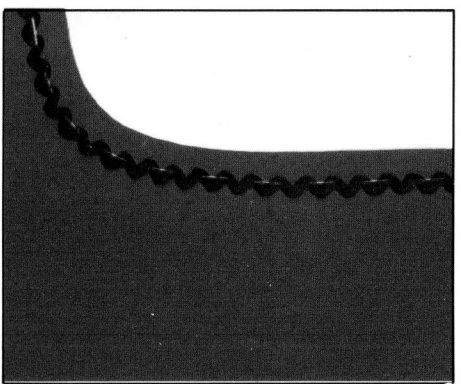

1 Mark the seamline of the edge to be decorated. Center the rickrack over the seamline of this edge on the right side and baste down. Ease gently over curved edges, and miter corners.

2 If decorating a faced opening, spread out the opening to make a straight line and cross the rickrack over at the ends before basting the facing, right side down, on top. The raw ends of the rickrack will go toward the raw ends of the facing. The rickrack and the seam will be tapered at the end of the opening.

continued

Simon Butcher

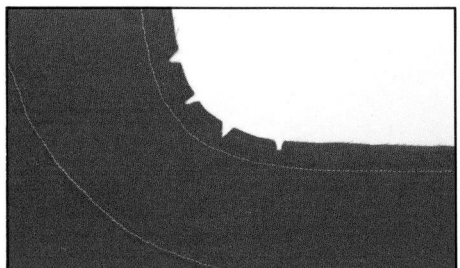

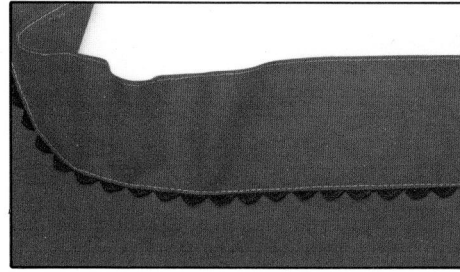

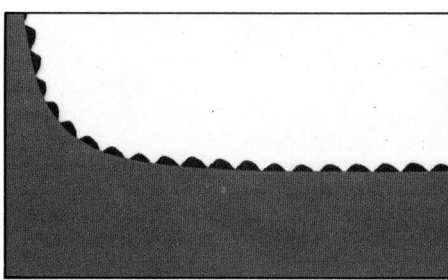

3 Make the facing and finish the outer edge. Baste and stitch to the main garment on the inner edge seamline through all thicknesses, right sides together. Clip and grade seam.

4 Understitch the facing, keeping the rickrack clear of the stitching. On an opening, check that the end is lying flat before understitching.

5 Press the piece; turn facing to the inside and press again so that the rickrack stands up along the edge. Catch-stitch the facings to the garment over seam allowances.

Five embroidery stitches

These are some of the most often-used embroidery stitches. Chain stitch can be used either for outlines or for fillings; many folk embroideries are worked entirely in chain stitch. The related lazy daisy stitch makes flower petals, with French knots often used for the centers. Scattered French knots give little pinpoints of color; massed together, they give a nubby texture to the surface. Stem stitch is ideal for outlines. The angle at which it is worked can be varied slightly to produce lines of varying thickness. Long and short stitch is used for fillings, as for large petals and leaves, and is often worked in two or more shades of one color. A good deal of practice is needed in order to work it successfully, especially if the area has a rounded shape.

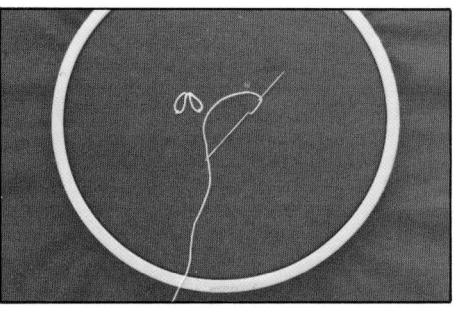

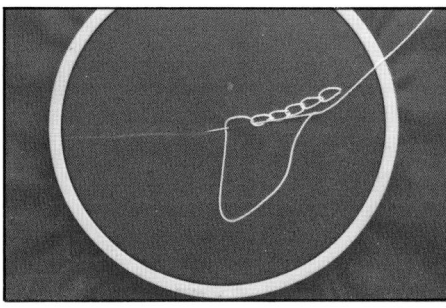

1 To work a lazy daisy stitch, bring the needle through to the right side of the fabric at the base of the first petal. Make a loop and hold it down with the left thumb. Insert needle into the same point from the right side and bring the needle out at the tip of the petal and secure with a small stitch. Work each petal in the same way so that the base of each one forms a small ring.

2 To work chain stitch: start on the wrong side; leave a long thread to work with and bring the needle through on the outline. Holding the loop down with the left thumb, insert the needle into the line at the same point as it came out, bringing it out a short distance along the line and over the loop. Pull needle to tighten stitch. Repeat, inserting needle just inside last chain.

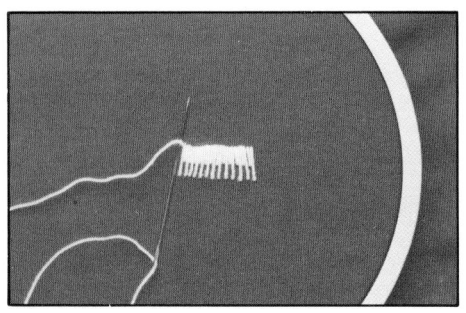

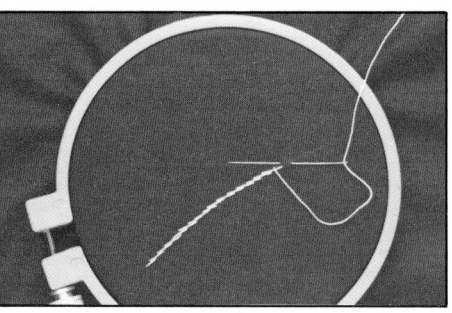

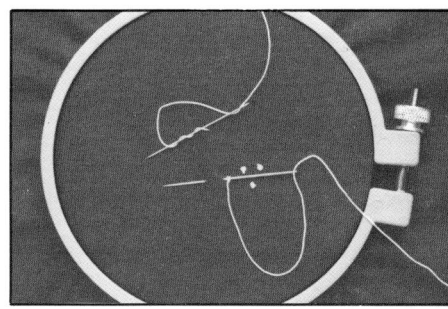

3 Work the first row of long and short stitch on the outer edge of the area to be filled. Alternately work long stitches— about $\frac{3}{8}$-$\frac{1}{2}$in (1-1.2cm)—and shorter ones, about three-quarters the length of the others, across the row. On the next and following rows work long stitches only, bringing the needle up through the ends of the stitches in the previous row. In the last row the stitches will again vary in length, in order to fill the remaining space.

4 To work stem stitch: start on wrong side, leave a long thread and bring needle out to right side. Keeping thread to bottom of work, take needle to right and insert. Bring out to left halfway along previous stitch. Pull needle to tighten. Insert needle again to right, bring out at left, near end of previous stitch. Always keep stitches even, keep thread below work and work from left to right.

5 To make a French knot, leave a long thread and bring the needle out to the right side in the chosen position. Wind the thread twice around the needle, then insert the needle into the fabric and pull the thread through the loops quickly and smoothly. Work French knots in groups for the best effect.

Hand-worked eyelets

Eyelets are used with buckles on belts and straps. They can also be used to thread cord and ties through. They must be stitched so that they are strong enough to to be functional and decorative at the same time.

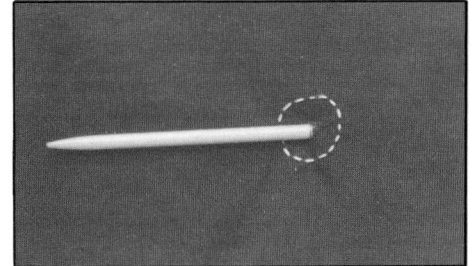

1 Make a small hole in the fabric with a punch or fine knitting needle. Using ordinary sewing thread, make a row of running stitches around the edge close to the hole.

2 Using buttonhole twist or pearl cotton, bring the needle through the fabric from the wrong side just behind the row of running stitches, leaving a long thread at the back to be sewn in later.
Work around the hole with closely-spaced blanket stitch (see Volume 2, page 62) covering the line of running stitches.
Fasten threads on wrong side with small stitches.

Embroidered overblouse

Free and easy fashion in a country style. This peasant-style blouse is hand-embroidered in bright-colored embroidery floss and has contrasting rickrack trim.

Stuart MacLeod

Adapting the pattern

The blouse is made by adapting the pattern for the basic shirt from the Stitch by Stitch Pattern Pack, available in sizes 10 to 20, which correspond to sizes 8 to 18 in ready-made clothes.

Materials
3 sheets of tracing paper 27 x 40in (70 x 100cm)
Flexible curve; yardstick

1 Pin the front yoke to the shirt front, overlapping ⅝in (1.5cm) seam allowances so that the seamlines are aligned. Trace both complete pattern pieces, leaving extra paper at the center front edge.
2 Raise the shoulder line by ¼in (5mm) at armhole edge only and taper the cutting line into the original cutting line at the neck edge. To widen the neckline, take ½in (1.3cm) from front neck edge. Mark the new seamline.
3 Lower the armhole by measuring ½in (1.3cm) down the side seamline from the armhole cutting line. Re-draw the curve using a flexible curve, tapering the line into the original cutting line at the notch.

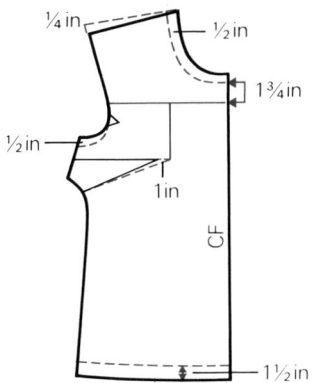

4 For the new length, measure up 1½in (4cm) from the lower edge of the pattern and draw a line across. To mark the yoke line, measure down the center front edge from neck cutting line 1¾in (4.5cm) and draw a line across the pattern at a right angle to the center front. Extend top dart line 1in (2.5cm). Re-draw the lower dart line to the new point. From the new point, draw a vertical line up to the yoke line.

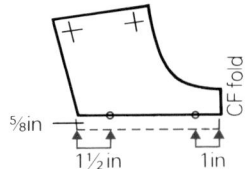

5 Cut along the yoke line to separate the pattern. Add ⅝in (1.5cm) seam allowance to the lower edge of the yoke. Mark the gathering positions on the lower seamline, 1in (2.5cm) in from center front edge and 1½in (4cm) in from the armhole cutting line.

6 On the front, slash down the vertical line from the top edge and close the bust dart and tape in place. This will open the pattern. Insert paper behind slash. Add ⅝in (1.5cm) to top edge and 1¾in 4.5cm) to center front edge, for the extra gathering.

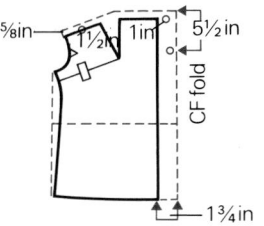

7 Mark the gathering positions on the top seamline 1in (2.5cm) in from center front edge and 1½in (4cm) in from armhole cutting line. Mark the length of the center front opening 5½in (14cm) below the top edge. Straighten the side seam as shown. Mark the positioning line for the elastic at the waistline. Indicate that center front is on a fold.

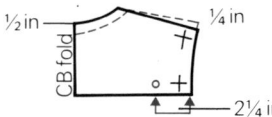

8 On the back yoke pattern, raise the shoulder line, at the armhole edge only, by ¼in (5mm). Taper the line into the original cutting line at the neck edge. To widen the neckline, take ½in (1.3cm) off back neck edge, measuring in from the neck cutting line. Mark the new seam allowance. Mark the gathering position on the bottom seamline 2¼in (5.5cm) in from the armhole cutting line.
9 For the back pattern, trace the basic shirt pattern, leaving extra paper at the center back edge. Lower the armhole and shorten the pattern using the same measurements and directions as for the front. For the gathering allowance add 4in (10cm) to center back edge. Indicate that center back is on a fold.

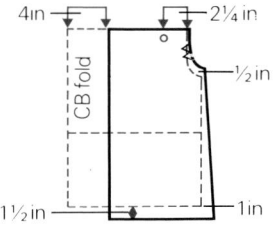

10 Mark the gathering position on the top seamline as directed for the back yoke. Straighten the side seam by measuring in along the lower edge from side cutting line 1in (2.5cm) and re-draw the cutting line from this point, tapering into the original cutting line at the armhole. Mark the positioning line for the elastic at the waistline, checking that this corresponds to the front.

11 For the sleeve pattern, trace the basic sleeve. To mark the new length, measure up from the lower edge 11½in (29.5cm) and draw a line across the pattern. Extend the grain line to the top edge of the sleeve. Raise the sleeve cap in the center by ¼in (5mm).
12 Lower the underarm curve at underarm seam by ⅝in (1.5cm) and measure out ⅝in (1.5cm) at side edges. Mark this point on both sides of the sleeve. Using a flexible curve, re-draw the underarm curves and sleeve cap.

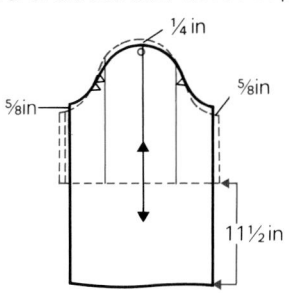

13 Straighten the underarm seamlines and add ⅝in (1.5cm) seam allowance to these edges. At the lower edge of the sleeve divide the sleeve into two equal parts on each side of the grain line. Draw vertical lines up to the sleeve cap from the lower edge at these points.
14 Cut the pattern to the new length. Lay the pattern over a large piece of paper. Slash along the three lines to separate the pattern into four parts. At the lower edge, spread the pattern by 2¾in (7cm) between each section and at the top edge by 2in (5cm) between each section. Tape the pattern in place.

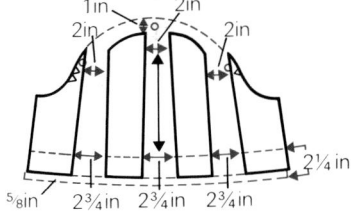

15 At the lower edge, re-draw the hemline and add ⅝in (1.5cm) hem allowance as shown. Raise the center of the sleeve cap by 1in (1.5cm). Using a flexible curve, re-draw the top part of the sleeve cap to the outer sections as shown. The sleeve cap is gathered between the two outer sections. Mark the elastic line 2¼in (6cm) up from lower edge.

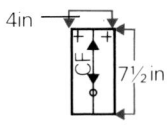

16 For the front facing pattern, cut a rectangle 4 x 7½in (10 x 19cm). Mark the length of the center front opening along the center. This is the straight grain.

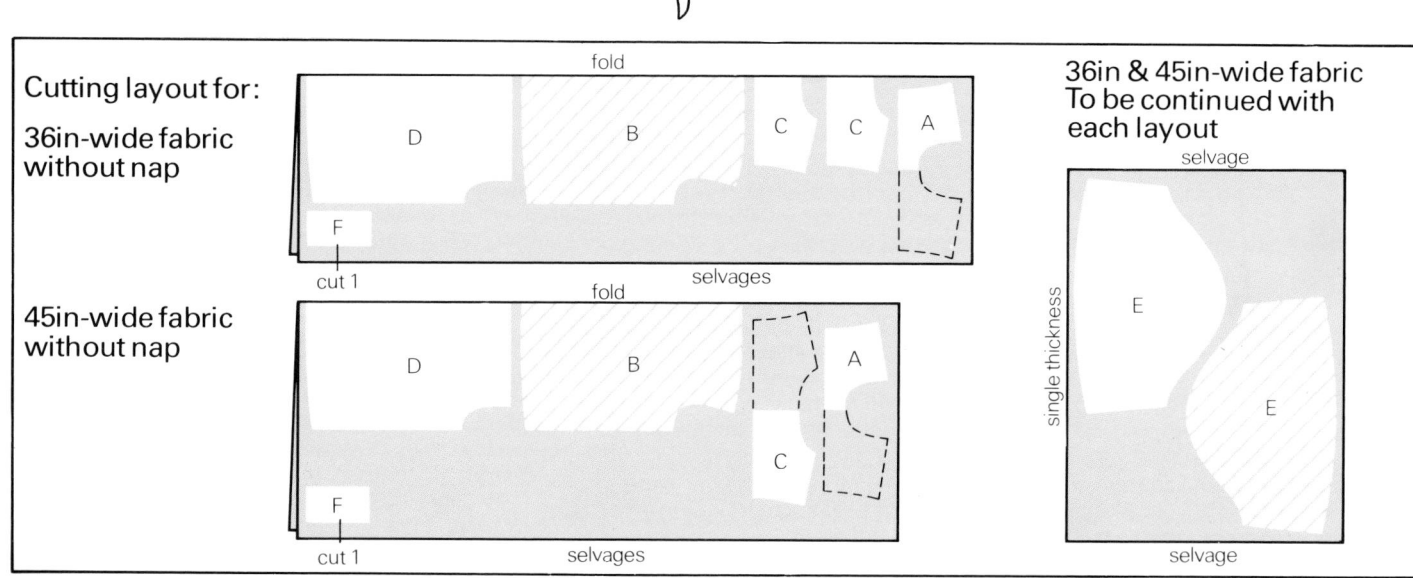

Cutting layout for:

36in-wide fabric without nap

fold

D

F
cut 1

B

C C A

selvages

45in-wide fabric without nap

fold

D

B

A

C

F
cut 1

selvages

**36in & 45in-wide fabric
To be continued with each layout**

selvage

single thickness

E

E

selvage

Directions for making

Suggested fabrics

Fine poplin, cotton satin, lawn, batiste, challis, chambray, fine linen.

Materials

36in (90cm)-wide fabric without nap:
Sizes 10, 12: $2\frac{5}{8}$yd (2.4m)
Size 14: $2\frac{3}{4}$yd (2.5m)
Size 16: $2\frac{7}{8}$yd (2.6m)
Sizes 18, 20: 3yd (2.7m)
45in (115cm)-wide fabric without nap:
Sizes 10-14: $2\frac{3}{8}$yd (2.1m)
Sizes 16-20: $2\frac{5}{8}$yd (2.4m)
Matching thread
Stranded embroidery floss in shades
of pink, green and yellow
$\frac{1}{4}$in (5mm)-wide elastic to fit waist and upper arm
$3\frac{7}{8}$yd (3.5m) rickrack
1yd (1m) narrow decorative cord or ribbon
Shoulder pads

Key to adapted pattern pieces

A Front yoke and yoke
  facing   Cut 2 on fold
B Front   Cut 1 on fold
C Back yoke and yoke
  facing   Cut 2 on fold
D Back   Cut 1 on fold
E Sleeve   Cut 2
F Center front facing   Cut 1

Note If making an embroidered version of the blouse as on page 78, you should transfer the embroidery motifs to the relevant garment sections and complete the embroidery before assembling the blouse. For information on tracing and transferring embroidery patterns see Volume 8, page 80. We have included a trace pattern for the embroidery—use the whole design for each sleeve, centering the design below the seam allowance of the sleeve cap, and part of the design for each front yoke. Make sure the design is reversed when tracing the second sleeve and second yoke. For a rich effect use several brilliant colors for both flowers and leaves.

1 Run two rows of gathering stitches between the marks at the top edge of the blouse front and back. Mark the center front opening line with basting.

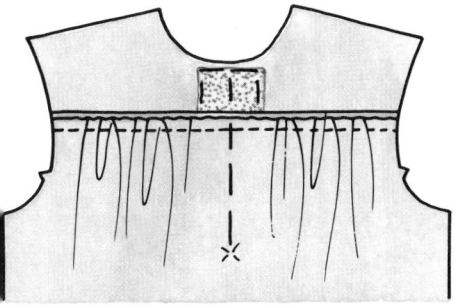

2 Cut a 2¼in (6cm) square of interfacing and baste it to the wrong side of the front yoke at the center front as shown. With right sides together, pin the front yoke to the front and the back yoke to the back, pulling up the gathering threads until they fit the yokes. Baste, spreading the gathers evenly across the yokes. Stitch the seams. Trim the seams and interfacing. Press seams upward.

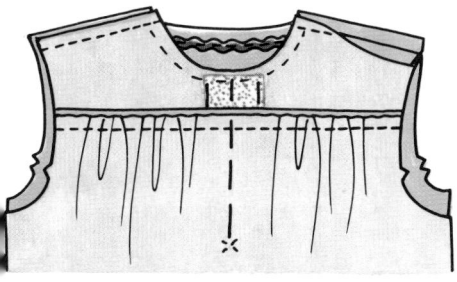

3 With right sides together, baste and stitch front and back yokes and yoke facings together at the shoulder seams. Press seams open. Cut a piece of rickrack and apply it to the front and back neck and center front opening as shown on page 75.

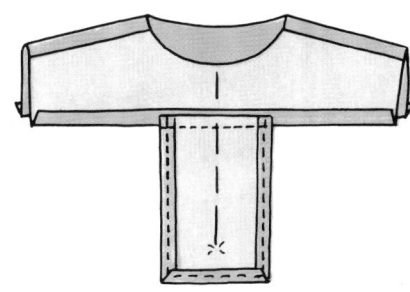

4 Finish the outer edge of the front opening facing by turning under ¼in (5mm) and machine-stitching. Press. With right sides together and center fronts matching, stitch front opening facing to front yoke facing. Press seam upward. Mark the center front line of the facing with a row of basting.

5 With right sides together and center front, center back and shoulders matching, pin and baste yoke facing to yoke around neck and front opening edge.

Starting at the center back, stitch around the neck edge and down the center front. Stitch ¼in (5mm) away from center front at the neck edge and taper down to the point, then up the other side to the center back.

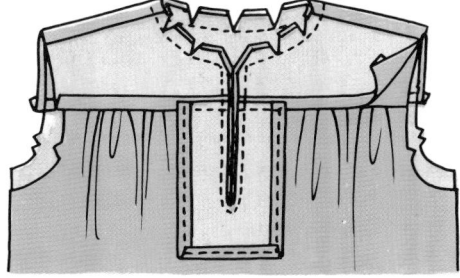

6 Check that the ends of rickrack are stitched into the seam allowance as shown on page 75. Trim seam, clip curves. Cut down center front to the point of the stitching without cutting the stitches. Clip corners.

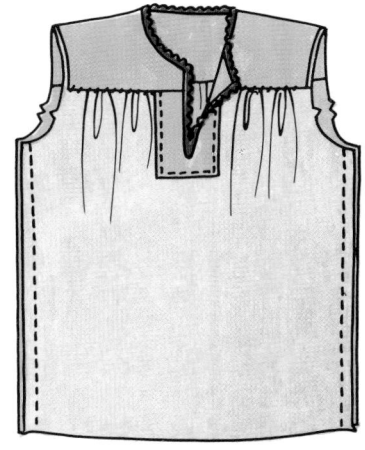

7 Turn the yoke facings and front facings to the inside and baste around stitched edges. Press. On the inside, turn under the seam allowance along the lower edges of the yoke facings and slip stitch to the stitching lines. Press. With right sides together, baste and stitch the side seams. Press seams open.

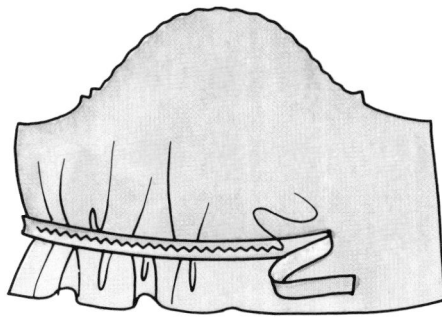

8 Run two rows of gathering stitches around the sleeve cap between the marks indicated on the pattern. Cut two lengths of ¼in (5mm)-wide elastic to fit the upper arm comfortably, and stitch them to sleeves 2¼in (6cm) above hem edge, as shown on page 68.

9 With right sides together, baste and stitch the underarm seams of the sleeves. Press seam open. To finish the lower edge of the sleeve and decorate with rickrack, see directions on page 75.

10 With right sides together and notches, seams and shoulder points matching, pin the sleeve into the armhole, pulling up the gathering threads until the sleeve fits the armhole. Baste, spreading the gathers evenly over the sleeve cap. Stitch the sleeve in place with the sleeve lying on top on the machine.

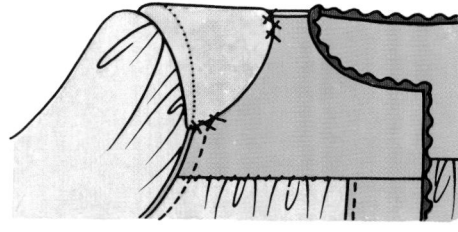

11 Trim the seam and clip the curved edges. Press seam toward sleeve and finish edges together. Sew shoulder pads to inside of shoulders as shown in Volume 9, page 61.

12 At the lower edge of the blouse finish and apply rickrack as shown on page 75. Cut a length of ¼in (5mm)-wide elastic to fit comfortably around waist plus about an inch (a few centimeters) extra and stitch to waistline on wrong side as directed on page 68.

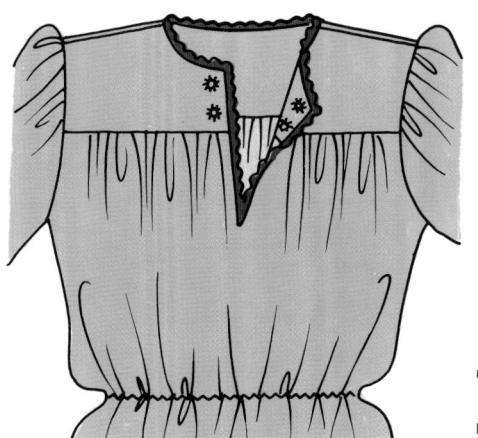

13 Make two hand-worked eyelets at the center front on each side of the yoke as shown on page 77. Thread cord through eyelets to tie at front.

Terry Evans

*Cutwork embroidery
*Working cutwork
*Chain and twisted chain stitches
*Pattern for a camisole trimmed with cutwork

Cutwork embroidery

There are various kinds of cutwork. One of the most familiar and popular is eyelet lace, which dates from the middle of the 19th century and is of English origin— hence its other name, **broderie anglaise**. Much earlier, in the 16th century, the Italians had developed a kind of cutwork called **punto tagliato** (from the words for "stitch" and "cut"), in which areas of fabric were cut away and the resulting spaces filled with stitches. This work became progressively more open and intricate, ultimately evolving into needle lace, in which the surrounding fabric was dispensed with altogether.

Still another type of cutwork—the kind we are introducing here—is sometimes called Richelieu work, after the 17th-century French cardinal and prime minister who did so much to encourage the textile industry, including lace and embroidery, in his country. This name has given rise to a belief that Richelieu work dates from that period, but in fact it came into fashion in the late 19th century, when it was widely used to decorate household linen. Many of the early examples are very elaborate and reminiscent of the opulent lace worn in the 17th century,

which may account for the name "Richelieu work." Modern cutwork is usually simpler, but it still makes an attractive embellishment not only for linens but also for blouses and other garments, especially lingerie.

The technique is essentially quite simple: Cutwork is a type of embroidery in which motifs are outlined with buttonhole stitch and the background areas then cut away. Often bars are worked across the spaces to strengthen the fabric and add interest to the design. The stitched motif may also be enhanced with other free embroidery stitches, such as stem, chain and French knots.

In all embroidery, the spaces left between the motifs are virtually as important as the motifs themselves, and this is particularly true of cutwork. If you are designing your own cutwork, shade in the areas to be cut away to get an idea of the finished effect; modify the design as necessary until you get a pleasing balance. In some cutwork the design is formed in reverse, as in a stencil: the edges outside the motif are stitched and the motif is then cut out. For practice, take a simple stencil design—such as the tulip shown below,

transfer it to fabric and work the buttonhole stitch as shown in the steps below, but turn the stitches to the edges on the outside of the motif.

Materials

The most suitable fabrics for cutwork are closely-woven, medium-weight linen and cotton. Some natural/synthetic blends are also suitable. Examine a cut edge of the fabric to make sure that it does not fray easily. White is the traditional color for this type of embroidery, but any color can be used.

The thread may be in a matching color or slightly darker, which gives a richer effect; or it can be in one or more contrasting colors. Multi-color cutwork has a more informal appearance than one-color work. Stranded embroidery floss, pearl cotton, *coton à broder* and silk twist are the most often-used threads for cutwork.

Use a crewel needle of an appropriate size for your thread and fabric. Mount the work in an embroidery frame to keep it taut while you work the stitches. Remove it from the frame before cutting away the background areas of the design.

Working cutwork

The effectiveness of cutwork depends to a great extent on a willingness to take pains. Stitches must be uniform and evenly spaced. The underside should be as neat as possible, as the work is not usually lined.

Transfer the design with a water-soluble marking pen or dressmaker's carbon. A dotted line will suffice and is easier to remove if you should make a mistake. Mark the areas to be cut away with Xs or some other mark.

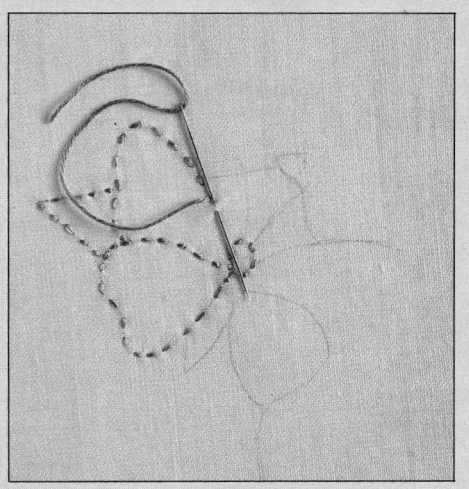

1 Using the embroidery thread—here *coton à broder*—work close running stitch close to the edges. This strengthens the edges and makes it easier to work the buttonhole stitch later.

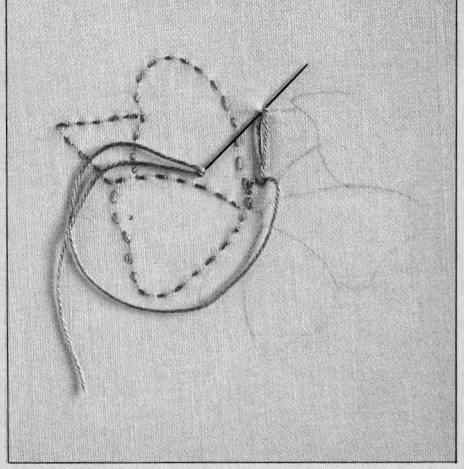

2 When you reach a bar (during the running stitch outlining), take the thread to the opposite edge, take a small stitch, return to the first edge and take a stitch there, then take another stitch on the opposite side. You now have three threads as a foundation for the bar.

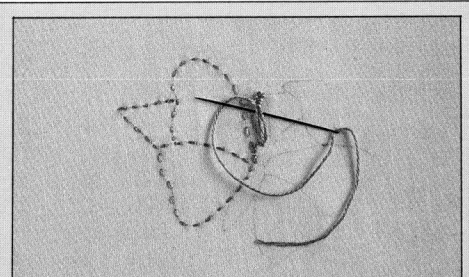
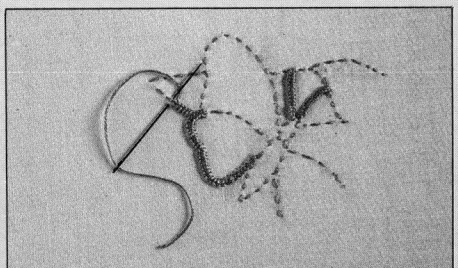
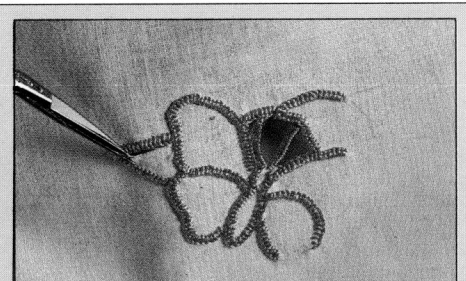

3 Now work buttonhole stitch over the threads, back toward starting edge. To work buttonhole stitch (or *blanket stitch*), slip the needle under the threads, loop the working thread under the needle and pull the needle through. Work stitches close together without twisting them. The knots should all lie on the same side.

4 When the outlining and bars are complete, work buttonhole stitch closely around all the edges, covering the running stitch. Make sure that the knots lie next to the areas to be cut away. Sometimes an outline will cross the fabric. Then you must decide which part of the design overlaps the other and work stitches with the knots on the "overlapping" edge.

5 When all the stitching is complete, cut away the areas marked with an X, using very sharp-pointed scissors and working on the right side. Be very careful not to cut the stitches.

Chain and twisted chain stitches

The basic chain stitch makes a fairly thick outline and can also be used for fillings. Bring the needle up through the fabric, make a small loop, take the needle down at the point where it emerged and bring it up inside the loop a short distance along the stitching line. Pull the thread through, but not too tautly. For the following stitches, take the needle down inside the loop where it emerged. Anchor the last loop by taking a tiny stitch over it.

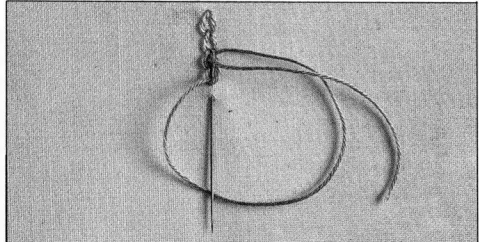

Twisted chain stitch makes a pleasingly textured outline.
1 Make a small loop as for ordinary chain, but take the needle down slightly to the left of the loop, a short distance below the point where it emerged. Then bring it out inside the loop, as usual, and pull the thread through.

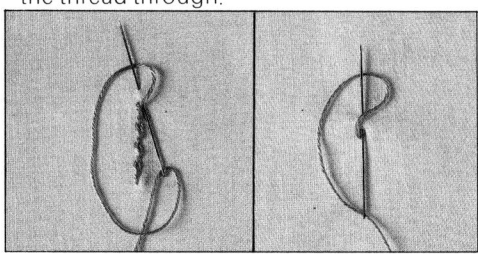

2 On following stitches continue to re-insert the needle to the left of the loop being formed. Fasten the last loop as in ordinary chain stitch.

Camisole with cutwork motif

Ron Kelly

Butterflies and fuschias

The camisole shown on page 83 features a charming cutwork motif, which could also be used on a slip, nightgown or blouse.

Size
The camisole illustrated is a size 10 (corresponding to a size 8 in ready-made clothes). Alterations for sizes 12, 14 and 16 are given with the pattern. (If you prefer, you can use a similar commercial pattern.)

Materials
$\frac{1}{2}$yd (.5m) of 45in (115cm)-wide (or wider) soft, closely-woven fabric (for all sizes)
1 skein of fine pearl cotton or silk twist in a slightly darker shade
Medium-size crewel needle
Matching sewing thread
$\frac{1}{2}$yd (.4m) of $\frac{1}{4}$in (5mm)-wide elastic
8in (20cm)-diameter embroidery hoop
Sharp-pointed embroidery scissors
Graph paper
Tracing paper
Dark felt-tip pen
Water-soluble marking pen

Working the embroidery
1 Enlarge the two pattern pieces given on page 85 using the graph paper. (See Volume 4, page 76 for how to enlarge a design.)

Cut out the enlarged patterns.
2 Fold the fabric so that the two selvages meet slightly to one side of the middle. Place the pattern pieces on the fabric (the back on the narrower fold of fabric) with center front and center back on the fold. (If you are using wider fabric, you can fold it with the selvages exactly in the middle.)
3 Pin the pieces in place and cut out the back only. Mark around the front with the marking pen. Mark the center front and both back and front foldlines with lines of basting, and transfer the small dots onto the fabric.
4 Trace the embroidery motif with the dark felt-tip pen. Place the tracing right side up on a flat surface and lay the camisole front on top, also right side up,

with the upper straight edge of the motif $1\frac{1}{4}$in (3.5cm) down from the foldline and the center mark on the center front. (If you have difficulty seeing the design through the fabric, tape the tracing to a window.) Trace the motif onto the fabric using the marking pen. The areas marked X will be cut away; copy these marks on the fabric.
5 Mount the fabric in the embroidery hoop. Using the embroidery thread, work the preliminary running stitch around the outlines of the motif (see page 82). Make sure that the stitches lie just inside the edge to be covered with buttonhole stitching.
6 When you reach one of the butterflies' antennae, interrupt the running stitch and work a bar.
7 Now work buttonhole stitch around the design (except for the veins of the leaves and the fuschia stamens). Make sure that the knotted edge of the stitching is next to the area to be cut away. Work a few back stitches at the point marked by the arrow on the trace pattern to link these parts of the design. Do not stitch through the fabric.
8 Work the veins of the leaves in twisted chain stitch (see page 83), making each stitch just under $\frac{1}{8}$in (3mm) long.
9 Work the stamens of the fuschias with long straight stitches and French knots (see Volume 5, page 76).
10 Remove the work from the frame. Using sharp-pointed embroidery scissors, carefully cut away the parts of the design marked X.
11 Press the work on the wrong side over a thick towel.
Assembling the camisole
1 Trim away the excess fabric around the edges of the camisole front.
2 Cut two strips of fabric, each $\frac{3}{4}\times14$in (2×36cm), for straps.
3 Place the front and back sections together with right sides facing and foldlines and small dots aligned. Pin,

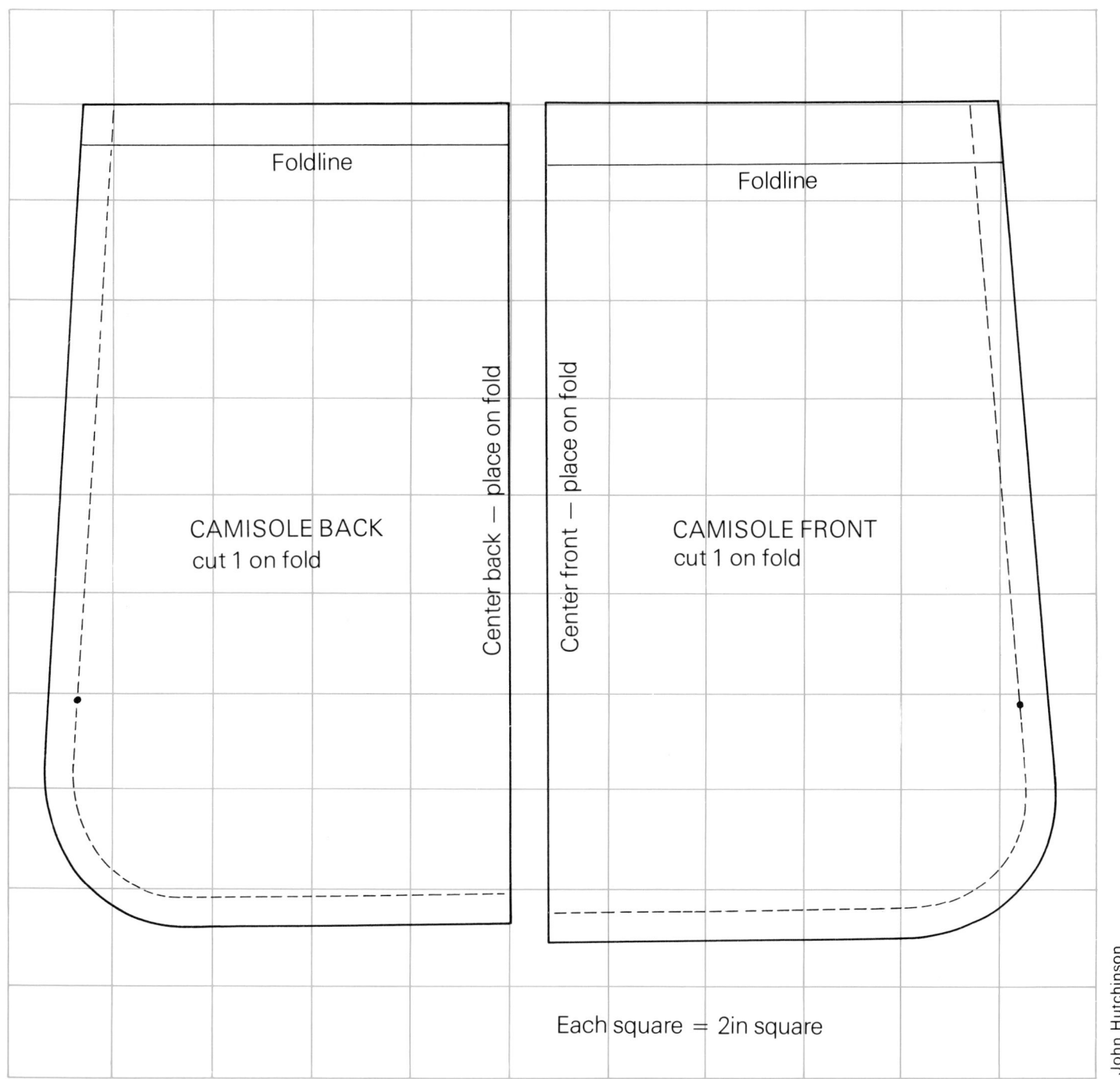

Foldline

Foldline

Center back — place on fold

Center front — place on fold

CAMISOLE BACK
cut 1 on fold

CAMISOLE FRONT
cut 1 on fold

Each square = 2in square

John Hutchinson

baste and stitch from dots up to the upper edge of the back, taking $\frac{5}{8}$in (1.5cm) seam allowance. Press seams open.
4 Finish the raw edges by turning under $\frac{1}{8}$in (3mm) and stitching. Continue this narrow hem around the lower edges.
5 Turn up the lower edge a further $\frac{1}{2}$in (1.2cm). Pin and baste in place, easing the fullness around the curves. Topstitch or hand-hem in place.
6 Turn under and stitch $\frac{1}{4}$in (5mm) along both front and back upper edges. (You will need to cut a few stitches in the side seam in order to turn under the back edge.)
7 Turn under the entire upper edge along the foldline; press. Baste the finished

Each square on this grid corresponds to 2 square inches (5 square centimeters) on your graph paper. The pattern as shown here is, when enlarged, a size 10 (corresponding to size 8 in ready-made clothes). To make it a larger size:
Size 12 Add $\frac{3}{8}$in (1cm) to side and lower edges.
Size 14 Add $\frac{7}{8}$in (2.2cm) to side and lower edges.
Size 16 $1\frac{3}{8}$in (3.5cm) to side and lower edges.

edges in place. Hand-hem the front edge. Topstitch the back edge over the first line of stitching—leaving a small opening at each side—and again about $\frac{1}{16}$in (2mm) down from the fold, forming a casing.
8 Insert elastic in the casing in the back and pin it in place at the sides. Try on the camisole and check it for fit. Trim elastic as desired; sew ends firmly in place by hand or machine.

9 Fold under $\frac{1}{8}$in (3mm) on both long edges of each strap; press. Fold again, aligning the turned-under edges. Baste and stitch.
10 Pin the straps to the top edge of the camisole and try it on. Adjust the positions of the straps if necessary. Hand-sew them in place on the wrong side, taking care not to catch in the elastic on the back and the outer layer of fabric on the front.

CROCHET

Fur and feathers

Add a touch of whimsy to an outfit with these frankly fake accessories.

"Leopard skin" hat and muff

Sizes
Hat To fit average size head.
Muff 11 × 12½in (28 × 32cm).

Materials
Hat *2oz (50g) of a lightweight mohair-type yarn in main color (A) and 2oz (50g) in contrasting color (B)*
Size G (4.50mm) crochet hook
Muff *4oz (100g) in main color (A), 2oz (50g) in contrasting color (B)*
Lining material and batting as required
1¾yd (1.5m) of thick cord
Size G (4.50mm) crochet hook

Gauge
14½ sts and 10½ rows to 4in (10cm) on size G (4.50mm) hook with yarn double.

Note
When changing color finish preceding hdc in the new color (yo, draw through last 3 loops on hook), and then work required number of hdc, finishing last hdc in the new color. Do not cut yarn but work over it in the other color.

Hat
To make
Use yarn double throughout. Using size G (4.50mm) hook and A, make 74 ch.
Base row 1 hdc into 3rd ch from hook, 1 hdc into each ch to end. Turn. 73 sts.
Next row 2 ch to count as first hdc, 1 hdc into each st to end. Turn.
Rep last row twice more.
Cont in hdc, working in patt from chart 1. Work 15 rows.
Shape crown
1st row 2 ch, *work next 2 hdc tog, patt 6, rep from * to end. Turn. 64 sts.
2nd row 2 ch, *patt 5, work next 2 hdc tog, rep from * to end. Turn. 55 sts.
3rd row 2 ch, *work next 2 hdc tog, patt 4, rep from * to end. Turn. 46 sts.
Cont with A only as foll:
4th row 2 ch, 1 hdc into each of next 2 sts, *work next 2 hdc tog, 1 hdc into each of next 3 sts, rep from * to last 3 sts, work next 2 hdc tog, 1 hdc into last hdc. Turn. 37 sts.
5th row 2 ch, *work next 2 hdc tog, 1 hdc into each of next 2 sts, rep from * to end. Turn. 28 sts.

CHART 1   CHART 2

✕ = A   ● = B

6th row 2ch, *work next 2hdc tog, 1hdc into next st, rep from * to end. Turn. 19 sts.
7th row 2ch, *work next 2hdc tog, rep from * to end. Turn. 10 sts.
8th row 1ch, keeping loop of each st on hook work 1sc into each st to end, yo and draw through all loops on hook. Fasten off.
Join seam. Turn first 4 rows to WS and slip stitch in place.

Muff
To make
Use yarn double throughout. Using size G (4.50mm) hook and A, make 53 ch.
Base row 1hdc into 3rd ch from hook, 1hdc into each ch to end. Turn. 53 sts.
Cont in hdc, working in patt from chart 2 until the 3rd row of the 11th patt from beg has been worked.
Fasten off.
Join edges of first and last rows. Line and pad as desired. Join side edges for 5½in (14cm). Sew cord to top of side edges for strap.

"Fox" stole

Materials
9oz (250g) of a chenille yarn
Size H (5.00mm) crochet hook
1 pair ⅜in (10mm) toy eyes
1 furrier's hook and loop
Suitable stuffing
Small amount of black yarn

Gauge
12sc and 12 rows to 4in (10cm) on size H (5.00mm) hook.

Under face
Using size H (5.00mm) hook make 4ch.
Base row 1sc into 2nd ch from hook, 1sc into each of next 2ch. Turn. 3sc.
1st row 1ch, 1sc into each sc to end. Turn.
2nd row 1ch, 1sc into first sc, 2sc into next sc−1sc increased−, 1sc into last sc. Turn. 4sc.
3rd row 1ch, 1sc into each sc to end. Turn.
4th row 1ch, inc 1sc, 1sc into each of next 2sc, inc 1sc. Turn. 6sc.
5th row 1ch, 1sc into each sc to end. Turn.
Cont to inc in this way until there are 16sc. Work 1 row. Fasten off.

Upper face and body
Work as for under face but do not fasten off; work 9ch.
Using a separate ball of yarn make 8ch and leave aside.
This completes upper face.
17th row 1sc into 2nd ch from hook, 1sc into each of next 7ch, 1sc into each sc to end, then work 1sc into each of the 8ch. Turn. 32sc.
18th and 19th rows 1ch, 1sc into each sc to end. Turn.
20th row 1ch, 1sc into each of next 8sc, inc 1sc, 1sc into each of next 14sc, inc 1sc, 1sc into each of next 8sc. Turn. 34sc.
21st and 22nd rows 1ch, 1sc into each sc to end. Turn.
23rd row 1ch, 1sc into each of next 8sc, inc 1sc, 1sc into each of next 16sc, inc 1sc, 1sc into each of next 8sc. Turn. 36sc.
24th and 25th rows 1ch, 1sc into each sc to end. Turn.
26th row 1ch, 1sc into each of next 8sc, inc 1sc, 1sc into each of next 18sc, inc 1sc, 1sc into each of next 8sc. Turn. 38sc.
27th to 30th rows 1ch, 1sc into each sc to end. Turn.
31st row 1ch, 1sc into each of next 8sc, inc 1sc, 1sc into each of next 20sc, inc 1sc, 1sc into each of next 8sc. Turn. 40sc.
Cont in sc, without shaping, until work measures 26in (66cm) from completion of upper face.
Next row 1ch, 1sc into each of next 10sc, turn.
Next row 1ch, work next 2sc tog−1sc decreased−, work to end. Turn. 9sc.
Next row 1ch, work to end. Turn. Cont to

dec in this way on next and every foll alternate row until 5sc rem, ending at side edge. Fasten off.
Return to where sts were left. Join yarn to next sc, 1sc into each of next 20sc, turn.
Next row 1ch, dec 1sc, work to within last 2sc, dec 1sc. Turn.
Next row 1ch, work to end. Turn.
Cont to dec in this way on next and every foll alternate row until 10sc rem. Fasten off. Return to where sts were left. Join yarn to next sc and work to end. Turn.
Complete to match first side reversing shaping.

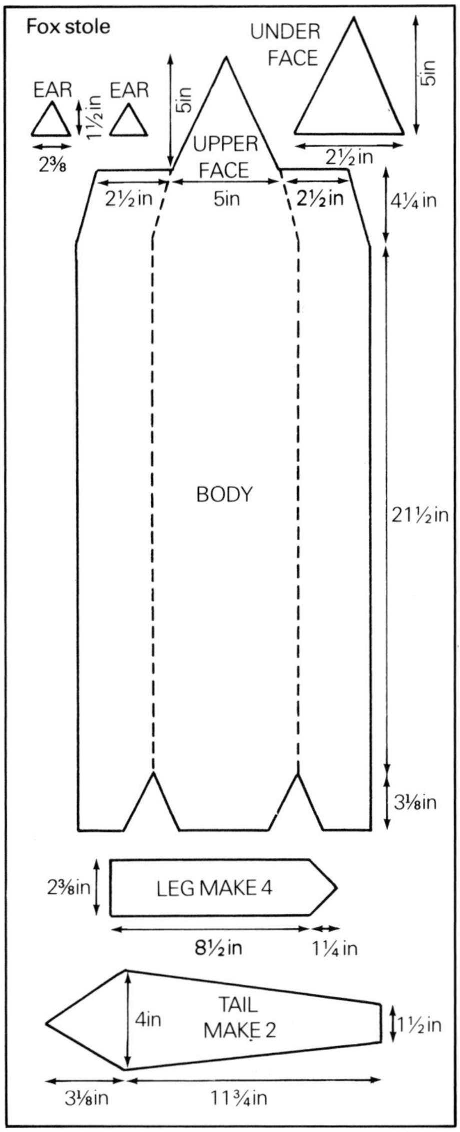

Tail
Using size H (5.00mm) hook make 6ch.
Base row 1sc into 2nd ch from hook, 1sc into each of next 4ch. Turn. 5sc.
1st to 6th rows 1ch, 1sc into each sc to end. Turn.
7th row 1ch, inc 1sc, 1sc into each of next 3sc, inc 1sc. Turn. 7sc.
8th to 13th rows 1ch, 1sc into each sc to end. Turn.
14th row 1ch, inc 1sc, 1sc into each of next 5sc, inc 1sc. Turn. 9sc.
15th to 26th rows 1ch, 1sc into each sc to end. Turn.
27th row 1ch, inc 1sc, 1sc into each of next 7sc, inc 1sc. Turn. 11sc.
28th to 37th rows 1ch, 1sc into each sc to end. Turn.
38th row 1ch, dec 1sc, 1sc into each of next 7sc, dec 1sc. Turn.
39th and 40th rows 1ch, 1sc into each sc to end. Turn.
Rep last 3 rows until 1sc rem.
Fasten off.
Make another piece in the same way.

Ears (make 2)
Using size H (5.00mm) hook make 9ch.
Base row 1sc into 2nd ch from hook, 1sc into each ch to end. Turn. 8sc.
1st row 1ch, dec 1sc, 1sc into each of next 4sc, dec 1sc. Turn.
2nd row 1ch, dec 1sc, 1sc into each of next 2sc, dec 1sc. Turn.
3rd row 1ch, 1sc into each sc to end. Turn.
4th row 1ch, (dec 1sc), twice. Turn.
5th row 1ch, dec 1sc. Fasten off.

Legs (make 4)
Using size H (5.00mm) hook make 9ch.
Base row 1sc into 2nd ch from hook, 1sc into each ch to end. Turn. 8sc.
1st row 1ch, 1sc into each sc to end. Turn.
Rep last row until work measures 8½in (22cm) from beg.
Next row 1ch, dec 1sc, 1sc into each sc to within last 2sc, dec 1sc. Turn. Rep last row 3 times more. Fasten off.

To finish
Join side edges of upper face and under face. Place the eyes in the upper face

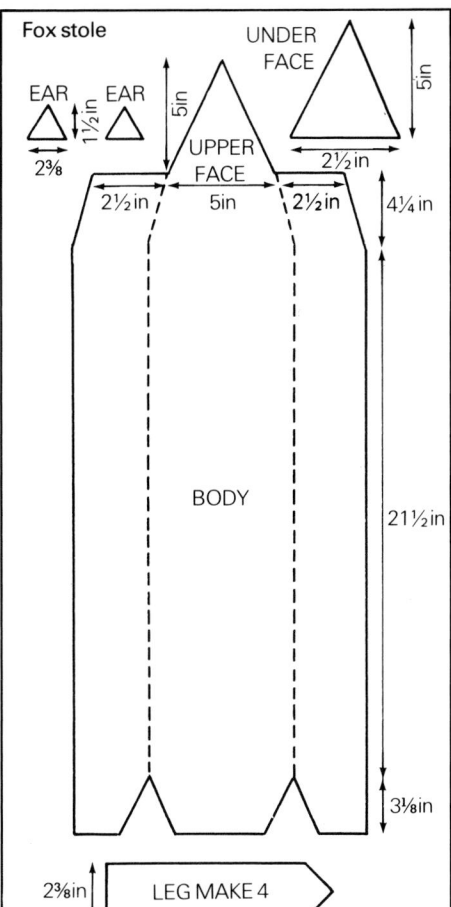

Fox stole

EAR 2⅜ | EAR 1½in | UNDER FACE 5in 2½in | UPPER FACE | 2½in 5in 2½in | 4¼in | BODY 21½in | 3⅛in

2⅜in LEG MAKE 4 | 8½in 1¼in

4in TAIL MAKE 2 1½in | 3⅛in 11¾in

Ian Stephen

87

and fix firmly at back. Turn under side flaps and join to under face. Join center seam of body. Join the two tail pieces tog. Stuff head and tail firmly but not too hard, then lightly stuff the body. Join end of body, sewing in the tail at the same time. Sew the ears to upper head approx 2in (5cm) behind the eyes, curving them to give shape and to push forward. To pull eyes tog, sew from behind one eye through head to other eye, pulling slightly to give shape to face. Sew the long edges of legs tog, leaving shaped edge open for foot. Attach one leg to each side approx 5½in (14cm) behind ears and one each side at beg of back shaping.

Embroider nose on face and 4 claws on each foot.

Attach hook to under face and loop to side of tail.

"Feather" boa

Size 4in × 2⅔yd (10cm × 2.5m) long.

Materials
15oz (425g) of a fine mohair-type yarn
Size H (5.00mm) crochet hook

Gauge
13 sts to 4in (10cm) on size H (5.00mm) hook.

To make
Using size H (5.00mm) hook make 27 ch.
Base row 1sc into 2nd ch from hook, 1sc into each ch to end. Turn.

1st patt row 1sc into first sc, *insert hook into next sc, place yarn over first and second fingers and extend yarn to a length of 3in (7.5cm) by lifting second finger, draw a loop through leaving loop 3in (7.5cm) long, yo and draw through both loops on hook, remove second finger from loop, rep from * to end. Turn.
2nd patt row 1sc into first st, 1sc into each st to end. Turn.
Rep these 2 rows until work measures 2⅔yd (2.5m) from beg, ending with a 2nd patt row. Fasten off.
Fold in half with RS tog and join bottom and center back seams to form a tube. Turn RS out and slip stitch top seam.

Technique tip
Single loop stitch

The boa is simply made with alternating rows of single loop stitch—formed at the back of the work with the WS facing—and single crochet. Before working the first loop stitch row work a base row of single crochet. Turn and work 1 single crochet into the first stitch in the usual way.

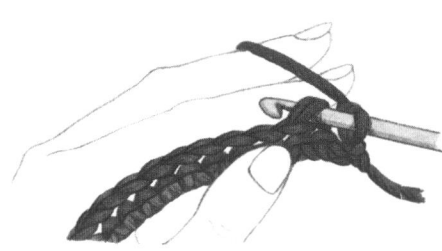

Insert the hook into the next stitch. Wind the yarn around the fingers so that it lies over the index finger and middle finger of the left hand.

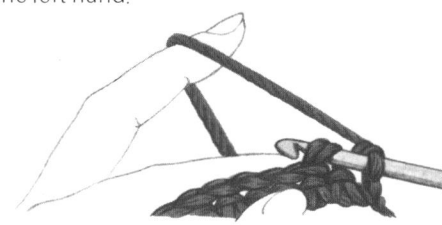

Extend the yarn to a length of 3in (7.5cm) by lifting the middle finger. This finger controls the length of the loop, so always raise it to the same height.

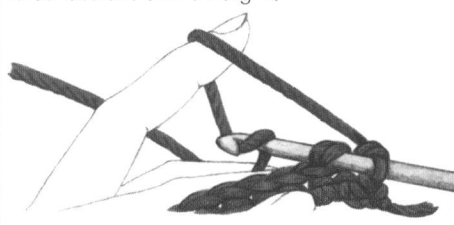

Take the hook under and behind the middle finger of the left hand and draw through a loop. Keep the yarn around the fingers at the back of the work to make sure the loop stays firmly in place.

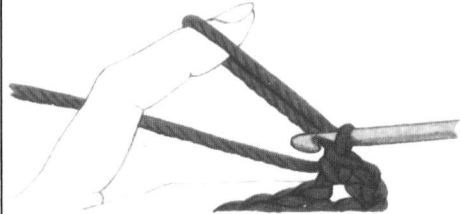

To secure the loop, finish as usual for single crochet—yarn over hook and draw through both loops on hook. Drop the loop from the second finger. Repeat these four steps to end of row.

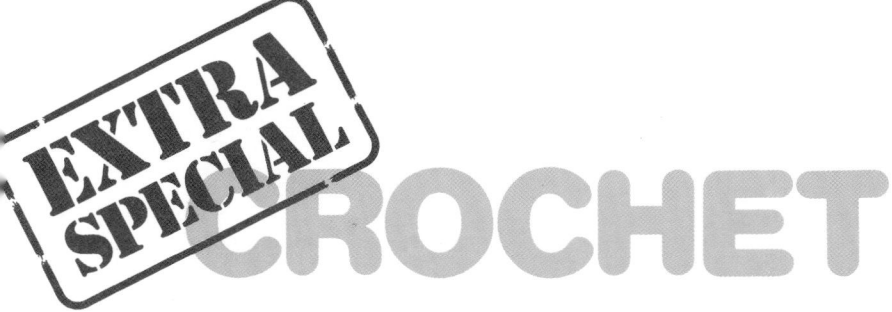

EXTRA SPECIAL CROCHET

Outer space

This chenille jacket is big enough to wear over a heavy sweater when you want a little extra warmth.

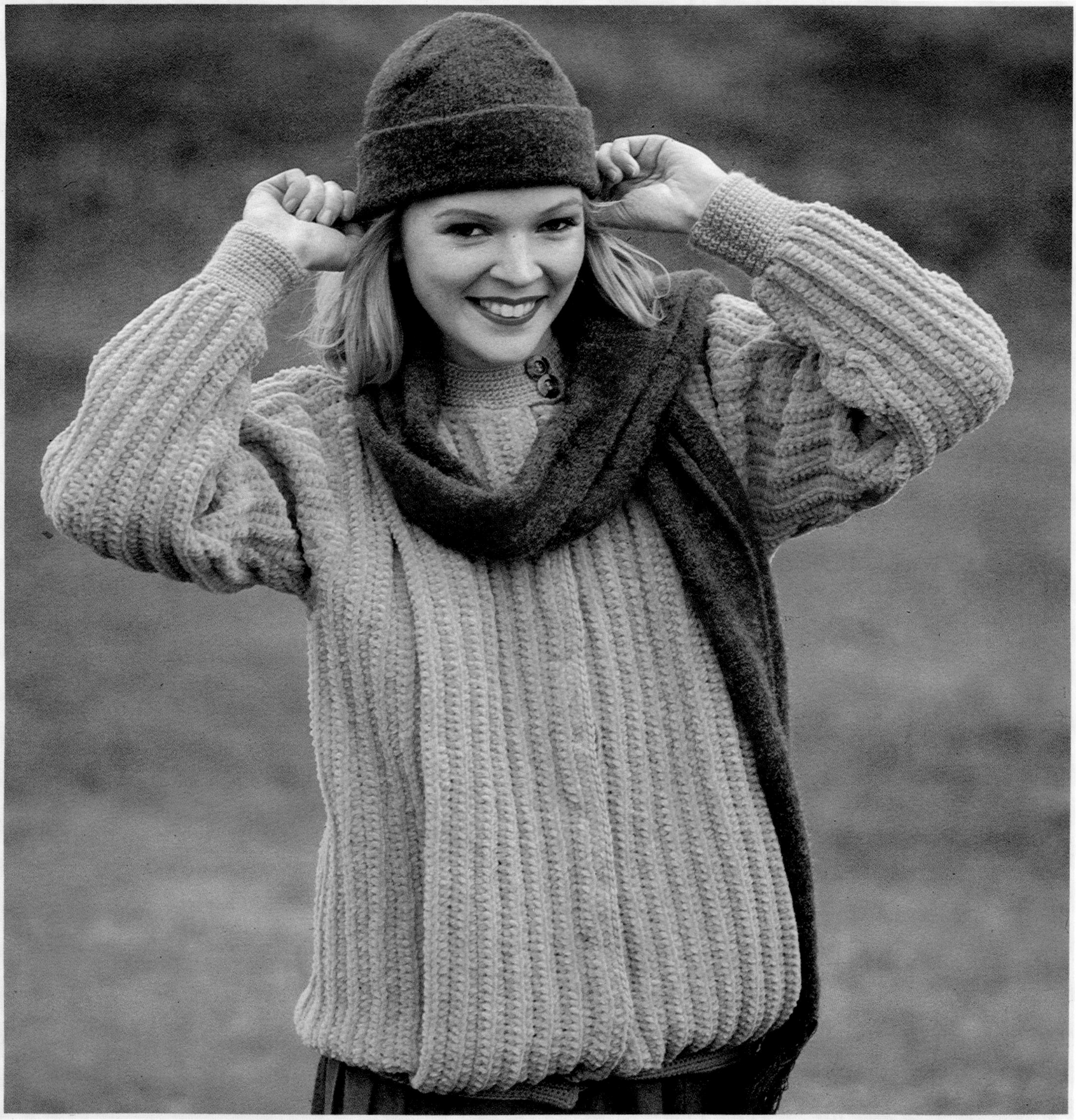

Rod Delroy

Sizes

To fit 34[36:38]in (87[92:97]cm) bust. Length, 24¼[24¾:25¼]in (60[62:63]cm). Sleeve seam, 20[20¾:20¾]in (51[53:53]cm).

Note Directions for larger sizes are in brackets []; if there is only one set of figures it applies to all sizes.

Materials

25[27:29]oz (700[750:800]g) of a lightweight chenille yarn
4oz (100g) of a knitting worsted
Sizes C, F, and G (3.00, 4.00 and 4.50mm) crochet hooks
8 buttons

Gauge

15hdc and 9 rows to 4in (10cm) worked on size G (4.50mm) hook.

Back

Using size G (4.50mm) hook and chenille, make 58ch for side edge.
Base row Work 1hdc into 3rd ch from hook, 1hdc into each ch to end. Turn. 57hdc.
Patt row 2ch, skip first hdc, working into back loop only of every st work 1hdc into each hdc to end, 1hdc into top of 2ch. Turn. Rep last row 3 times more.
Next row Make 27[29:31]ch for first armhole, work 1hdc into 3rd ch from hook, 1hdc into each of next 24[26:28]ch, then working into back loop only of each st, work 1hdc into each hdc to end, 1hdc into top of the 2ch. 83[85:87] sts. Patt 32[34:36] rows. Work across first 57 sts, turn and leave rem sts unworked for 2nd armhole. Patt 4 rows. Fasten off.

Right front

Work as for back until first armhole is complete. Work 4 more rows and mark each end of last row. Work a further 12 rows then mark each end of last row. Now cont in patt until 30[31:32] rows have been completed from armhole.
Fasten off.

Left front

Make 84[86:88]ch and work base row as for back. 83[85:87] sts.
Patt 29[30:31] rows.
1st and 3rd sizes only
Next row Fasten off. Skip first 26[30] sts, rejoin yarn to next st, 2ch, patt to end. Turn. Now work 4 more rows in patt. Fasten off.
2nd size only
Next row Work across first 57 sts, turn. Now work 4 rows in patt. Fasten off.

Left sleeve front

Using size G (4.50mm) hook and chenille, make 8[12:12]ch.
1st row Work 1hdc into 3rd ch from hook, 1hdc into each ch to end. Turn. 7[11:11]hdc.
2nd row Make 14ch. Fasten off. Skip first 7ch, rejoin yarn to next ch, 2ch to count as first hdc, then 1hdc into each of rem 6ch, 1hdc into each of back loops on each of rem 7[11:11]hdc (including 2ch at end), now work another hdc in 2ch at end. Turn. 15[19:19] sts.
3rd row 2ch, skip first hdc, 1hdc into back loop of each hdc to end, 1hdc into each of the 7ch. Turn. 22[26:26] sts.
4th row Make 14ch. Fasten off. Skip first 7ch, rejoin yarn to next ch, 2ch to count as first hdc, 1hdc into each of next 6ch, 1hdc into each 1hdc to within 2ch, 2hdc into top of 2ch. Turn. 30[34:34] sts.
5th row 2ch, skip first hdc, 1hdc into each hdc to ch at end, 1hdc into each of 7ch. Turn. 37[41:41] sts.

Rep 4th and 5th rows twice more. 67[71:71] sts.
Next row Patt to within last st, 2hdc into last st. 68[72:72] sts.
Next row Patt to end. Turn.
Rep last 2 rows once more.
Next row Patt to within last st, 2hdc into last st. Turn. 70[74:74] sts.
2nd size only
Next row Patt to end. Turn.
Next row Patt to within last st, 2hdc into last st. Turn. 75 sts.
3rd size only
Next row Patt to end. Turn.
Next row Patt to within last st, 2hdc into last st. Turn. 75 sts.
Rep last 2 rows once more. 76 sts.
All sizes
Next row Make 16[18:20]ch for yoke, 1hdc into 3rd ch from hook, 1hdc into each of next 13[15:17]ch, then 1hdc into the back loop of each st to end. Turn. 85[89:95] sts.
Next row Patt to end. Turn.
Rep last row 4 times more, make 24[26:28]ch, then fasten off.

Right sleeve front

Using size G (4.50mm) hook and chenille, make 14[18:18]ch. Fasten off.
1st row Skip the first 7ch, rejoin yarn to next ch, 2ch to count as first hdc, then 1hdc into each of rem 6[10:10]ch. Turn. 7[11:11] sts.
2nd row 2ch, 1hdc into back loop of first hdc, 1hdc into each hdc to end, 1hdc into each of 7ch. Turn.
3rd row Make 14ch. Fasten off. Skip first 7ch, rejoin yarn to next ch, 2ch, 1hdc into each ch, then 1hdc into each hdc to end, finishing with 1hdc into top of 2ch. Turn. 22[26:26] sts.
4th row As 2nd. 30[34:34] sts.
5th row As 3rd. 37[41:41] sts.
Rep 4th and 5th rows twice more. 67[71:71] sts.
Next row 2ch, 1hdc into first hdc, work to end. Turn. 68[72:72] sts.
Next row Patt to end. Turn.
Rep last 2 rows once more.
First size only
Next row Fasten off. Make 15ch, work 2hdc into first st, work to end. Turn. 70 sts.
Next row Patt to within the 15ch, 1hdc into each of the 15ch. Turn. 85sts.
2nd size only
Next row 2ch, 1hdc into first hdc, patt to end. Turn.
Next row Patt to end. Turn.
Next row Fasten off. Make 17ch, then work 2hdc into first st, patt to end. Turn.
Next row Patt to within last 17ch, 1hdc into each of the 17ch. Turn. 92 sts.
3rd size only
Next row 2ch, 1hdc into first hdc, patt to end. Turn.
Next row Patt to end. Turn.
Rep last 2 rows once more.
Next row Fasten off. Make 19ch, 2hdc into first hdc, then patt to end. Turn.
Next row Patt to within last 19ch, 1hdc

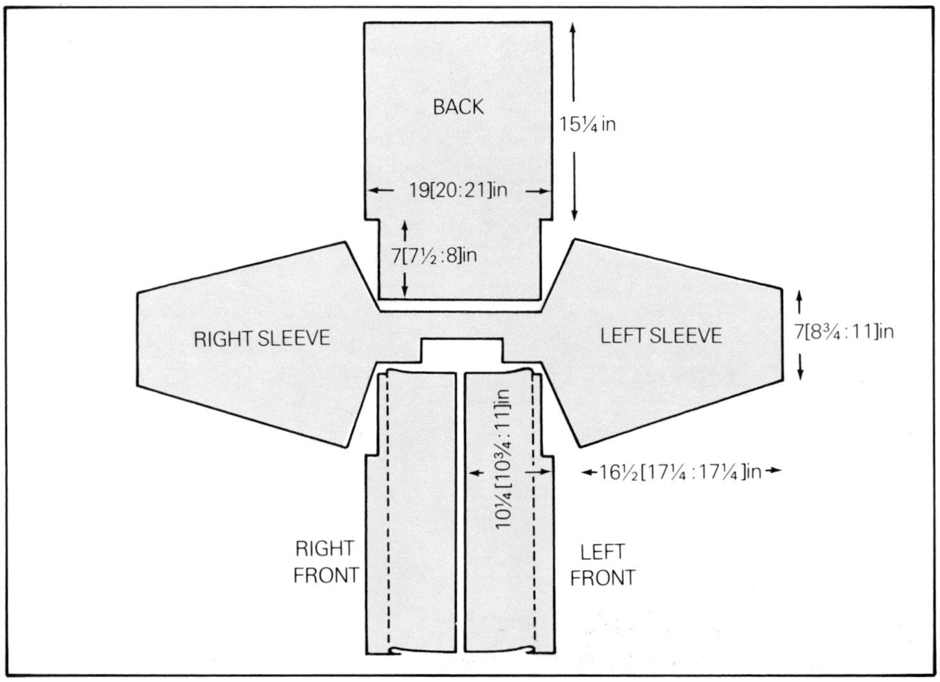

BACK
15¼ in
19[20:21]in
7[7½:8]in
RIGHT SLEEVE
LEFT SLEEVE
7[8¾:11]in
10¼[10¾:11]in
16½[17¼:17¼]in
RIGHT FRONT
LEFT FRONT

John Hutchinson

90

into each of the 19ch. Turn. 95 sts.
All sizes
Next row Patt to end. Turn.
Rep last row 4 times more. Fasten off.

Sleeve back and yoke
Next row Rejoin yarn to last fasten off point on left sleeve front and work across all sts on left sleeve, 1hdc into each of 24[26:28]ch for back neck, then 1hdc into each st of right sleeve. 194[210:218]sts.
Patt 5 rows across all sts.
Divide and complete first sleeve
1st row Work across first 70[75:76] sts, turn.
2nd row Dec 1, work to end. Turn.
3rd row Patt to end. Turn.
Rep 2nd and 3rd rows until 67[71:71] sts rem; end with a 2nd row.
Next row Sl st across first 7 sts, sl st into next st, 2ch to count as first hdc, work to end. Turn.
Next row Dec 1, work to within last 7 sts, turn.
Rep last 2 rows until 7[11:11] sts rem. Fasten off.
Divide and complete second sleeve
1st row Skip 54[60:66] sts for back yoke, rejoin yarn to next st, 2ch, 1hdc into each st to end. Turn. 70[75:75] sts.
2nd row Work to within last 2 sts, dec 1. Turn.
3rd row Patt to end. Turn.
Rep last 2 rows until 67[71:71] sts rem; end with a dec row.
Next row Patt to within last 7 sts, turn.
Next row Sl st across first 7 sts, sl st into next st, 2ch, work to within last 2 sts, dec 1. Turn. Rep last 2 rows until 7[11:11] sts rem. Fasten off.

To finish
Fold tuck in each of fronts, matching marked points at top and bottom. Work a row of sc along top edge to secure tuck. Work a row of sc along top back edge, then match back yoke with back top and sew in place. Insert back sleeves into back armholes. Insert front sleeves into front armholes, then sew across yoke leaving 7[8:9] rows free for front neck.

Collar
Using size F (4.00mm) hook, knitting worsted and with RS facing make 9ch, 1sc into 2nd ch from hook, 1sc into each of rem 7ch, then work 1sc into each st along right front neck, then work 2sc into each row end up neck edge of yoke, 1sc into each st along back neck, 2sc into each row end down left neck edge of yoke and then 1sc into each st along left front neck edge. Turn.
Next row 1ch, 1sc into each sc to end. Turn.
1st buttonhole row 1ch, 1sc into each of first 2sc, 2ch, skip next 2sc, 1sc into each sc to end. Turn.
2nd buttonhole row 1ch, 1sc into each

sc to within last 2ch sp, 2sc into 2ch sp, 1sc into each of last 2sc. Turn.
Next row 1ch, 1sc into each sc to end. Turn.
Next row 1ch, 1sc into each sc to end. Turn.
Work the 2 buttonhole rows once more.
Next row 1ch, 1sc into each sc to end. Fasten off.
Cuffs (alike)
With RS facing, using knitting worsted and size G (4.50mm) hook and working into the row ends of sleeve, work *1sc into each of next 2 row ends, 2sc into next row end, rep from * to end. Turn.
Next row 1ch, 1sc into each sc to end. Turn.
Rep last row 15 times. Fasten off.
Join underarm and side seams.

Waistband
With RS facing, using knitting worsted and size F (4.00mm) hook, work 2sc into each row end all along lower edge of fronts and back, securing tucks in place on fronts. Turn. Change to size C (3.00mm) hook and work 1sc into each sc to end. Turn. Work a further 8 rows in

sc. Fasten off. Using knitting worsted and size F (4.00mm) hook, work a row of sc along each front edge, working 1sc into each st and 1sc into each row end of waistband.

Concealed buttonhole band
Using knitting worsted and size F (4.00mm) hook make 96[98:100]ch.
1st row 1sc into 2nd ch from hook, 1sc into each ch to end. Turn. 95[97:99]sc.
2nd row 1ch, 1sc into each sc to end. Turn.
3rd row 1ch, 1sc into each of first 3[4:5]sc, *3ch, skip next 3sc, 1sc into each of next 14sc, rep from * to within last 7[8:9]sc, 3ch, skip next 3ch, 1sc into each sc to end. Turn.
4th row 1ch, 1sc into each sc and 3sc into each 3ch sp to end. Turn.
Rep 2nd row twice more. Fasten off.
Attach buttonhole band to inside of right front edge, sewing at inner edge only.
Now sew buttonhole band to right front edge, halfway between each buttonhole and secure at top and bottom.
Sew buttons on left front and collar edge to correspond with buttonholes.

Classic pullover

Here's a handsome sweater a classic V-neck made in a fashionable bouclé yarn. It is easy to work in plain Tunisian crochet with knitted ribbings.

Sizes
To fit 36[38:40]in (92[97:102]cm) chest.
Length, 29¾[30:31]in (76[77:79]cm).
Sleeve seam, 18¾in (48cm).
Note Directions for larger sizes are in brackets []; if there is only one set of figures it applies to all sizes.

Materials
20[20:22]oz (550[550]g) of a lightweight bouclé yarn
Size G (4.50mm) Tunisian crochet hook
1 pair No. 5 (4mm) knitting needles

Gauge
17 sts and 16 rows (i.e. 8 vertical loops) to 4in (10cm) worked on size G (4.50mm) Tunisian crochet hook.

Back
Using size G (4.50mm) Tunisian crochet hook make 84[88:94]ch.
1st row Insert hook into 2nd ch from hook, yo and draw a loop through, *insert hook into next loop, yo and draw a loop through, rep from * to end. 84[88:94] loops on hook.
2nd row Yo and draw through first loop on hook, *yo and draw through next 2 loops on hook, rep from * to end.
3rd row *Insert hook from right to left through next vertical loop, yo and draw a loop through, insert hook from left to right through next vertical loop, yo and draw a loop through, rep from * to end, insert hook from right to left into end st, yo and draw a loop through. Do not turn work. 84[88:94] loops on hook. The 2nd and 3rd rows form patt. Cont in patt until work measures 16[16:16½]in (41[41:42]cm); end with a 2nd row.
Shape raglan armholes
Next row Sl st across first 4 loops, patt to within last 4 loops, then work back.
Dec one loop (by working 2 loops tog) at each end of next and every foll loop row until 32[34:38] sts rem; end with a 2nd row. Fasten off.

Front
Work as back to beg of armhole shaping.
Shape raglan armholes
Next row Sl st across first 4 loops, patt to within last 4 loops, then work back.
Divide for neck
1st row Dec 1 loop, work 36[38:41]

loops, then work back.
2nd row Work 37[39:42] loops, then work back.
Dec 1 loop at armhole edge on next and every foll loop row, **at same time** dec 1 loop at neck edge on next and every foll alternate loop row until 16[17:19] dec have been worked at neck edge. Cont to dec at armhole edge only until one loop rems.
Fasten off.
Rejoin yarn to inner edge of sts that were left and work to match first side.

Sleeves
Using size G (4.50mm) Tunisian hook make 52[52:58]ch. Work first row as for back. 52[52:58] loops on hook.
Cont in patt inc 1 loop (by working 1st into first loop and 2 sts into last loop) at each end of every foll 9th loop row until there are 66[66:72] loops. Cont straight until work measures 16½in (42cm); end with a 2nd row.
Shape raglan armhole
Work as given for back raglan armhole until 14[12:16] loops rem. Fasten off.

Cuffs
With RS facing and using No. 5 (4mm) needles pick up and K 52[52:58] sts along lower edge. Work 18 rows K1, P1 ribbing. Bind off in ribbing.

Waistbands (alike)
With RS facing and using No. 5 (4mm) needles pick up and K 84[88:94] sts along lower edge.
Work 18 rows K1, P1 ribbing. Bind off in ribbing.

Neckband
Join raglan seams. With RS facing and using No. 5 (4mm) needles join yarn to center back neck and pick up and K 27 sts along neck, 10[10:12] sts from top of sleeve and 62[62:64] sts along front neck to center. 99[99:103] sts. Work 8 rows K1, P1 ribbing, dec one st at center front edge on every other row. Bind off in ribbing. Work 2nd side to correspond.

To finish
Block the work. Join side, sleeve and neckband seams.

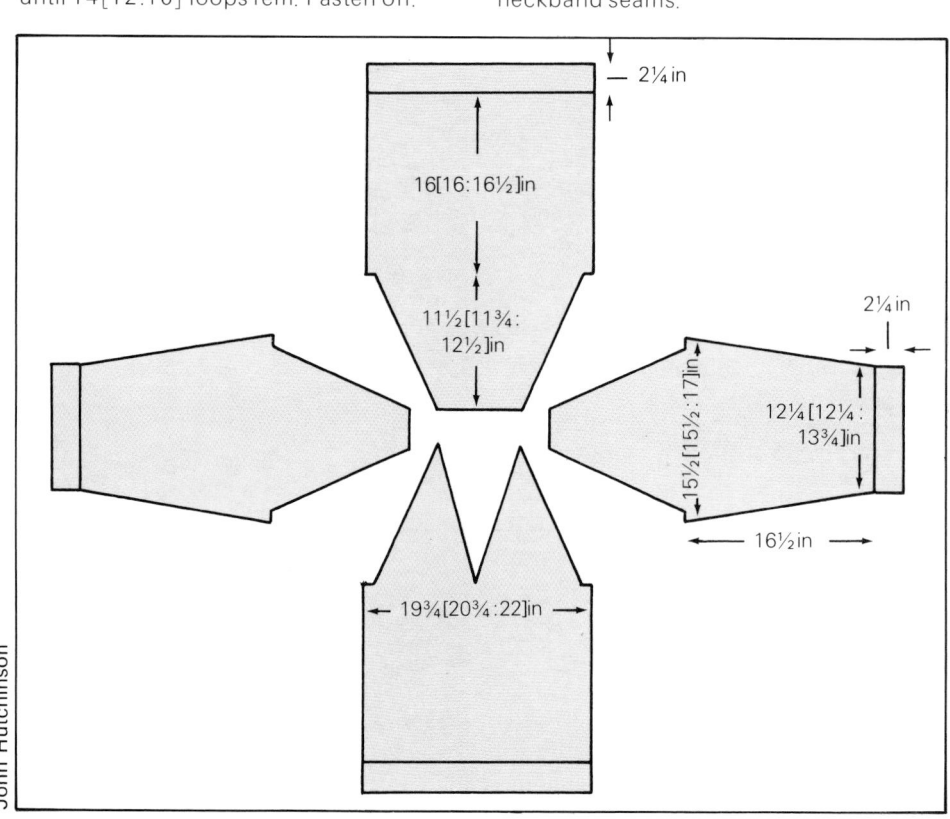

John Hutchinson

Knit-wit!

This sleeveless sweater is a real puzzle. Wear it with a black sweater and everyone will think you didn't have time to finish it.

Sizes

To fit 34[36:38]in (87[92:97]cm) bust. Length, 23½[24:24½]in (60[61:62]cm). **Note** Directions for larger sizes are in brackets []; if there is only one set of figures it applies to all sizes.

Materials

13[13:15]oz (350[350:400]g) of a knitting worsted in main color (A)
2[2:4]oz (50[50:100]g) of a sport yarn in 1st contrasting color (B)
2oz (50g) of a sport yarn in 2nd contrasting color (C)
1 pair each Nos. 2, 3, 8 and 10 (2¾: 3¼, 5½ and 6½mm) knitting needles
Knitting spool
Stuffing

Gauge

15 sts and 20 rows to 4in (10cm) in stockinette st using No. 10 (6½mm) needles and A.
26 sts and 34 rows to 4in (10cm) in stockinette st using No. 3 (3¼mm) needles and B.

Front

*Using No. 8 (5½mm) needles and A, cast on 69[73:77] sts.
1st ribbing row K1, (P1, K1) to end.
2nd ribbing row P1, (K1, P1) to end.
Rep these 2 rows for 2¼in (6cm); end with a 2nd ribbing row. Change to No. 10 (6½mm) needles. Beg with a P row, cont in reverse stockinette st until work measures 15¾in (40cm); end with a K row.*

Shape armholes and divide for neck

Next row Bind off 5, P until there are 27[29:31] sts on right-hand needle, P2 tog, turn and leave rem sts on a spare needle. Complete this side of neck first. Dec one st at armhole edge on every row, **at the same time** dec one st at neck edge on every foll 4th row until 18[19:20] sts rem. Keeping armhole edge straight cont to dec one st at neck edge on every 4th row until 10[10:11] sts rem. Cont straight until armhole measures 7¾[8¼:8¾]in (20[21:22]cm); end at armhole edge.

Shape shoulder

Bind off 3 sts at beg of next and foll alternate row. Work 1 row. Bind off. Return to sts on spare needle. With RS facing place next st on a safety pin, join yarn to next st and P to end of row. Complete as first side reversing shaping.

Back

Work as for front from * to *.
Next row P37[39:41], do **not** cut off yarn but wind a small ball of yarn. Cut off yarn. Leave all sts on a spare needle. Using No. 3 (3¼mm) needles and B, cast on 119 sts. Work in stockinette st for 2in (5cm); end with a P row.

Shape armholes

Bind off 8 sts at beg of next 2 rows. Dec one st at each end of every row until 73[76:79] sts rem. Cont straight until armholes measure 7¾[8¼:8¾]in (20[21: 22]cm); end with a P row.

Shape shoulders

Bind off 6 sts at beg of next 4 rows and 7 sts at beg of foll 2 rows. 35 sts. Rep 2 ribbing rows of front for ¾in (2cm); end with a 2nd ribbing row. Bind off loosely in ribbing.

Pocket

Using No. 10 (6½mm) needles and A, cast on 17 sts. Beg with a P row, cont in stockinette st for 3¼in (8cm); end with a K row. Change to No. 8 (5½mm) needles and work 2 ribbing rows of back twice. Bind off in ribbing.

Armhole borders (alike)

Front With RS facing join on A and using No. 8 (5mm) needles, pick up and K 49[51:53] sts evenly along armhole edge. Beg with 2nd ribbing row, work 2 ribbing rows of front for 1in (2.5cm); end with a 2nd ribbing row. Bind off in ribbing.
Back With RS facing join on B and using No. 2 (2¾mm) needles pick up and K 69[73:77] sts evenly along armhole edge. Work as for front armhole borders.

Neckband

Join right shoulder seam. With RS facing join A to top of left front at shoulder and using No. 8 (5½mm) needles, pick up and K 44[46:48] sts along left front neck, K center st from safety pin, then pick up and K 44[46:48] sts along right front neck. 89[93:97] sts.
1st row (P1, K1) to within 2 sts of center st, P2 tog, P center st, P2 tog tbl, (K1, P1) to end.
2nd row (K1, P1) to within 2 sts of center st, K2 tog tbl, K center st, K2 tog, (P1, K1) to end.
Rep these 2 rows for 1in (2.5cm); end with a first row. Bind off in ribbing dec each side of center st.

Knitting needles

Using knitting spool and C, and stuffing strip as you work, make a strip of spool knitting 10in (25cm) long. Bind off.
Using No. 2 (2¾mm) needles and C, cast on 3 sts for knob. K 1 row.
Next row P1, (pick up loop lying between needles and P into back of it—called make 1 or M1—, P1) twice.
Next row K to end.
Next row P1, M1, P3, M1, P1.
Next row K to end.
Next row P2 tog tbl, P to last 2 sts, P2 tog.
Next row K to end.
Rep last 2 rows once more. Bind off. Gather edge of knob and sew to spool knitting.
Make another needle in the same way.

To finish

Press or block, according to yarn used. Join left shoulder and neckband seam. Sew lower edge of top of back to lower part of back overlapping for 2in (5cm). Join side seams. Sew on pocket. Insert knitting needles into sts on back, secure first and last sts on each needle. Take yarn over shoulder and insert ball of yarn in pocket. Sew yarn to sweater at regular intervals to secure.

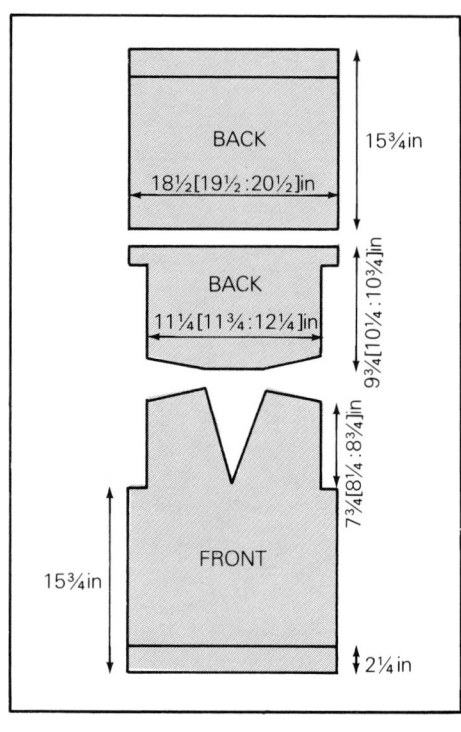

BACK 15¾in
18½[19½:20½]in

BACK
11¼[11¾:12¼]in

9¾[10¼:10¾]in

7¾[8¼:8¾]in

FRONT

15¾in

2¼in

Ian Stephen

KNITTING

A little romance

Try knitting these pretty camisoles in soft muted colors.

Sizes
To fit 32[34:36:38]in (83[87:92:97] cm) bust.
Front-opening camisole length at side seam, 13¾[14¾:15¾:16¾]in (36[38:40: 42]cm).
Lace-trimmed camisole length from back neck to hem, 16[16½:17:17½]in (41[42: 43:44]cm).
Ribbon-threaded camisole length at side seam, 21½[22½:23½:24½]in (55[57:59: 61]cm).
Note Directions for the larger sizes are in brackets []; if there is only one set of figures it applies to all sizes.

Materials
   Fine, soft sport-weight yarn
   Front-opening camisole 4[5:6:7]oz
      (100[125:150:175]g)
   1 pair each Nos. 1 and 3 (2½ and
      3¼mm) knitting needles
   1yd (1m) narrow satin ribbon
   3 buttons
   Lace-trimmed camisole 5[6:7:8]oz
      (125[150:175:200]g)
   1 pair each Nos. 2 and 3(2¾ and
      3¼mm) knitting needles
   Size B (2.50mm) crochet hook
   1½yd (1.3m) narrow lace
   Ribbon-threaded camisole 5[6:7:8]oz
      (125[150:175:200]g)
   1 pair each Nos. 1 and 3 (2½ and
      3¼mm) knitting needles
   2yd (2m) narrow satin ribbon

Gauge
Front-opening camisole 30 sts and 40 rows to 4in (10cm) in patt on No. 3 (3¼mm) needles.
Lace-trimmed and ribbon-threaded camisoles 32 sts and 40 rows to 4in (10cm) in stockinette st on No. 3 (3¼mm) needles.

Front-opening camisole

Back
Using No. 1 (2½mm) needles cast on 115[121:129:137] sts.
1st row *K1, P1, rep from * to last st, K1.
2nd row *P1, K1, rep from * to last st, P1.
Rep last 2 rows for 2¼in (6cm); end with a 2nd row and dec one st at end of row on first and 4th sizes only. 114[121:129: 136] sts. Change to No. 3 (3¼mm) needles. Beg patt.
1st row (RS) K6[1:5:0], *K8, yo, sl 1, K1, psso, K7, rep from * to last 6[1:5:0] sts, K6[1:5:0].
2nd and foll alternate rows P to end.
3rd row K6[1:5:0], *K6, K2 tog, yo, K1, sl 1, K1, psso, K6, rep from * to last 6[1:5:0] sts, K6[1:5:0].
5th row K6[1:5:0:], *K5, K2 tog, yo, K3, yo, sl 1, K1, psso, K5, rep from * to last 6[1:5:0] sts, K6[1:5:0].
7th row K6[1:5:0], *K4, K2 tog, yo, K5, yo, sl 1, K1, psso, K4, rep from * to last 6[1:5:0] sts, K6[1:5:0].

8th row P to end.
These 8 rows form patt. Cont in patt until work measures 13[14:15:16]in (34[36:38:40]cm); end with a WS row, inc 1 st at end of row on first and 4th sizes only. 115[121:129:137] sts.
Change to No. 1 (2½mm) needles. Beg with a K row, work 6 rows stockinette st.
Next row K1, *yo, K2 tog, rep from * to end.
Beg with a P row, work 6 more rows stockinette st. Bind off.

Front
Work as for back to 9[9¾:10½:11¼]in (23[25:27:29]cm) from beg; end with a WS row.
Divide for front opening
Next row Patt 53[56:60:63] sts, sl next 8[9:9:10] sts onto a safety pin, patt to end.
Cont in patt, working 3 sts in garter st at front edge, on last set of 53[56:60:63] sts for right side of opening until work measures 13[14:15:16]in (34[36:38:40]cm); end with a WS row and dec one st at end of last row on 2nd and 3rd sizes only, 53[55:59:63] sts. Change to No.1 (2½mm) needles. Work picot hem as for back, keeping 3 sts in garter st at front edge. Bind off. Rejoin yarn to sts at left side of opening. Complete to match first side.

To finish
Fold picot hem in half and sew in place on WS of work.
Front border
Using No. 3 (3¼mm) needles and with RS facing, rejoin yarn to sts on safety pin. Cont in garter st until border fits up left front edge to picot edging. Bind off. Sew border in place along left front. Sew 3 evenly-spaced buttons onto border. Make ribbon button loops to correspond with buttons on opposite edge. Join side seams. Sew on satin ribbon straps.

Lace-trimmed camisole

Back
Using No. 2 (2¾mm) needles cast on 137[145:153:161] sts.
1st row K1, *P1, K1, rep from * to end.
2nd row P1, *K1, P1, rep from * to end.
Rep last 2 rows for 1¼in (3cm); with a 2nd row.
Change to No. 3 (3¼mm) needles. Beg with a K row, cont in stockinette st, dec one st at each end of 21st and every foll 20th row until 123[131:139:147] sts rem. Cont straight until work measures 16[16½:17:17½]in (41[42:43:44]cm); end with a P row.
Shape armholes
Bind off 5 sts at beg of next 2 rows, 4 sts at beg of foll 2 rows and 3 sts at beg of foll 2 rows. 99[107:115:123] sts.
Shape neck
Next row K2 tog, K38[40:42:44], bind off 19[23:27:31] sts, K38[40:42:44] sts, K2 tog.
Cont on last set of sts. Dec one st at each end of next and every foll alternate row until 17 sts rem. Cont straight until armhole measures 6¾[7:7¼:8]in (17[18:19:20]cm); end with a P row. Bind off. Rejoin yarn to neck edge of rem sts. Complete to match first side.

Front
Work as for back until 125[133:141:149] sts rem. Cont straight until work measures 13[13½:14:14½]in (33.5[34.5:35.5:36.5]cm); end with a P row. Cont to dec at sides before, **at same time** beg patt. Note that when 123[131:139:147] sts rem, K1 is omitted at each end of odd-numbered rows and P1 at each end of even-numbered rows.
1st row K1, *yo, P2 tog*, rep from * to * 23[25:27:29] times, K27, rep from * to * 24[26:28:30] times, K1.
2nd row P1, *yo, P2 tog*, rep from * to * 23[25:27:29] times, P27, rep from * to * 24[26:28:30] times, P1.
3rd row K1, *yo, P2 tog*, rep from * to * 25[27:29:31] times, K19, rep from * to * 26[28:30:32] times, K1.
4th row P1, *yo, P2 tog*, rep from * to * 25[27:29:31] times, P19, rep from * to * 26[28:30:32] times, P1.
5th row K1, *yo, P2 tog*, rep from * to * 26[28:30:32] times, K15, rep from * to * 27[29:31:33] times, K1.
6th row P1, *yo, P2 tog*, rep from * to * 26[28:30:32] times, P15, rep from * to * 27[29:31:33] times, P1.
7th row K1, *yo, P2 tog*, rep from * to * 27[29:31:33] times, K11, rep from * to * 28[30:32:34] times, K1.
8th row P1, *yo, P2 tog*, rep from * to * 27[29:31:33] times, P11, rep from * to * 28[30:32:34] times, P1.
9th row K1, *yo, P2 tog*, rep from * to * 28[30:32:34] times, K7, rep from * to * 29[31:33:35] times, K1.
10th row P1, *yo, P2 tog*, rep from * to * 28[30:32:34] times, P7, rep from * to * 29[31:33:35] times, P1.
11th row K1, *yo, P2 tog*, rep from * to * 29[31:33:35] times, K3, rep from * to * 30[32:34:36] times, K1.
12th row P1, *yo, P2 tog*, rep from * to * 29[31:33:35] times, P3, rep from * to * 30[32:34:36] times, P1.
13th row K1, *yo, P2 tog *, rep from * to * 29[31:33:35] times, K2 tog, K1, rep from * to * 30[32:34:36] times, K1.
14th row P1, *yo, P2 tog*, rep from * to * 29[31:33:35] times, P2, rep from * to * 30[32:34:36] times, P1.
15th row P1, *yo, P2 tog *, rep from * to * to last st, P1.
Cont in patt until front measures same as back to underarm; end with a WS row.
Shape armholes
Keeping patt correct, bind off 5 sts at beg of next 2 rows, 4 sts at beg of foll 2 rows and 3 sts at beg of next 2 rows.

98[106:114:122] sts.
Shape neck
Next row K2 tog, patt 38[40:42:44], bind off 18[22:24:26] sts, patt 38[40:42:44], K2 tog.
Dec one st at each end of next row.
Next row Patt to center 4 sts, yo, P4 tog, yo, patt to end.
Cont in patt, work 9 rows, dec one st at each end of next and foll alternate rows.
Next row Patt to center 6 sts, yo, P6 tog, yo, patt to end.
Cont in patt, dec as before until 11 sts rem. Cont straight until front matches back to shoulder; end with a WS row. Rejoin yarn to neck edge of rem sts. Complete to match first side.

To finish
Join side and shoulder seams. Work 1 row sc around neck and armholes. Sew lace around neck edge.

Ribbon-threaded camisole

Back
Using No. 1 (2½mm) needles cast on 145[153:161:169] sts.
1st row K1, *P1, K1 rep from * to end.
2nd row P1, *K1, P1, rep from * to end.
Rep last 2 rows for 4in (10cm); end with a 2nd row. Change to No. 3 (3¼mm) needles. Beg with a K row, cont in stockinette st, dec one st at each end of 21st and every foll 20th row until 129[137:145:153] sts rem. Cont straight until work measures 20½[21½:22½:23½]in (52[54:56:58]cm); end with a P row.
Next row (eyelet hole row) K3, *yo, K2 tog, K2, rep from * to last 2 sts, K2.
Beg with a P row, work 5 rows stockinette st. Work 6 rows garter st. Bind off.

Front
Using No. 1 (2½mm) needles cast on 145[153:161:169] sts. Rib 4in (10cm) as for back. Change to No. 3 (3¼mm) needles. Beg patt.
Next row K39[41:43:45], K2 tog, yo, K63[67:71:75], yo, K2 tog tbl, K39[41:43:45].
Work 3 rows stockinette st. Cont in patt as set on next and every foll 4th row until work measures 14¾[15:15½:16]in (37.5:38.5:39.5:40.5]cm); end with a 4th row, **at same time** dec one st at each end of 21st and every foll 20th row.
Shape bust
1st row K31[33:35:37], K2 tog, yo, K3, yo, K2 tog tbl, K57[61:65:69], K2 tog, yo, K3, K2 tog tbl, K31[33:35:37].
2nd and foll alternate rows P to end.
3rd row K30[32:34:36], K2 tog, yo, K5, yo, K2 tog tbl, K55[59:63:67], K2 tog, yo, K5, yo, K2 tog tbl, K30[32:34:36].
5th row K29[31:33:35], K2 tog, yo, K7, yo, K2 tog tbl, K53[57:61:65], K2 tog, yo, K7, K2 tog tbl, K29[31:33:35].
Cont in patt as set, dec at side edges as

before until 129[137:145:153] sts rem, until row ''K1, K2 tog, yo, K59[63:67 71], yo, K2 tog tbl, K1, K2 tog, yo, K59[63: 67:71], yo, K2 tog tbl, K1'' has been worked. P1 row.
Next row (eyelet hole row) K3, *yo, K2 tog, K2, rep from * to last 2 sts, K2, Beg with a P row, work 5 rows stockinette st. Work 6 rows garter st. Bind off.

To finish

Join side seams. Cut 1 yd (1m) ribbon; thread through eyelet holes to tie in bow at front. Cut ribbon for shoulder straps and sew to top edge.

Technique tip
Ribbon button loops

The buttons on the front-opening camisole are fastened with ribbon button loops, which are ideal for delicate garments, especially when used with small shanked buttons.

Use ribbon approximately $\frac{1}{4}$in (5mm) wide. Place it in front of you on the table. To form the loop, fold about 2in (5cm) from the short, right-hand end toward you to make a diagonal fold.

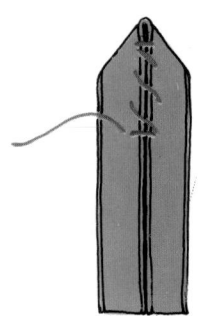

Then fold the long end toward you so that it is parallel with the short end and the ribbon forms a point. This is the right side of the loop. Secure the point with a few slip stitches. Trim the long end to match the short. Sew on buttons and pin loops to opening to match. Remove slip stitches and make sure that buttons fasten easily. Alter position of loops if necessary and sew them to opening. Trim ends of ribbon.

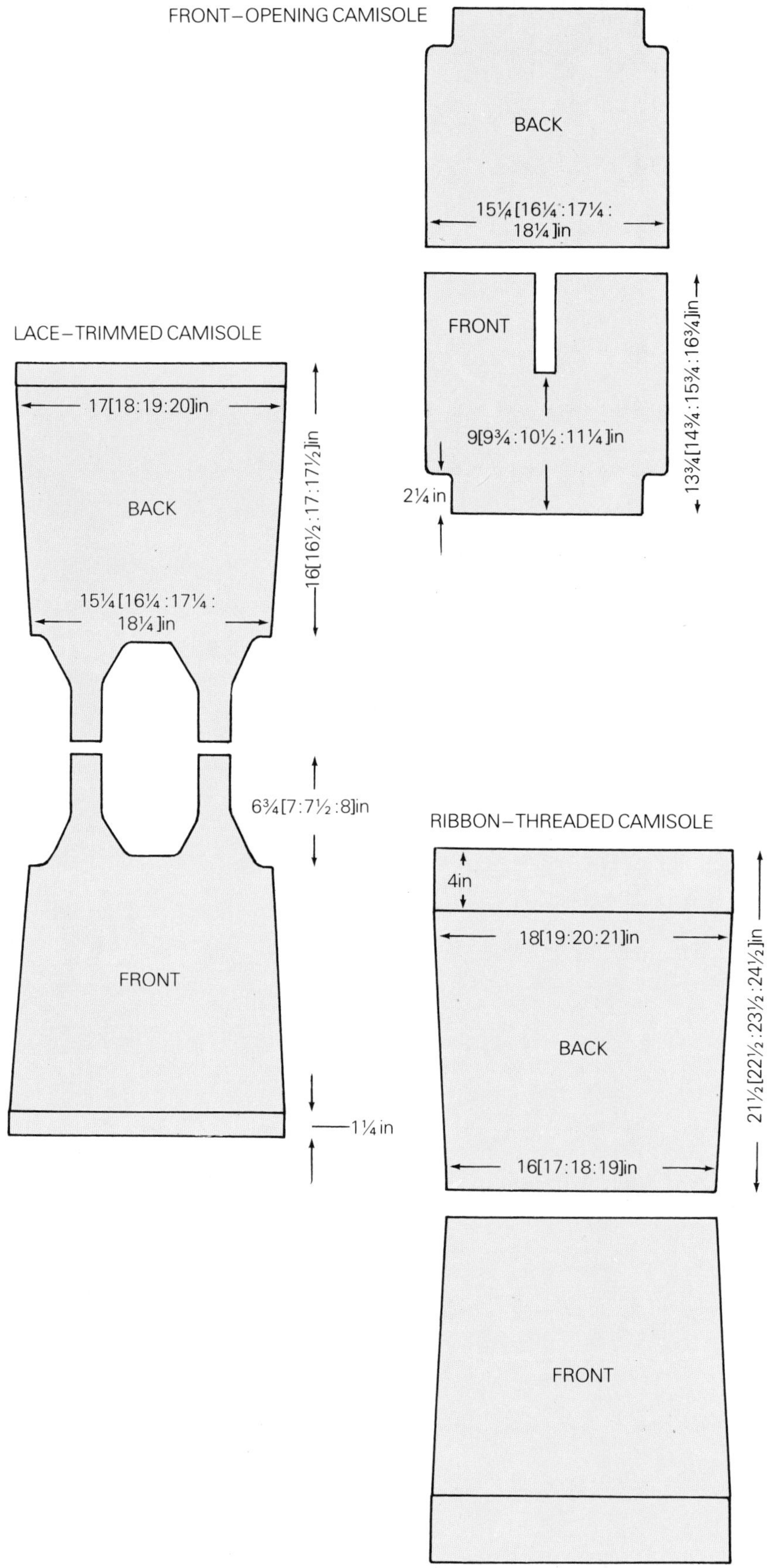

FRONT–OPENING CAMISOLE

BACK

15¼[16¼:17¼: 18¼]in

FRONT

9[9¾:10½:11¼]in

2¼ in

13¾[14¾:15¾:16¾]in

LACE–TRIMMED CAMISOLE

17[18:19:20]in

BACK

16[16½:17:17½]in

15¼[16¼:17¼: 18¼]in

6¾[7:7½:8]in

FRONT

1¼ in

RIBBON–THREADED CAMISOLE

4in

18[19:20:21]in

BACK

21½[22½:23½:24½]in

16[17:18:19]in

FRONT

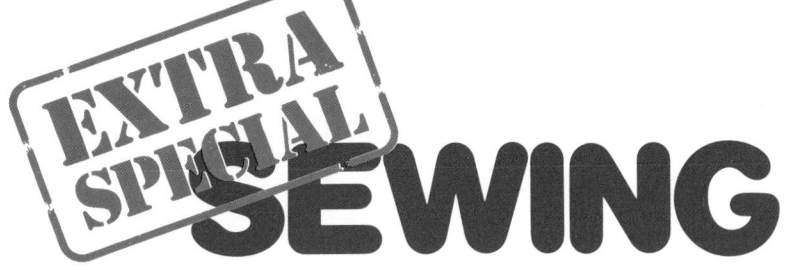

EXTRA SPECIAL SEWING

Two-faced

This coat leads a double life. It is completely reversible and trimmed with contrasting binding around the edge.

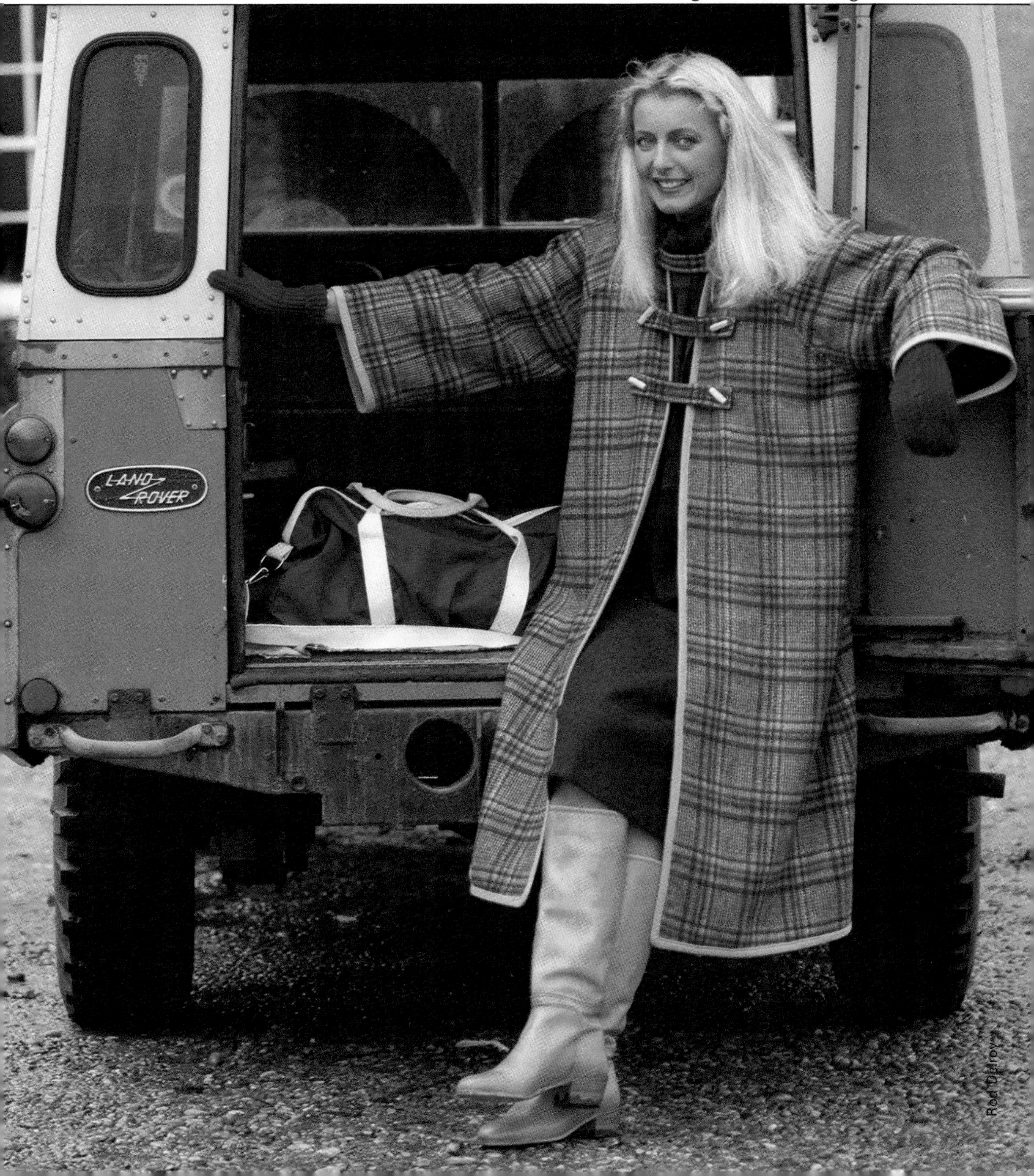

Rod Delroy

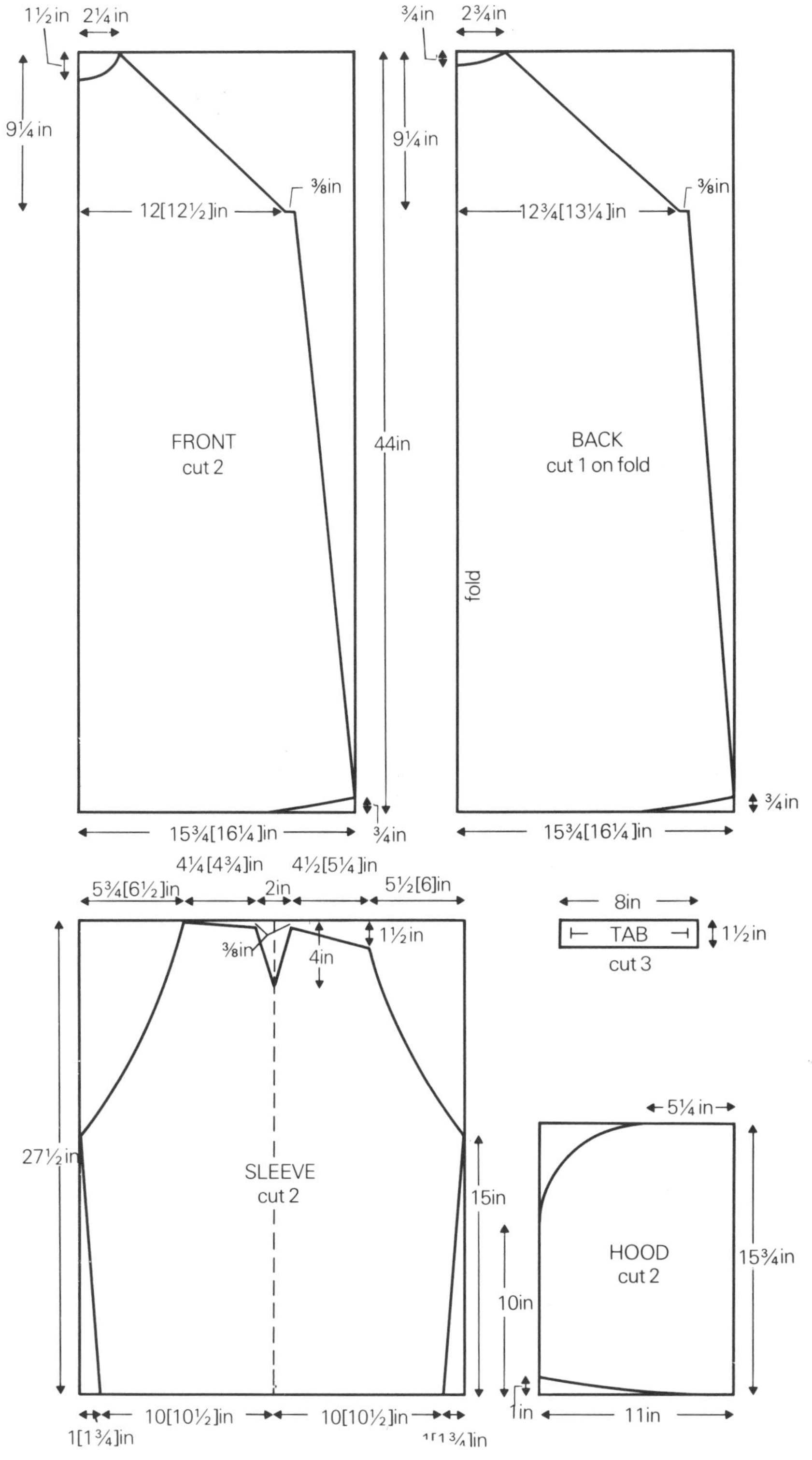
1½in 2¼in
9¼in
12[12½]in
⅜in
FRONT
cut 2
15¾[16¼]in
¾in
¾in 2¾in
9¼in
44in
12¾[13¼]in
⅜in
BACK
cut 1 on fold
fold
¾in
15¾[16¼]in
4¼[4¾]in
4½[5¼]in
5¾[6½]in
2in
5½[6]in
⅜in
1½in
4in
27½in
SLEEVE
cut 2
15in
10[10½]in
10[10½]in
1[1¾]in
1[1¾]in
8in
TAB
cut 3
1½in
5¼in
HOOD
cut 2
15¾in
10in
1in
11in

Cutting layout–60in-wide fabric

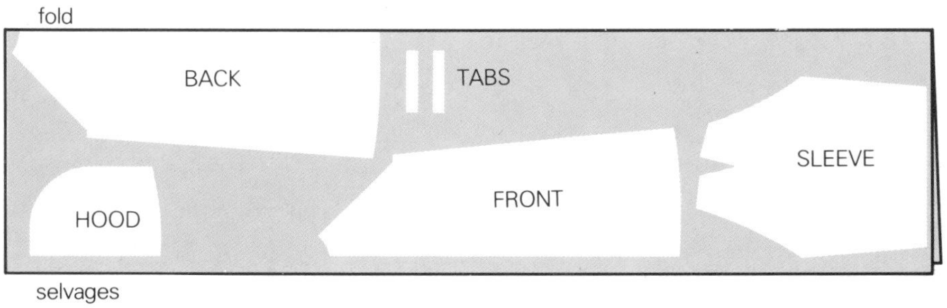
fold
BACK
TABS
SLEEVE
FRONT
HOOD
selvages

Brian Mayor

Measurements
To fit sizes 10/12[14/16].
Finished length: 44in (112cm).

Note Measurements are given for size 10/12. Figures for the larger size are in brackets. If only one figure is given, it applies to both sizes. ⅝-¾in (1.5-2cm) seam allowances have been included, as appropriate (see Technique tip). Check length before buying and cutting fabric.

Suggested fabrics
Reversible coatings, tweed, fur fabric.

Materials

LAND ROVER

$3\frac{1}{4}$yd (2.9m) of 54/60in (140/
150cm)-wide reversible fabric
(or twice this amount of
conventional fabric)
7m (6.5m) of 1in (2.5cm)-wide wool
braid
Matching thread
12 toggles or buttons
Yardstick, tailor's chalk
Flexible curve, paper for patterns

1 Following the measurement diagrams, make pattern pieces. Check that the edges of the raglan seams are even and that the base of the hood fits around the neckline. Cut out, following layout.

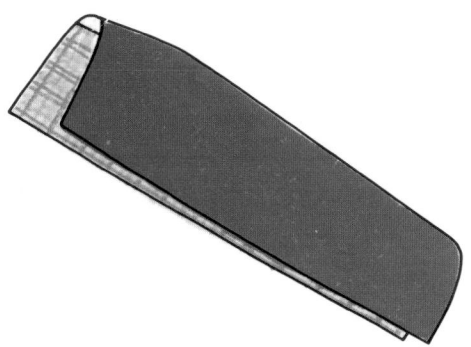

2 Pin, baste and stitch shoulder darts on each sleeve (see Technique tip if using reversible fabric). Press.

3 Stitch sleeve seams, using a flat felled seam, pressing seam allowance toward back (see Technique tip).

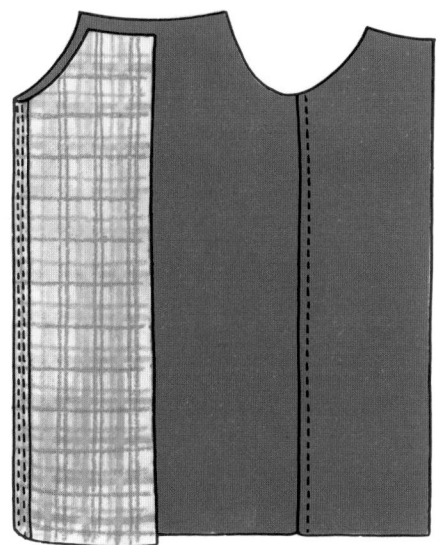

4 Stitch side seams of coat with a flat felled seam, pressing seam allowance toward back as on sleeves.

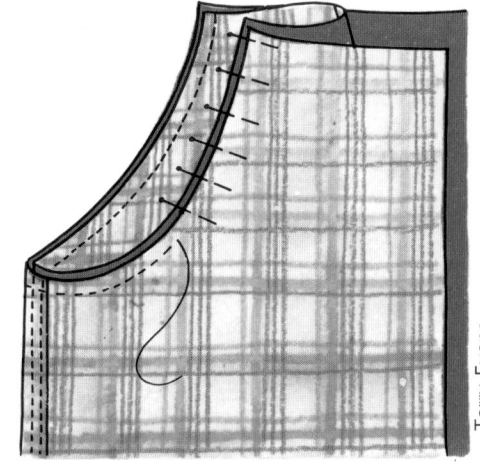

5 Set sleeves into armholes, matching sleeve seams and side seams, using a plain seam (see Technique tip).

Rod Delroy

Terry Evans

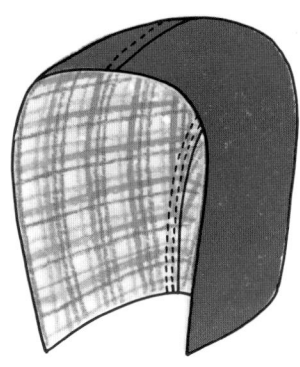

6 Stitch the center seam of the hood, using a flat felled seam.

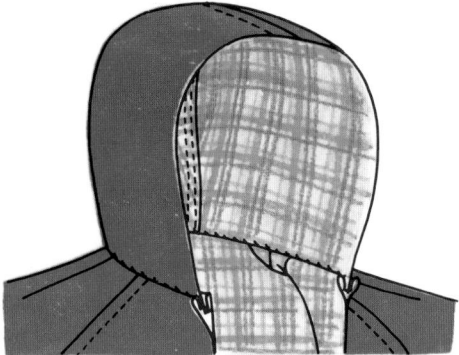

7 Attach hood by slipping raw edge of hood between the layers of the coat fabric, turning under raw edges of coat and slip stitching to hood along seamline.

8 Bind around edge of coat with braid, using the easy binding method (see Volume 16, page 56), mitering the corners neatly (see Volume 7, page 71). Start at one of the side seams and bind in a continuous strip around one front lower edge, up the front, around the hood, back down the other front and around the rest of the lower edge.

9 Bind the cuff edges in the same way, starting and finishing at the seam.

10 Work a ¾in (2cm) buttonhole ¾in (2cm) from each end of each tab piece. Bind edges and miter corners.

Note Alternatively, tab can be cut twice, with seam allowances added, and the pieces joined, right sides facing, turned right side out and topstitched.

11 Try on coat and pin the tabs in place, spacing them evenly, about 8in (20cm) apart. Take off coat and sew buttons in place to match buttonholes. Turn coat to reverse side and sew on six more buttons.

Note To make the coat in a conventional fabric with a lining, make the coat twice, once in coating fabric and once in lining. Turn lining wrong side out, slip it inside the coat and baste around all raw edges. Bind the edges to hold lining to coat.

Technique tip

Working with reversible fabrics

Reversible fabrics are usually made from two layers of woven fabric, either of which can be used as the top fabric of a garment. They may be two contrasting colors or one patterned and one solid color fabric. The layers are held together by threads which connect the inner surfaces. A few simple techniques enable you to finish both sides neatly, so that the garment is completely reversible.

Flat felled seam

This type of seam is suitable for long, straight sections. Stitch a flat seam, taking a $\frac{3}{4}$in (2cm) seam allowance. Press the seam open, then press both seam allowances to one side.

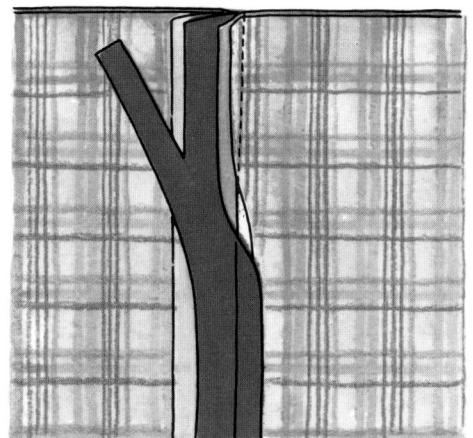

Separate the two layers of fabric, trimming the binding threads with scissors or a sharp craft knife. Grade the seam allowances of the four layers of fabric, leaving the top layer $\frac{3}{4}$in (2cm) wide and trimming the under layer to $\frac{1}{4}$in (5mm).

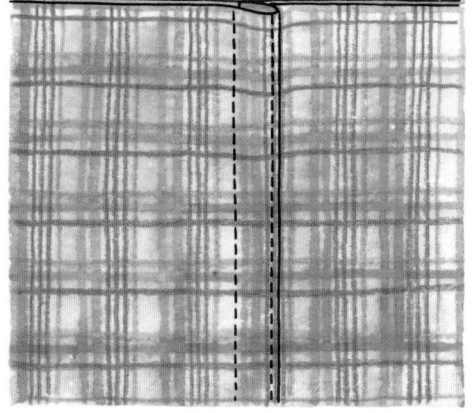

Turn under the free edge of the top layer of fabric. Pin, baste and stitch it in place, at the same time enclosing the other three layers of fabric.

Plain seam

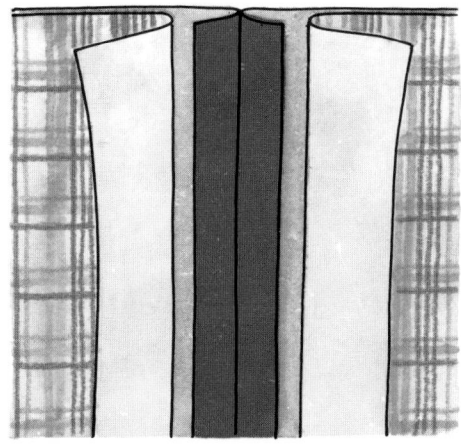

Separate the layers of fabric to a width of $1\frac{1}{2}$in (4cm) on each side of the seamline. Pin, baste and stitch a matching layer from each side of the seam, right sides facing. Press seam open.

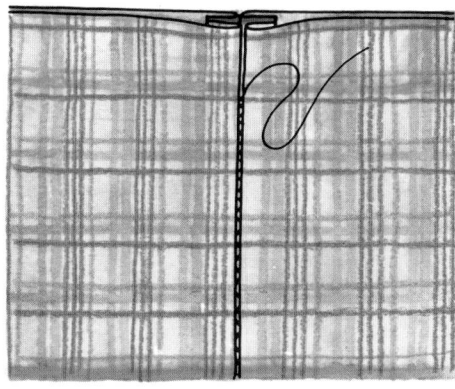

Turn seam allowances under on remaining free edges. Slip stitch folded edges together.

Darts

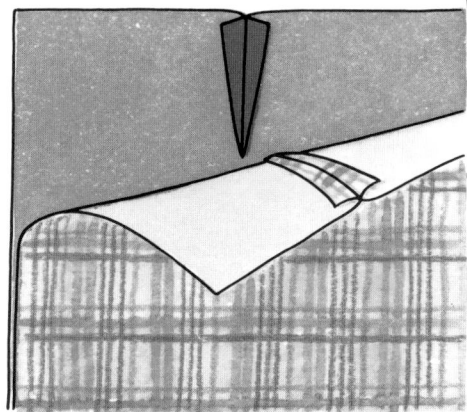

Separate the layers of fabric as far as the point of the dart. Stitch the dart on the inside of each fabric layer and press open, cutting the dart open if necessary.

Hems

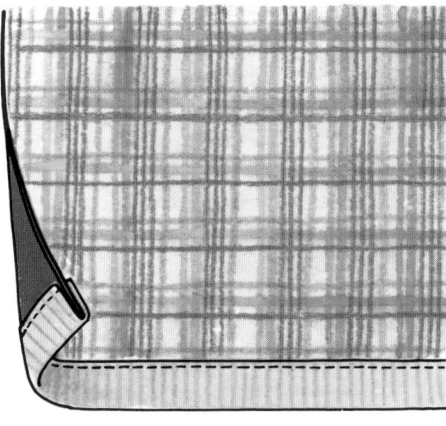

The simplest way to finish a hem is to bind it with braid.

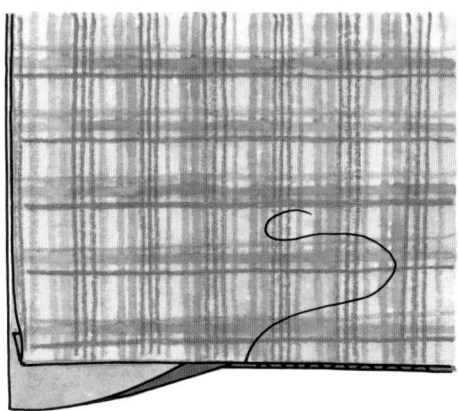

Alternately, the layers can be separated for $1\frac{1}{2}$in (4cm) then $\frac{3}{4}$in (2cm) can be turned in on each side and the edges slip stitched together. Topstitch for a crisp finish.

Dreaming of summer

These separates are designed to go together, but could be split up. The sashed tunic top is trimmed with a patch pocket to match the skirt, and the neck, armhole and hem edges are finished with topstitching.

Measurements
To fit ages 8[10:12].
Tunic length, 19½[21:22]in (50[53:56] cm).
Skirt length, 19¼[20:21½]in (49[51: 55]cm).
Waist, 24[25:26]in (61[63:66]cm).

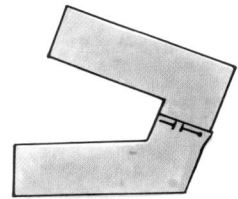

Note Measurements are given for age 8. Figures for larger sizes are in brackets []. If only one figure is given, it applies to all sizes.
A ⅝in (1.5cm) seam allowance has been included except where otherwise stated. A 2in (5cm) hem allowance is included.

Suggested fabrics
Cotton, lightweight wool, denim, gingham, wool/synthetic blends.

Tunic

Materials
1¾[1⅞:2]yd (1.6[1.7:1.8]m) of 36in (90cm)-wide fabric or 1[1:1⅛]yd (.9[.9:1]m) of 60in (150cm)-wide fabric
Small piece of contrasting fabric for pocket
Matching thread
One 5in (13cm) zipper; hook and eye
Two sheets of pattern paper, 20×24in (50×60cm)
Pencil; yardstick; flexible curve; tailor's chalk

1 Remember that children's measurements vary considerably. To fit the pattern pieces together accurately, first make a paper pattern, following the measurement diagram on page 108. The back and front, which are alike, and the sleeve pieces are drawn on folded paper as shown. Note the 90° angle of neckline and fold of paper.
Cut out all pattern pieces. Make separate patterns for neck, hem and cuff facings; these are all 1in (2.5cm) wide and shown as red broken lines.

2 Following the appropriate fabric layout, cut out back, front, sleeves, cuffs, facings and tie belt in fabric. Note that the center front is placed on a fold. Add a ⅝in (1.5cm) seam allowance along the center back edge.
To eliminate a shoulder seam on the neck facing, pin the front facing pattern to the back, overlapping the ⅝in (1.5cm) shoulder seam allowance as shown. Place the pattern with center front on fold of fabric and cut out a single piece from fabric.

3 Cut out pocket in contrasting fabric.
4 Stay-stitch front and back necklines of tunic. With right sides together and raw edges even, pin, baste and stitch shoulder seams. Press seams open.

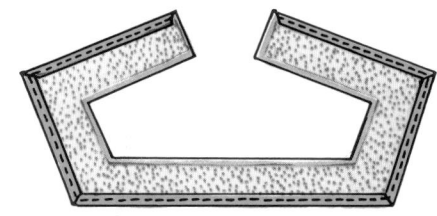

5 Turn up a ¼in (5mm) hem all around outer edge of neck facing; baste. Press.

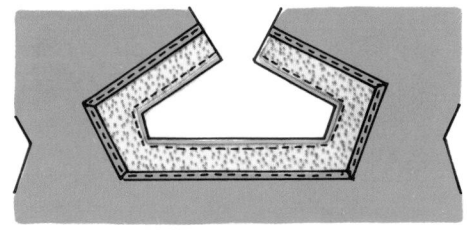

6 With right sides together and raw edges

even, pin, baste and stitch facing to neckline around inner edge, taking a ¼in (5mm) seam. Clip into corners and press the facing upward. Turn the facing to the wrong side and baste close to neck edge. Topstitch all around, close to inner and outer edges of facing.
7 With right sides together, pin, baste and stitch back seam to within 6in (15cm) of neckline.
Press seam open. Finish edges with zig-zag stitch or overcasting.

106

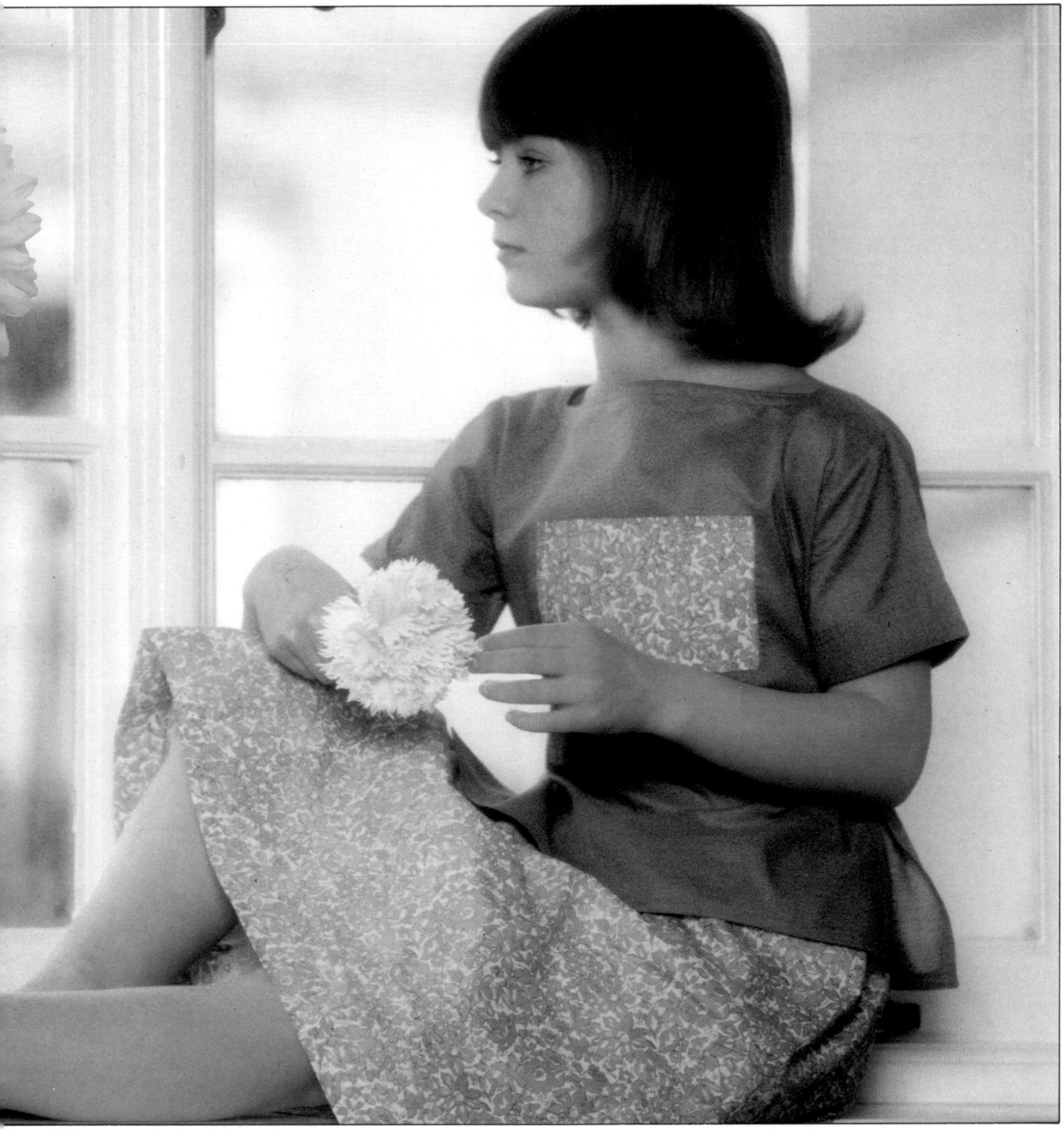

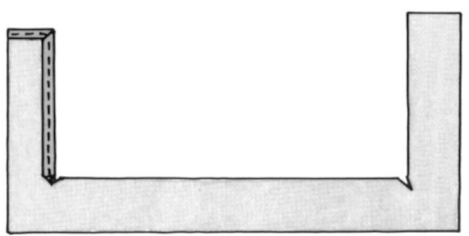

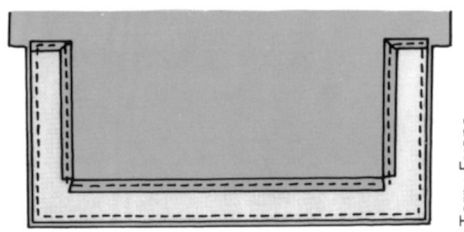

Rod Delroy

Terry Evans

8 Measure $6\frac{1}{4}$in (16cm) up from hem of tunic. Trim $\frac{3}{8}$in (1cm) from side seam allowances to this point.

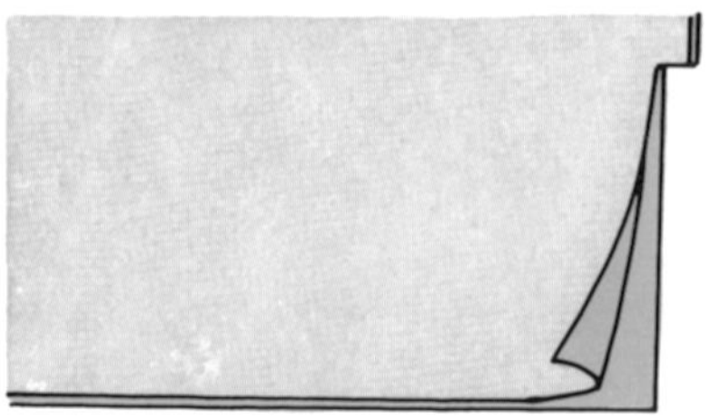

9 Clip $\frac{1}{4}$in (5mm) into corners of hem facing. Baste and press a $\frac{1}{4}$in (5mm) hem around inner and top edges as shown.

10 With right sides together and raw edges even, pin, baste and stitch outer edge of facing to front tunic hem, taking

Measurement diagram

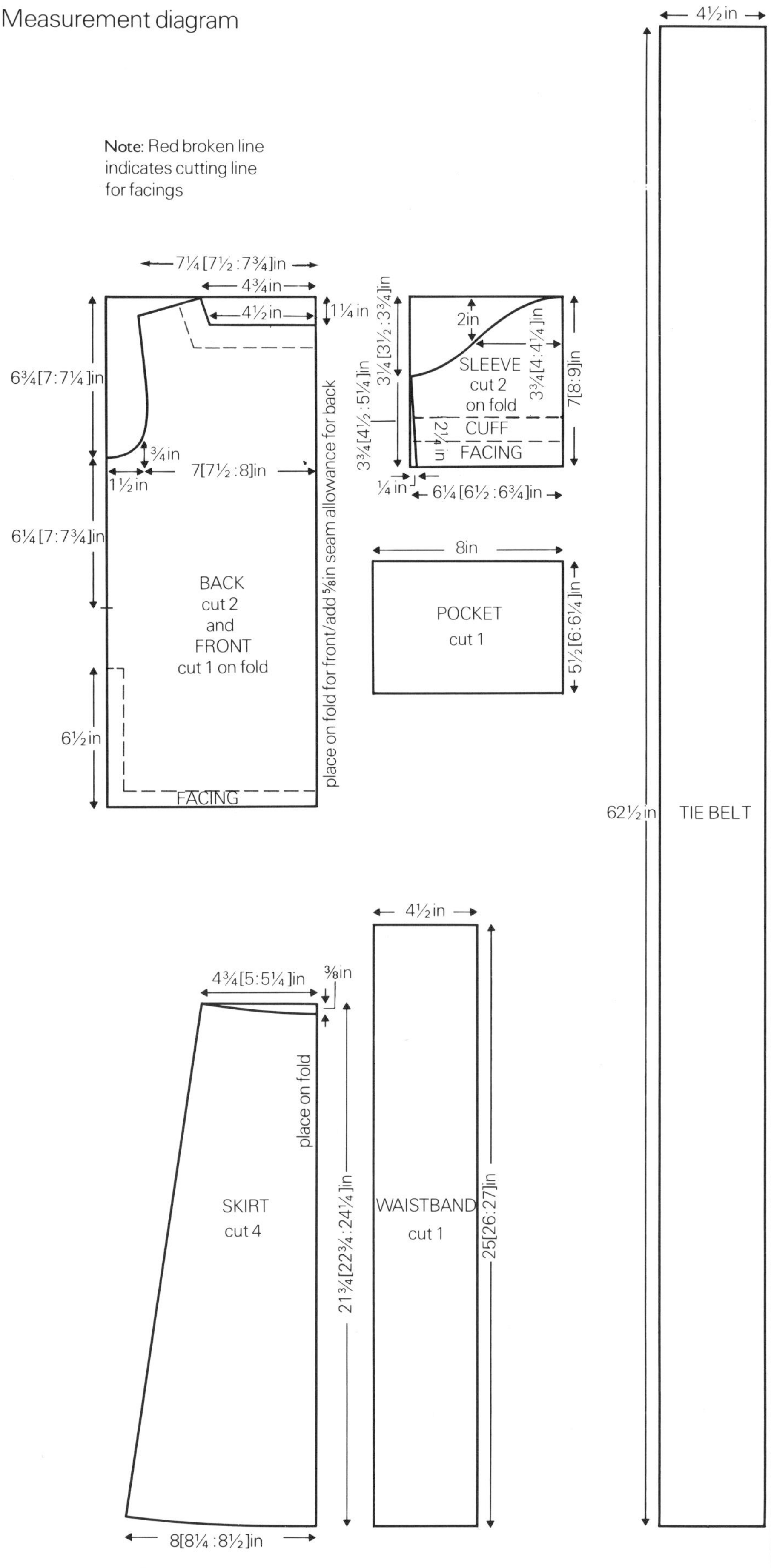

Note: Red broken line indicates cutting line for facings

← 7¼ [7½ : 7¾]in →

← 4¾in →

← 4½in →

1¼in

6¾[7:7¼]in

¾in

1½in

7[7½ : 8]in

6¼[7:7¾]in

BACK
cut 2
and
FRONT
cut 1 on fold

place on fold for front/add ⅝in seam allowance for back

6½in

FACING

2in

← 4½ [4½ : 5¼]in →

3¾ [4½ : 5¼]in

3¼ [3½ : 3¾]in

SLEEVE
cut 2
on fold

3¾ [4 : 4¼]in

7 [8 : 9]in

CUFF

FACING

2¼in

¼in

← 6¼ [6½ : 6¾]in →

← 8in →

POCKET
cut 1

5½ [6 : 6¼]in

4½ in

← 4¾ [5 : 5¼]in →

⅜in

place on fold

SKIRT
cut 4

← 4½in →

WAISTBAND
cut 1

21¾ [22¾ : 24¼]in

25 [26 : 27]in

← 8 [8¼ : 8½]in →

62½in | TIE BELT

4½ in

Brian Mayor

a ¼in (5mm) seam. Clip corners and turn facing to wrong side. Repeat for back tunic hem.

11 Baste around outer edge of facings and topstitch as for neck.

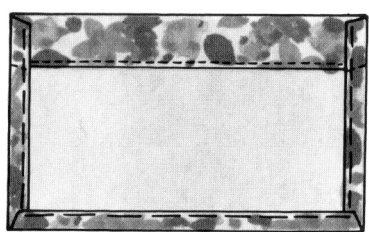

12 Turn under and stitch a ¼in (5mm) hem at top of pocket. Turn under another ¾in (2cm) and topstitch. Turn under and baste ⅝in (1.5cm) hems around remaining edges. Press.

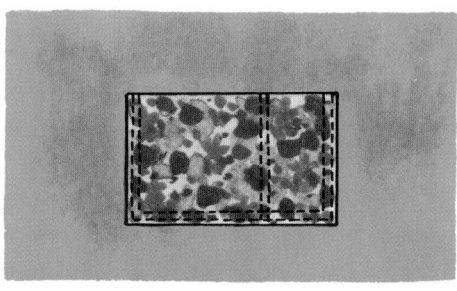

13 Position pocket on right side of tunic, matching center fronts. Topstitch around three sides. Add two vertical lines of topstitching 2in (5cm) from and parallel to left side of pocket.

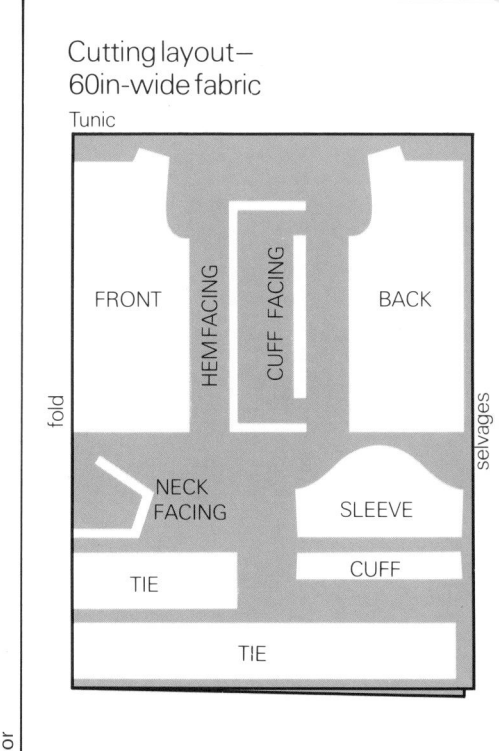

Cutting layout—60in-wide fabric

Tunic

fold

FRONT

HEM FACING

CUFF FACING

BACK

NECK FACING

SLEEVE

CUFF

TIE

TIE

selvages

14 With right sides together and raw edges matching, pin, baste and stitch side seams from facings to underarm. Finish and press.

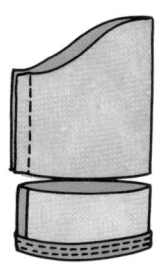

15 With right sides together and raw edges matching, stitch underarm seams of sleeves, cuffs and cuff facings. Take only ⅜in (1cm) seam allowance on cuffs to allow cuff to slip over sleeve comfortably. Apply the facings to inside of cuffs as for neck and hem.

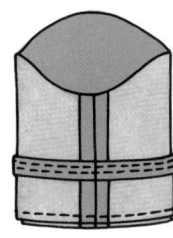

16 Matching seams, slip sleeve into cuff, with right side of cuff to wrong side of sleeve. Stitch and press, with seam allowance toward cuff. Turn up cuff over sleeve.

17 Starting and finishing 2in (5cm) to each side of center of sleeve cap, run a row of gathering stitches for easing the sleeve into the armhole.
Ease the sleeve cap, pulling up the gathering stitches until the sleeve fits the armhole. With right sides together and underarm seams matching, pin, baste and stitch the sleeves into the armholes. Finish and press the seam allowances toward the sleeves.

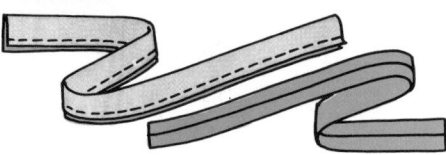

18 With right sides together, stitch long edge of tie belt, leaving ends open. Trim seam allowance. Turn right side out and press with seam in center of tie. Turn in and slip stitch ends.

Cutting layout—36in-wide fabric

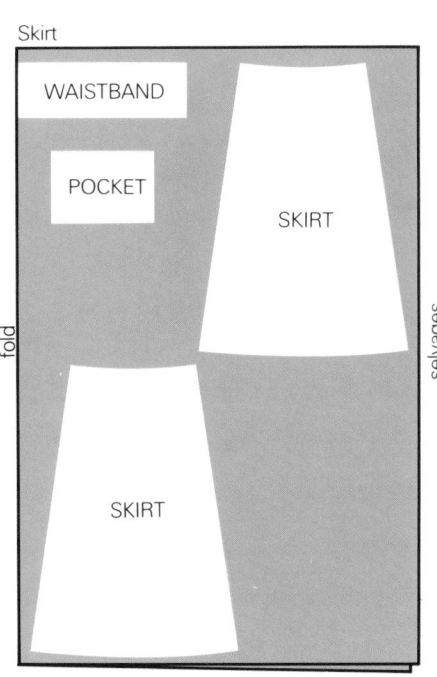

Skirt

| WAISTBAND |
| POCKET |
| SKIRT |
| SKIRT |

fold / selvages

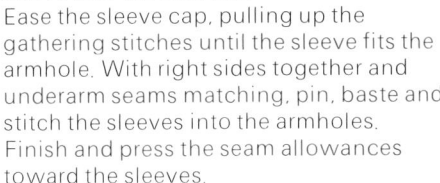

Tunic — fold

| TIE | TIE | CUFF | SLEEVE | HEM FACING | NECK FACING | FRONT |
| | | | | BACK | | CUFF FACING |

selvages

Skirt — fold

| WAISTBAND | SKIRT | POCKET | SKIRT |

selvages

Note: For larger sizes, allow extra fabric for pocket

Terry Evans

Brian Mayor

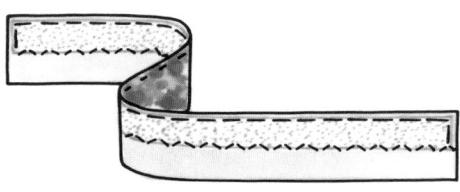

3 Baste interfacing to wrong side of waistband along outer edge and catch-stitch along inner edge.

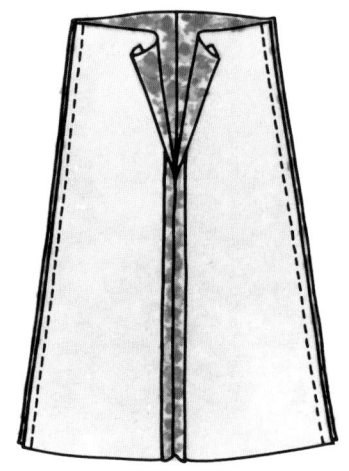

4 With right sides together and raw edges matching, pin, baste and stitch the four skirt seams, leaving 6¾in (17cm) open at center back seam for insertion of zipper. Press seams. Insert zipper.
5 Run a row of gathering stitches within seam allowance at waist. Pull up gathering thread until skirt fits waistband. Secure thread and adjust gathers.

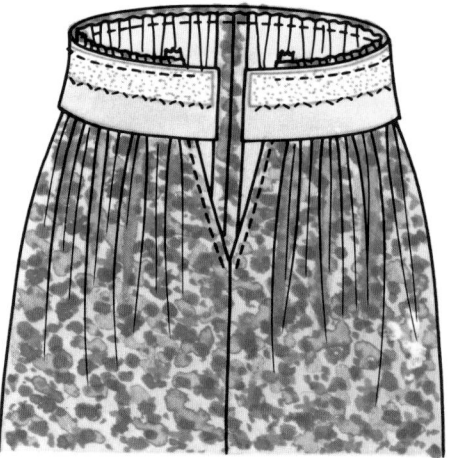

6 With right sides together and interfaced edge upward, pin, baste and stitch waistband to skirt. Stitch with gathers upward on machine. Trim seam allowances and press waistband. Turn under seam allowance on remaining long edge of waistband. Slip stitch edge of waistband over seamline on inside of skirt. Turn in ends of waistband and slip stitch. Sew hooks and eyes to waistband.
7 Turn up and complete hem. As skirt is slightly flared, use the method shown in Volume 6, page 106.

Skirt

Materials
1⅝[1⅝:1¾]yd (1.4[1.4:1.5]m) of
   36in (90cm)-wide fabric or
1¼[1⅜:1½]yd (1.1[1.2:1.3]m) of
   60in (150cm)-wide fabric
One 6in (15cm) zipper
Two hooks and eyes, thread
¼yd (25cm) of 36in (90cm)-wide
   interfacing
One sheet of pattern paper, 20×25in
   (50×65cm)
Pencil, yardstick, tailor's chalk

1 Folding paper as shown, make a paper pattern for skirt, following the measurements given. Cut out pattern.
2 Cut out four skirt sections and one waistband in fabric. Cut one waistband in interfacing to half waistband width.

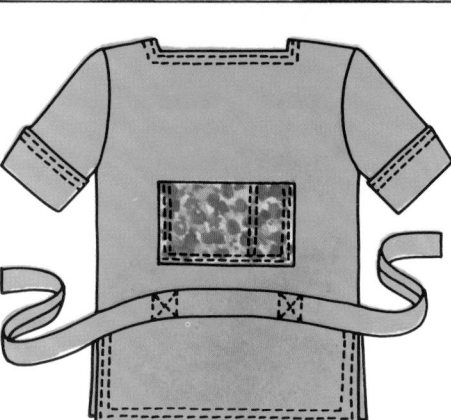

19 With center fronts matching and seam to the inside, position belt at marked waistline and topstitch parallel to pocket. Insert zipper in center back opening and finish with hook and eye.

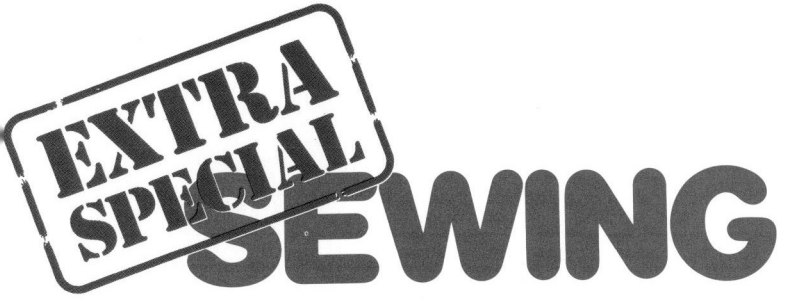

EXTRA SPECIAL SEWING

This simple two piece outfit is made special in two ways: it is made in silk and the vest and the pocket flaps are quilted.

Suited in silk

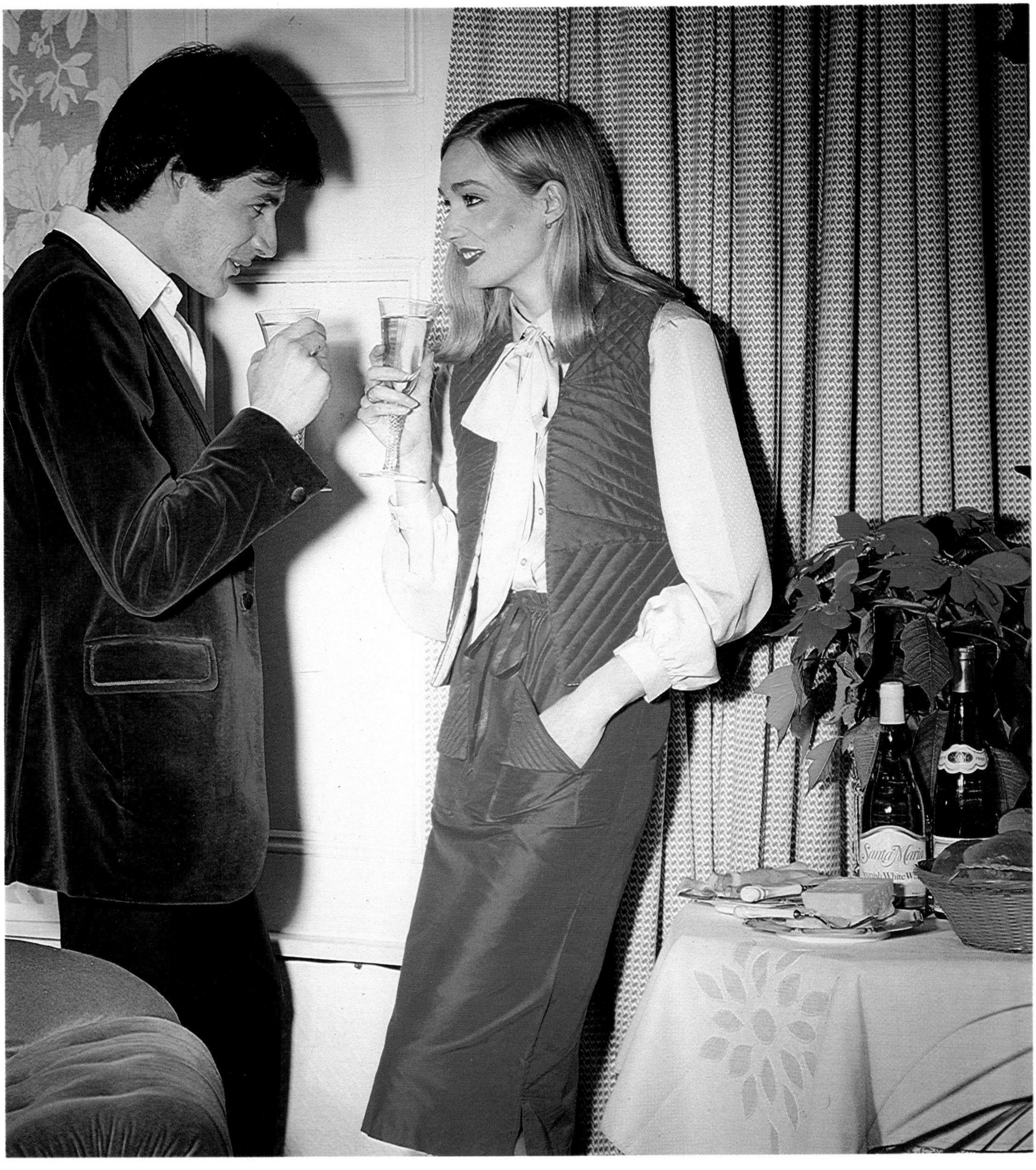

Stuart Macleod

Measurements

To fit sizes 8/10 [12/14].
Vest length, 23¼ [24]in (59[61]cm).
Skirt length, 27½ [28¼]in (70[72]cm).
Note Measurements are given for size 8/10 with measurements for the larger size in brackets []. If there is only one figure, it applies to all sizes. A seam allowance of ⅝in (1.5cm) and a skirt hem allowance of 1½in (3.5cm) are included.

Suggested fabrics

Medium-weight silk; lightweight silk or polyester for lining.

Materials

2⅛[2⅜]yd (1.9[2.1]m) of 45in (115cm)-wide silk or 3½yd (3.2m) of 36in (90cm)-wide silk
¾yd (.7m) of 45in (115cm)-wide lining or 1¾yd (1.5m) of 36in (90cm)-wide lining
1½yd (1.3m) of 36in (90cm)-wide muslin
1½yd (1.3m) of 36in (90cm)-wide lightweight batting
2¼yd (2m) of narrow ribbon or cord
Matching thread, pattern paper
Tailor's chalk, yardstick

Vest

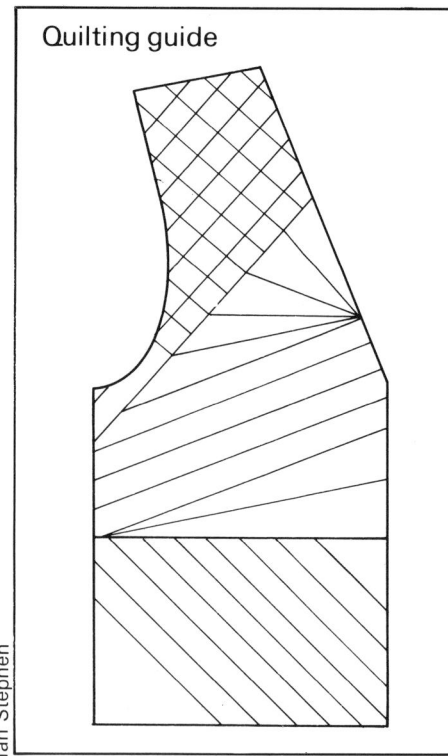

Quilting guide

1 Following the appropriate figures on the measurement diagram, draw the pattern for the vest and check it to make sure that it fits.
2 Cut out the pieces in the appropriate fabrics the number of times stated, cutting the silk slightly larger all around than the batting, muslin backing and lining.

3 Following the quilting guide, mark the design on the right side of the two fronts, drawing the lines with tailor's chalk. You need not follow the quilting guide exactly; draw your own design or, if you are using a patterned fabric, follow the design on the fabric.

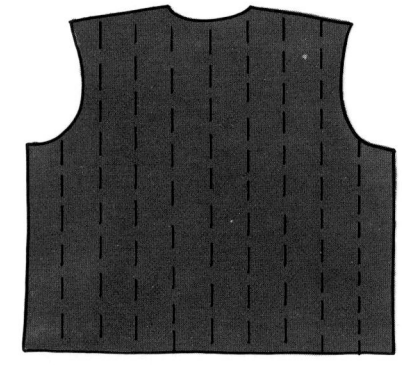

4 Starting from center back, mark quilting lines on the back of the vest, positioning them 1½in (4cm) apart all across the back.

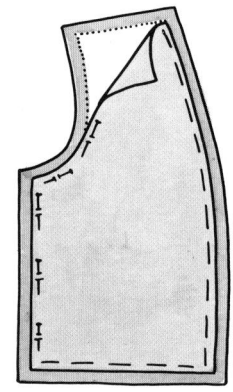

5 Pin batting and muslin vest pieces to wrong side of silk vest sections. Baste all around to secure. Baste the whole quilting design carefully along the marked lines.
6 Machine stitch along basted lines through all thicknesses. Trim quilted sections to match pattern pieces.

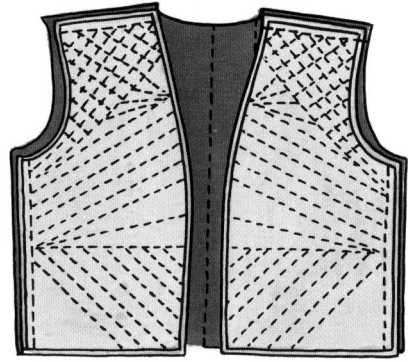

7 With right sides together and raw edges matching, pin, baste and stitch shoulder and side seams of quilted sections. Press seams open and trim batting from seam allowance.

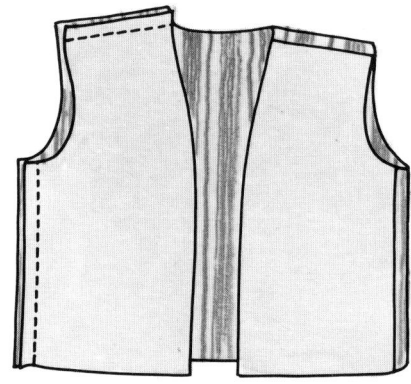

8 Repeat to join lining pieces.

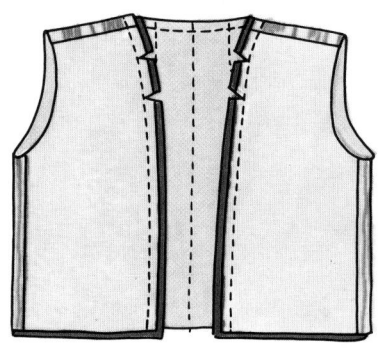

9 With right sides together, pin, baste and stitch lining to quilted section all around neck and front edges, taking ⅝in (1.5cm) seams. Clip and notch curves.
10 In the same way, stitch across the lower edges from the center front to the side seams.
11 Turn right side out. Turn in remaining openings on armhole and lower edges. Pin, baste, and slip stitch to close.

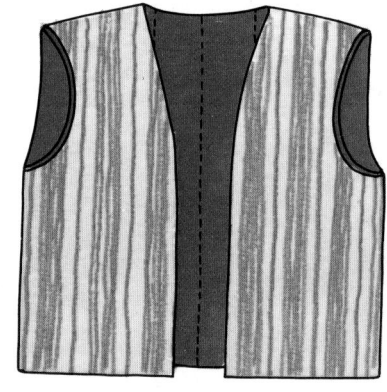

12 Press edges lightly. Work even running stitch all around the front, lower and armhole edges.

Skirt

1 Following the measurement diagram, mark the rectangular skirt sections on the fabric with tailor's chalk.
2 Cut out the two skirt sections, the waistband and the four pocket pieces.
3 From batting, cut out two triangles, following the measurement diagram. Cut two triangles from muslin.

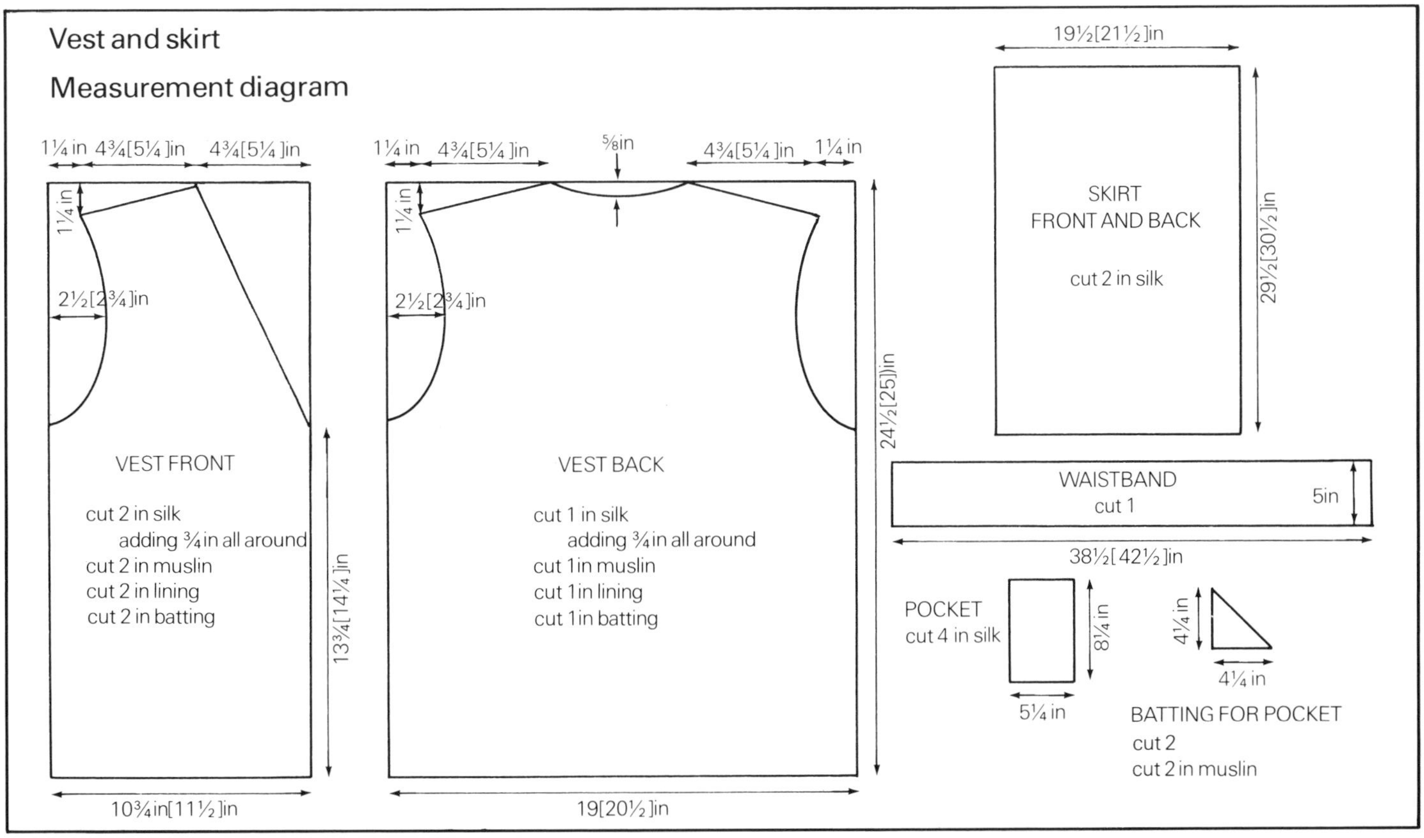

Vest and skirt
Measurement diagram

Ian Stephen

VEST FRONT

cut 2 in silk
    adding ¾in all around
cut 2 in muslin
cut 2 in lining
cut 2 in batting

1¼ in 4¾[5¼]in 4¾[5¼]in
1¼ in
2½[2¾]in
13¾in[14¼]in
10¾in[11½]in

VEST BACK

cut 1 in silk
    adding ¾in all around
cut 1in muslin
cut 1in lining
cut 1in batting

1¼ in 4¾[5¼]in ⅝in 4¾[5¼]in 1¼ in
1¼ in
2½[2¾]in
24½[25]in
19[20½]in

SKIRT FRONT AND BACK

cut 2 in silk

19½[21½]in
29½[30½]in

WAISTBAND
cut 1
5in
38½[42½]in

POCKET
cut 4 in silk
8¼ in
5¼ in

BATTING FOR POCKET
cut 2
cut 2 in muslin
4¼ in
4¼ in

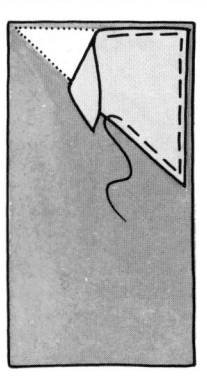
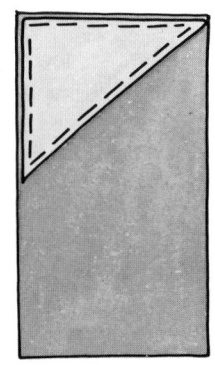

4 Place batting triangles on wrong side of pocket lining sections, positioning one triangle at the top right and the other triangle at the top left as shown. Cover with a piece of muslin. Pin, and baste all around the batting.

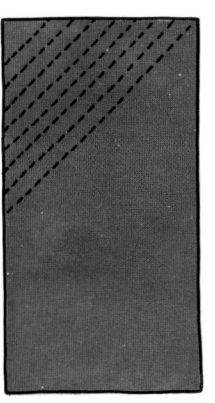

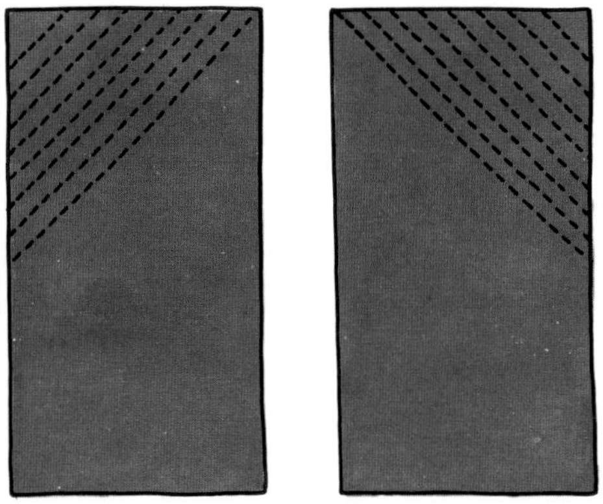

5 Starting from the corner and positioning the lines ⅜in (1cm) apart, mark eight lines across the corner to be quilted, parallel to the long edge of the batting section. Baste. along marked lines. Machine stitch through all three layers.

6 Place remaining pocket sections on quilted pocket sections, right sides together. Pin and baste all around. Machine stitch around three sides, leaving lower edge open. Trim batting and seam allowances and clip corners.

7 Turn right side out, turn in open edges and slip stitch together to close.

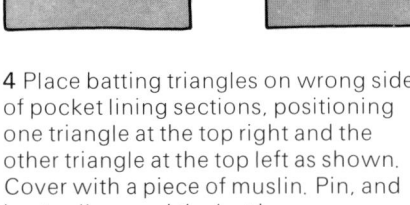

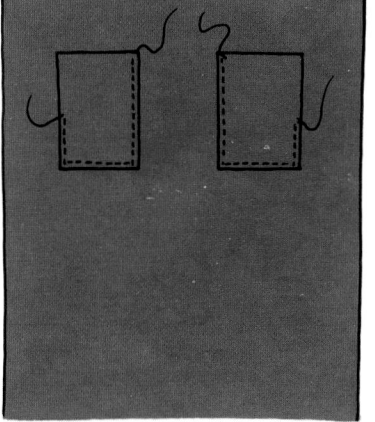

8 Pin and baste pockets, quilted side down, to skirt front, positioning them 4in (10cm) down from top edge and 3¼in (8cm) in from side edges. Topstitch in place from lower edge of the quilting, down outer side edge, across the lower edge and up the inside edge, stitching ⅛in (3mm) from edge of pocket.

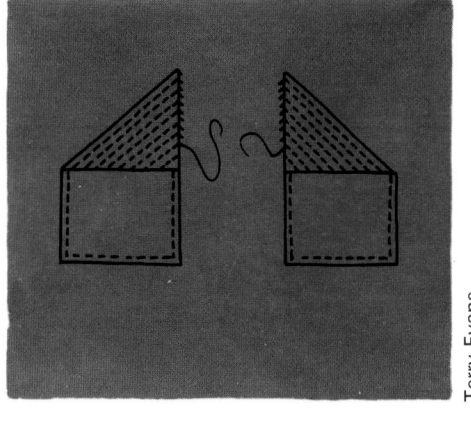
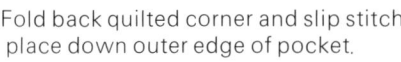

Terry Evans

9 Fold back quilted corner and slip stitch in place down outer edge of pocket.

Cutting layout for 45in-wide fabric

Smaller size

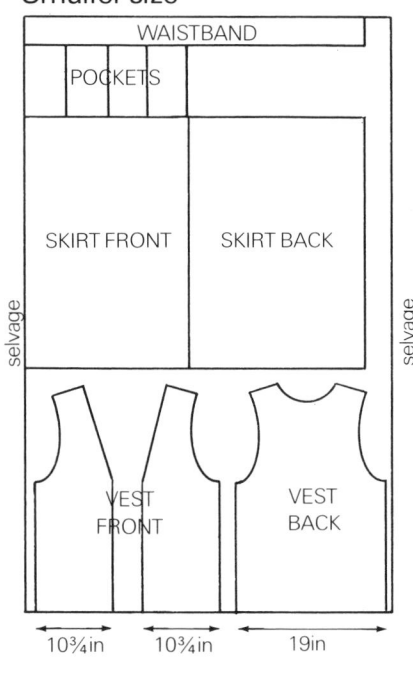

WAISTBAND

POCKETS

SKIRT FRONT

SKIRT BACK

selvage

VEST FRONT

VEST BACK

←10¾in→ ←10¾in→ ←19in→

Larger size

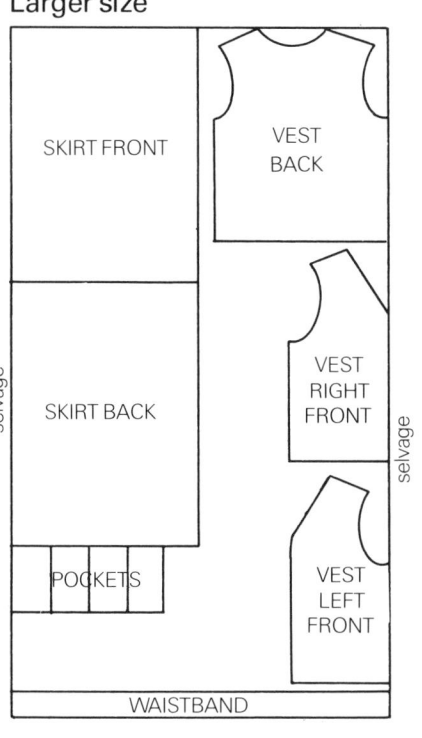

SKIRT FRONT

VEST BACK

selvage

SKIRT BACK

VEST RIGHT FRONT

selvage

POCKETS

VEST LEFT FRONT

WAISTBAND

Ian Stephen

Technique tip

More hints on quilting

It is generally advisable to quilt fabric before cutting out, since the process of quilting takes up a certain amount of fullness. However, on the vest featured here, the pattern is related to the shape of the garment, and so must be worked after it is cut out.

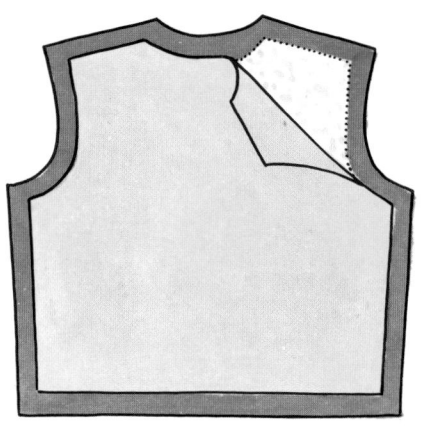

When cutting out the fabric, cut the top pieces ¾in (2cm) larger all around than the batting and backing. The design is fairly intricate, so instead of basting a grid on the fabric, it is a good idea to baste the whole design on the fabric.

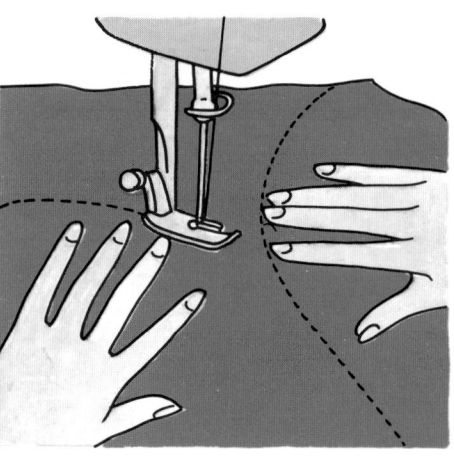

Stitch carefully, following the basted lines. Hold the fabric firmly as you stitch. On curved lines, lay your hands on each side of the foot, moving the fabric as the needle rises. On straight lines it is easier to produce even stitches if you hold the fabric in front of and behind the foot.

After stitching, pull top thread through to the back and secure all the threads neatly on the wrong side. Lay the pattern piece on the quilted section and trim the upper layer to fit. Trim away batting and backing from seam allowances if necessary.

Press quilting lightly on wrong side over a folded towel.

---

10 With right sides together and raw edges matching, pin, baste and stitch side seams of skirt, leaving 8in (20cm) open at lower edge on each side. Press seam open. Finish seam allowance and hem edge by turning under ¼in (5mm) and machine stitching.

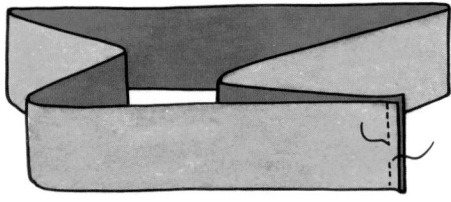

11 Join short ends of waistband, taking ¾in (2cm) seam and leaving a ⅜in (1cm)-wide gap ⅝in (1.5cm) from lower edge.

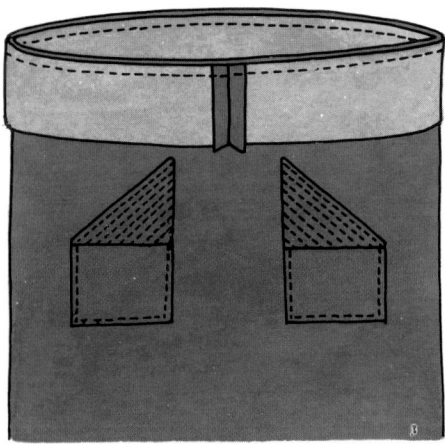

12 With right sides together and raw edges even, pin, baste and stitch

waistband around upper edge of skirt, taking a ⅜in (1cm) seam, positioning seam at center front of skirt. Press seam allowance upward.

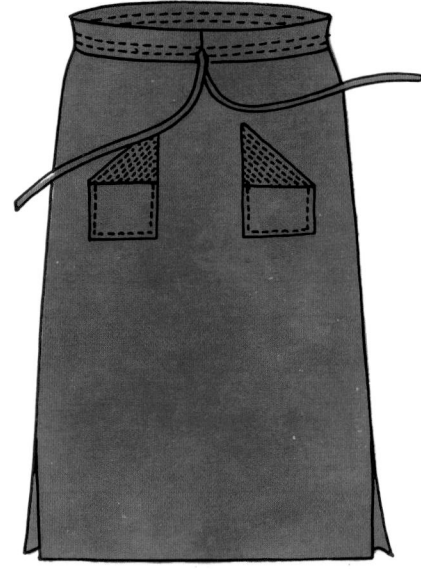

13 Turn under ⅜in (1cm) along free edge of waistband. Fold waistband in half so that folded edge matches seamline. Pin and baste in place. From right side, stitch through waistband ¼in (5mm) from existing seam; add a second line of stitching ⅜in (1cm) above the first.

14 Thread ribbon or cord through casing.

15 Turn under ¼in (5mm) on lower edge; machine stitch. Turn up another 1¼in (3cm) and sew by hand. Sew edges of side slits in place, mitering corners.

114

Needlework

These pretty bedroom accessories—one trimmed with embroidery, the other with sachets—have a practical function: they keep your nightgown tucked away till bedtime.

Sweet hearts

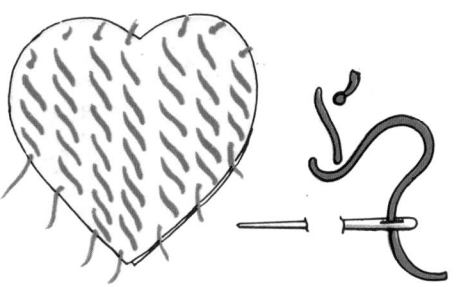

Spike Powell

Embroidered satin case

Finished size
18×19in (46×48cm).

Materials
1yd (.9m) of 36in (90cm)-wide pale green satin
½yd (.5m) square of white cotton
½yd (.5m) square of medium-weight interfacing
3⅜yd (3m) of 2¼in (6cm)-wide lace
2yd (1.8m) of ⅜in (1cm)-wide velvet ribbon
Stranded embroidery floss in shaded green, shaded pink, pale pink and peach
Sewing thread in shades of green
1in (2.5cm) of touch-and-close fastening
Tracing paper
Dressmaker's carbon in a light color
Small embroidery hoop
Medium-size crewel needle

1 Using tracing paper and a pen, trace the case pattern. Fold paper in half. Place the fold on the broken line and trace the pink lines. Open the paper flat and trace the green lines, matching lines at center. Cut out pattern.
2 Using the pattern cut out four case pieces from green satin, adding ⅜in (1cm) seam allowance all around. Cut out one case from white cotton fabric and one from interfacing, adding seam allowance.

3 On the right side of one satin piece lightly trace the floral design using dressmaker's carbon paper. Place the fabric right side up and place the dressmaker's carbon paper on top, shiny side down. Place the pattern on top of the carbon paper so that the seam allowance extends equally all around the pattern. Trace the design.

Janet Allen

4 Place this marked piece wrong side down on cotton fabric piece with edges matching. Pin and pad-stitch the two case pieces together as shown.

5 Set your sewing machine to satin stitch: zig-zag with a minimum stitch length and a width of just under $\frac{1}{8}$in (3mm).

6 Place a sheet of tracing paper under the fabric and, using different green threads, work the stems of the design. When stems are completed, remove the paper and discard it. Take all the loose threads to the wrong side and fasten off.

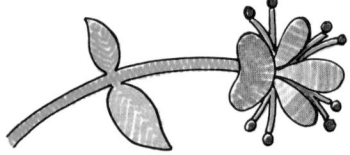

7 Place the stitched pieces in the embroidery hoop, making sure that it is taut, and hand-embroider the flowers and leaves, moving the fabric as necessary.

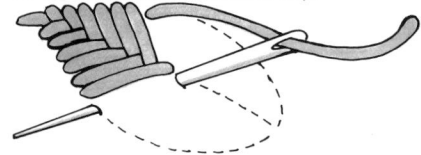

8 Work the leaves in fishbone stitch using three strands of shaded green embroidery floss.

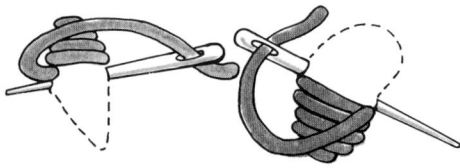

9 Work the three smaller petals in satin stitch, using three strands of shaded pink embroidery floss, and the main petal using three strands of peach.

10 Work the stamens in chain stitch using three strands of shaded green embroidery floss.

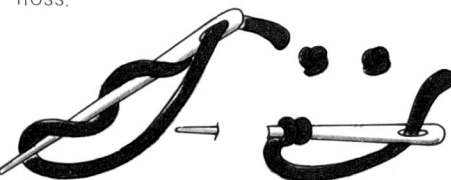

11 Work French knots at the stamen ends using six strands of pale pink embroidery floss.

12 When the embroidery is completed, remove all the pad stitching. Press the embroidery carefully on the wrong side, using a steam iron or damp cloth to ease out any wrinkles.

13 Mark the seamline on all the case pieces, $\frac{3}{8}$in (1cm) from the edge, with basting stitches. Mark the dots on the top edge.

14 Run a row of gathering stitches along the straight edge of the lace. Pull up threads to fit edge of heart; adjust gathers. Starting at the center top, pin the lace to the seamline of the embroidered piece, right sides together, as shown. Sew the short edges of the lace together and overcast the raw edges together.. Baste the lace along the seamline.

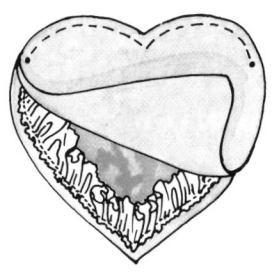

15 Place another satin case piece over embroidered piece with right sides facing and edges matching. Pin, baste and stitch around curved top edge between the dots. Trim seam allowance and clip curves at short intervals. This double section will form the outer and inner front of the case.

16 Place the interfacing piece on the wrong side of one of the remaining satin pieces. Pin and baste the two heart pieces together all around their edges.

17 Place the remaining satin piece and the interfaced piece together with right sides facing. Pin, baste and stitch them together around the curved top edge between the dots. Trim seam allowance and clip curves at frequent intervals. This section will be the outer and inner back of the case.

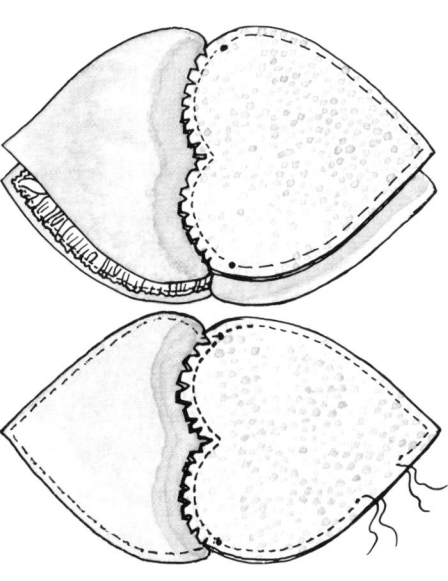

18 Open out the back and front pieces of each side of the case. Lay the outer front (embroidered) and the inner front with right sides facing up. Place the back section on top, with the interfaced inner back over the inner front and the outer back over the outer front. Match dots and seamlines. Pin, baste and stitch the sections together, leaving a small opening in one side of the inner case.

19 Trim seam allowance and clip the curves. Turn the case right side out. Turn in opening edges and slip stitch them neatly together.

20 Tuck the case lining inside the outer case.

21 Separate the touch-and-close fastening into two halves. Place one half at the bottom point of the heart on the inside of back opening. Pin, baste and hand-sew tape in place.

22 Place other half of fastening on inside front of opening to correspond. Pin, baste and hand-sew in place.

23 Cut the velvet ribbon into eight equal lengths. Tie each piece of ribbon into a neat bow. Snip ribbon ends into "V" shapes for a neat finish.

24 Place bows around the edge of the case, placing one bow at center top, one bow at center bottom and the remaining bows at equal intervals between these two. Neatly hand-sew all the bows in place.

Lavender case

Finished size
$17\frac{1}{4} \times 19$in (44×48cm).

Materials

1yd (.9m) of 36in (90cm)-wide dark
*   purple cotton*
½yd (.5m) of 36in (90cm)-wide
*   floral printed cotton*
¼yd (.2m) of 36in (90cm)-wide lilac
*   cotton*
½yd (.5m) square of medium-weight
*   interfacing*
3⅞yd (3.5m) of ⅜in (1cm)-wide lilac
*   satin ribbon*
Matching thread
1in (2.5cm) of touch-and-close
*   fastening*
Tracing paper; lavender

1 Trace pattern as for embroidered case, step 1, omitting the flower design. Trace pattern for sachet.
2 From dark purple cotton cut four case pieces, adding ⅜in (1cm) seam allowance all around. Cut out one case piece from interfacing, adding ⅜in (1cm) seam allowance all around.
3 From lilac cotton cut four sachet pieces, adding ⅜in (1cm) seam allowance all around.
4 For ruffles cut five strips, each $35 \times 3\frac{1}{4}$in (90×8cm), from printed fabric.
5 For the case ruffle, join three strips to make one long one, placing them

together at short ends, with right sides facing; pin, baste and stitch.
6 Make a narrow double hem along one long edge of ruffle. Turn under ¼in (5mm) and then another ¼in (5mm). Pin, baste and stitch hem.

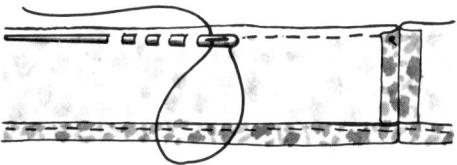

7 Run a line of gathering stitches along the remaining raw edges of ruffle.
8 Assemble the case as for the embroidered case, steps 13 to 22, substituting the floral printed ruffle for the lace ruffle.
9 Make two lavender sachets. First mark the seamline on each sachet piece, ⅜in (1cm) from the edge, with basting stitches.

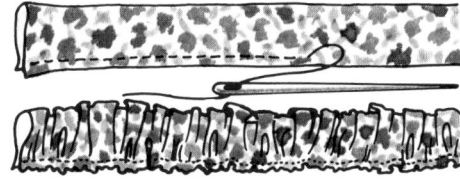

10 Fold one of the remaining ruffle pieces in half lengthwise, with wrong sides together and raw edges matching. Run a row of gathering stitches along double

raw edge of ruffle.
11 Place the ruffle on the right side of one sachet piece (folded edge of ruffle to inside); pull up thread to fit and distribute gathers evenly. Pin and baste ruffle in place. Pin, baste and sew short ends together.
12 Place another sachet piece on the ruffled piece with right sides facing and the ruffle sandwiched between them. Pin, baste and stitch the hearts together, catching in the ruffle and leaving a small opening in one side. Trim and clip into the seam allowance.
13 Turn sachet right side out. Fill it with lavender. Turn in opening edges and slip stitch them together neatly.
14 Make another lavender sachet in the same way, following steps 10 to 13.

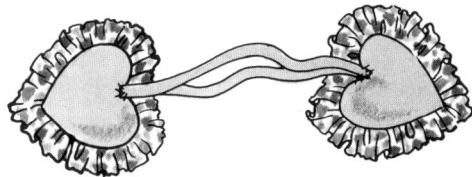

15 Cut a 27in (70cm) length of ribbon. Fold ribbon in half and sew the folded end to the center top of one sachet. Sew the cut ends to the center top of the other sachet.
16 Cut four 12in (30cm) lengths of ribbon. Place ribbons together in pairs and tie them in double bows to trim the sachets.

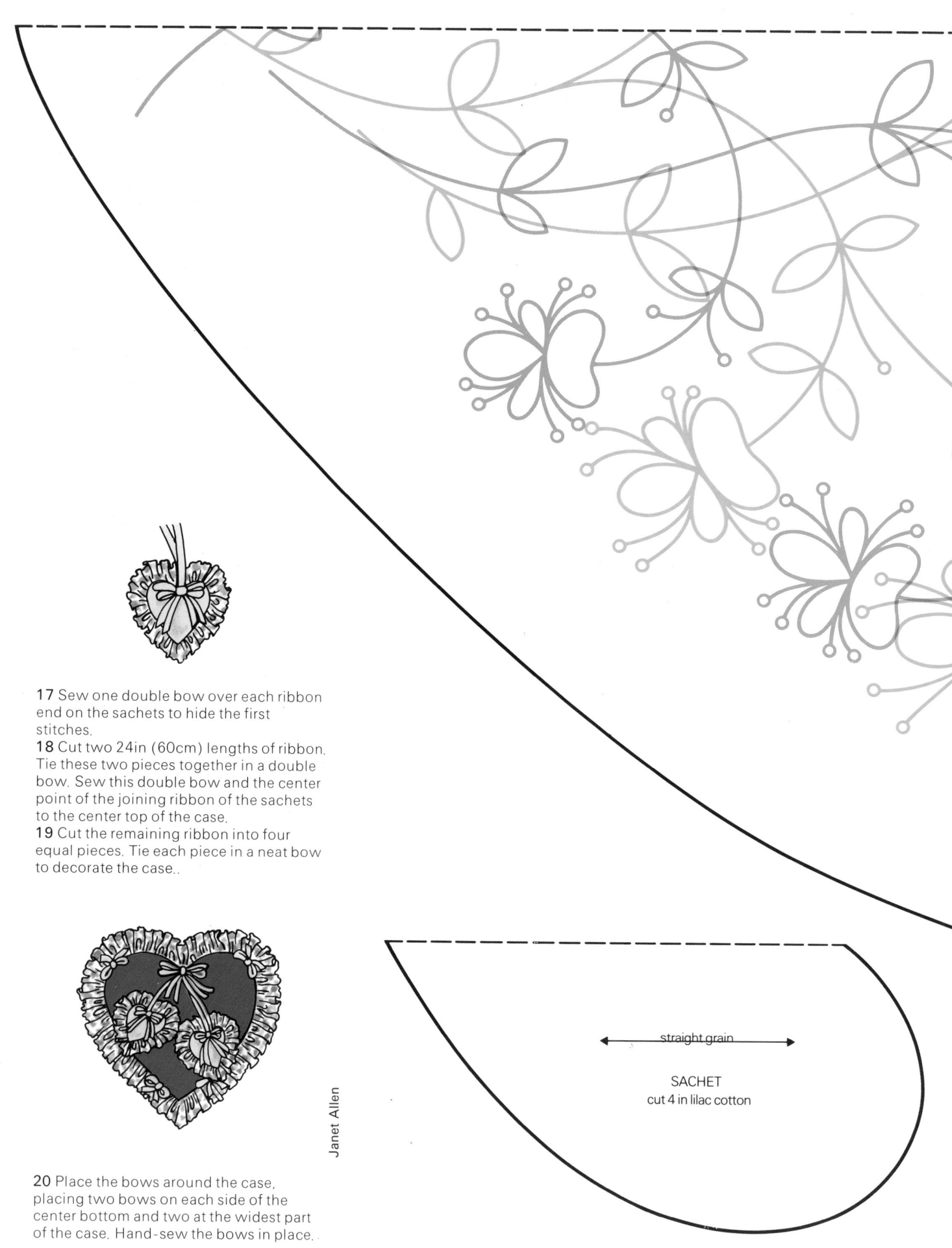

17 Sew one double bow over each ribbon end on the sachets to hide the first stitches.

18 Cut two 24in (60cm) lengths of ribbon. Tie these two pieces together in a double bow. Sew this double bow and the center point of the joining ribbon of the sachets to the center top of the case.

19 Cut the remaining ribbon into four equal pieces. Tie each piece in a neat bow to decorate the case..

20 Place the bows around the case, placing two bows on each side of the center bottom and two at the widest part of the case. Hand-sew the bows in place.

Janet Allen

straight grain

SACHET
cut 4 in lilac cotton

CASE
cut 4 in green satin, 1 in white cotton, 1 in interfacing
cut 4 in dark purple cotton, 1 in interfacing

Brian Mayor

Homemaker

Crochet-edged shade

The pretty answer for a small window is this window shade. Made in an attractive print, it is trimmed with crochet motifs.

Belinda

Finished size

The shade shown measures 32in (81cm) in width. A motif is 4 × 2⅜in (10×6.5cm).

Materials

1¼yd (1.1m) (or required length) of 36in (90cm)-wide printed fabric
2oz (50g) of a fine mercerized crochet cotton
2½yd (2.2m) of 1¼in (3cm)-wide fusible webbing
Matching thread
Window shade kit to fit 32in (81cm)-wide window
No. 4 (1.75mm) crochet hook
10in (25cm) of cord; shade pull
Small tacks

1 Trim fabric width to 34½in (87cm).
2 Fold 1¼in (3cm) to the wrong side down one long side. Pin and press in place.

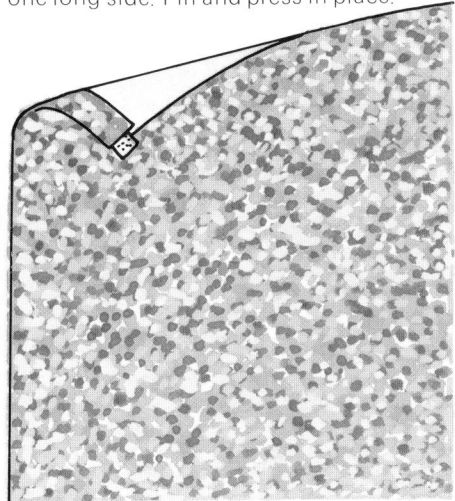

3 Cut a piece of fusible webbing the same length as the fabric. Place the webbing in the fold of the side hem. Iron the side hem in place.
4 Repeat steps 2 and 3 on the other long edge of the shade.

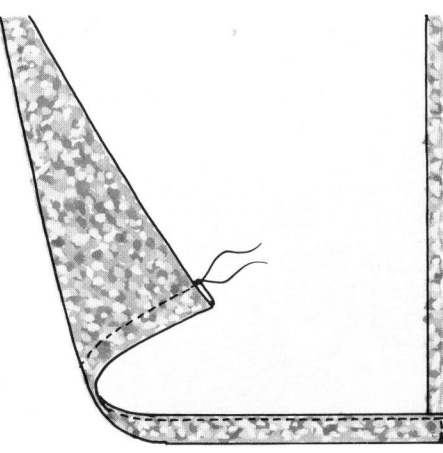

5 To form the hem casing, turn ¾in (2cm) to wrong side at bottom of shade, then turn up another 1½in (4cm). Pin, baste and stitch in place, along casing edge and down one short edge of hem.

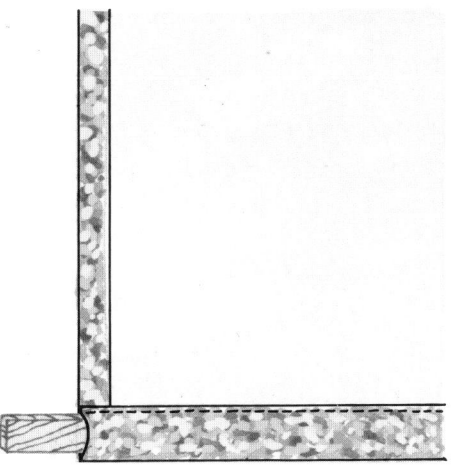

6 Cut the wooden lath from the window shade kit to measure 31½in (80cm) long. Slot the lath through the casing. Pin, baste and stitch (using zipper foot) the remaining side to enclose the lath.

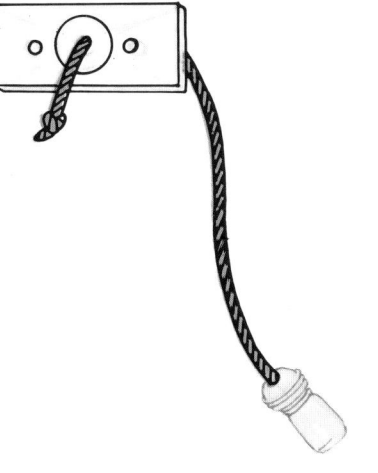

7 Thread one end of the cord through the shade pull and knot it to fix it in place. Thread the other end of cord through the cord holder as directed in kit and knot it at the back.

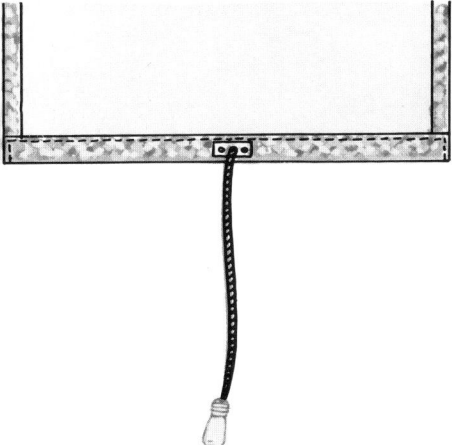

8 Screw the holder to the middle of the lath on the back of the shade, so that the cord hangs down straight.
9 Using No. 4 (1.75mm) hook make 34ch.

10 *Base row*: 1 sc into 2nd ch from hook, *2ch, skip next 3ch, 1dc, 2ch and 1dc all into next ch, 2ch, skip next 3ch, 1sc into next ch, rep from * to end of ch. Turn.
11 *1st patt row*: *2ch, 1dc into next dc, 4dc into next 2ch sp, 1dc into next dc, 2ch, 1sc into next sc, rep from * to end. Turn.
12 *2nd patt row*: Sl st into each of next 2ch and 3dc, 1sc into next sp between dc, *3ch skip next 2dc, 1dc into last dc of group, 1dc into first dc of next group, 3ch, skip next 2dc, 1sc into next sp between dc, rep from * to end, finishing with 1 sc into next sp between dc in the last group. Turn.
13 *3rd patt row*: * (2ch, 1dc into next dc) twice, 2ch, 1sc into next sc, rep from * to end. Turn.
14 Rep steps 11 to 13 twice more, working 3 groups on first rep and 2 groups on second rep, then rep steps 11 and 12 once more.

15 *Next row*: 2ch, 1dc into next dc, 4dc into next 2ch sp, 1dc into next dc, 2ch, 1sc into next sc. Fasten off.
16 Repeat steps 9 to 15 and make 7 more

motifs in the same way.

17 Join motifs together at base row to form a row of 8 motifs. Work 2 rows of sc along foundation ch.

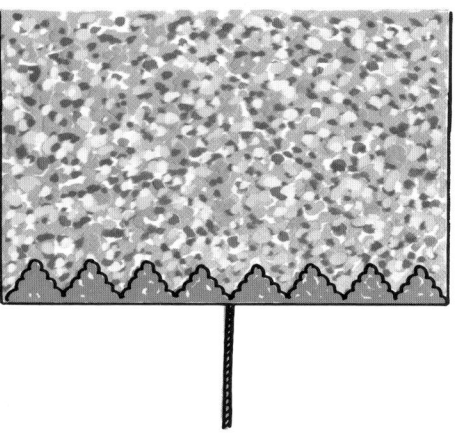

18 Repeat steps 9 to 17 and make 2nd row of motifs in the same way.

19 Position the first row of motifs along the lower edge of the shade, placing them right side up on the right side of the shade along the bottom edge. Pin, baste and hand-sew in place.

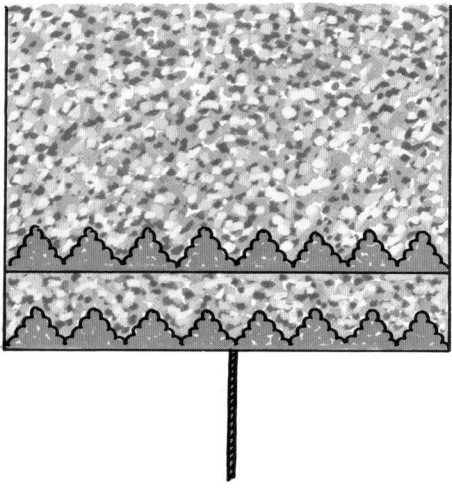

20 Place 2nd row of motifs on the shade right side up, $5\frac{1}{2}$in (14cm) from lower edge. Pin, baste and hand-sew in place.

21 The fabric is attached to the roller so that the fabric hangs next to the window. Cut the roller to fit the shade.

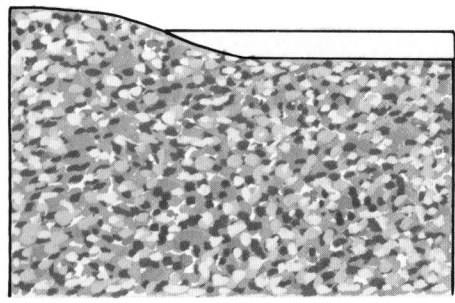

22 At the top of the shade turn a $\frac{5}{8}$in

(1.5cm) hem to the right side. Pin and baste in place.

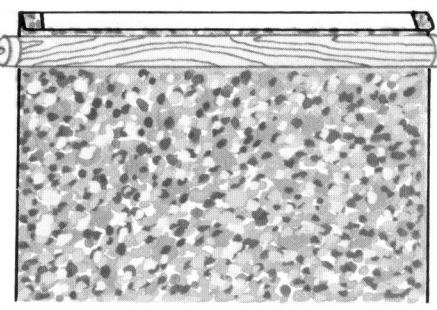

23 Place the prepared fabric shade right side up on a flat surface. Lay the roller across the top of the fabric, with the spring at the left-hand side, making sure that roller is at a right angle to fabric.

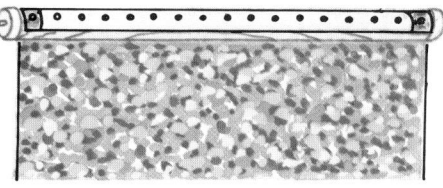

24 Attach the fabric to the roller with small tacks, working from the center out toward each end. Place the tacks at about $1\frac{1}{4}$in (3cm) intervals along the marked line of the roller.

25 Roll the fabric firmly and evenly around the roller before fixing the shade into the brackets. Fix shade into brackets. Pull shade down to test the spring tension. If the shade does not roll up smartly, pull it down again and remove it from brackets. Roll it up again and replace in brackets.

Homemaker

Perk up an old deck chair and recliner with colorful and comfortable new covers for the garden or the beach.

Sun set

Quilted recliner cover

Materials

7yd (6.5m) of 45in (115cm)-wide heavyweight cotton fabric
3⅜yd (3m) of ½in (1.2cm)-thick foam, at least as wide as the recliner
11yd (10m) of 1½in (4cm)-wide bias binding
Matching thread

Measuring and cutting out

1 Remove the old cover and rip out the stitching so that the cover lies flat in one piece.
2 Use this as a guide. Measure the length and width of the old cover and then add 6in (15cm) to each measurement for seam allowances and "take-up" in quilting.
3 Cut out two rectangles of fabric to these measurements and one rectangle the same size in foam.

To make the cover

1 Place the foam between the two pieces of fabric with wrong sides inside and edges matching. Pin and baste 1in (2.5cm) in from all edges to hold the three layers in place.

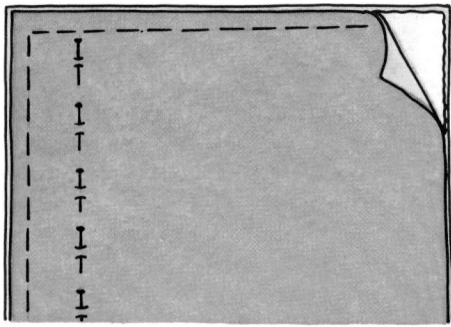

2 Divide the width of the fabric, between the basted lines, into equal sections, each about 4in (10cm) wide. Mark the divisions with pins in parallel lines running down the entire length of the cover.

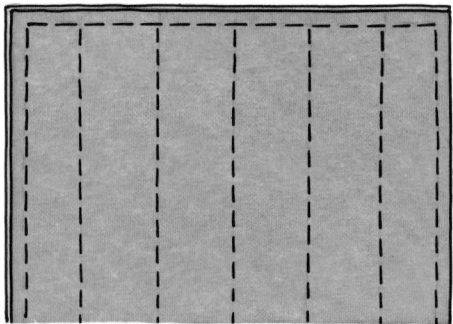

3 Baste along each marked line through all three layers. Stitch down each line, using the largest open zig-zag stitch on the machine.

4 Place the quilted fabric over the recliner. The overhang at each end will be turned under to form the end pockets.

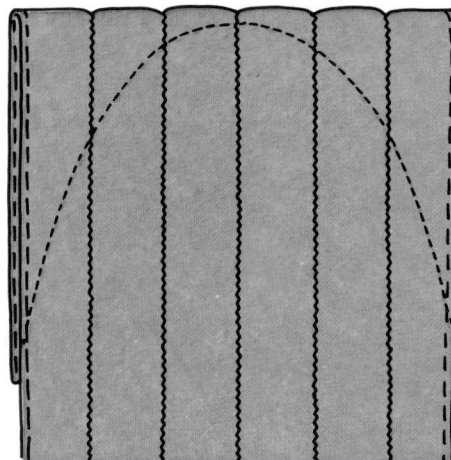

5 Completing one end at a time, pin, then baste the fabric to fit the shape of the recliner, turning under the ends to form pockets.
6 Repeat step 5 at other end of recliner.
7 Trim away any excess fabric from the straight edges of the pockets. Check that the cover fits smoothly when the ends are fully extended. It can easily be removed by closing both ends of the recliner.
8 Make any necessary alterations to the fit. Stitch pocket sides along the basted lines. Trim away any excess seam allowance. Finish the seam edges with an open zig-zag stitch.
9 The fabric must be cut from around the hinges to prevent unnecessary wear. Use the original cover as a guide in marking the positions. Place the old cover on top of the new one and mark where each hinge will be.

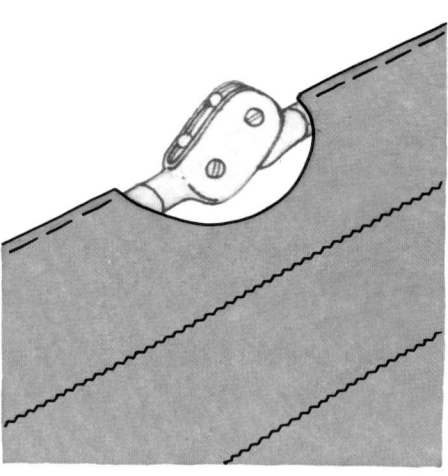

10 At one hinge mark cut away a semi-circle, starting ¾in (2cm) to each side of the mark, but cutting the fabric close to the hinge on the inside edge.
11 Repeat step 10 at the remaining hinge positions.
12 Trim side edges, if necessary, to fit recliner; re-baste layers together.

13 Bind the cut and unfinished edges, working the straight edges of the end pockets and along the side edges, including the indentations for hinges. Open out the bias binding. Place one edge of binding on underside of cover, with right sides facing. Pin, baste and stitch along the crease of the binding for the entire length. Stitch the ends of the binding together to fit.

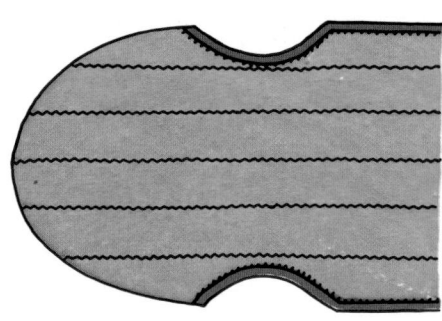

14 Turn binding over to right side of cover. Pin, baste and slip stitch binding to cover previous stitching line.

Deck chair cover

Materials

1½yd (1.3m) of 18in (45cm)-wide deck chair canvas
Upholstery tacks
Thumbtacks
Hammer

1 Remove the old cover from the deck chair. Make any necessary repairs to the deck chair; clean and re-paint it if necessary.
2 Turn ¾in (2cm) to the wrong side at one short end of the canvas. Press.

3 Set up the deck chair frame. Using two thumbtacks, temporarily tack the folded end of the canvas to the top rail of the frame on the edge where the original canvas was held. On the completed chair the canvas will be wrapped around the rail as shown.

4 Collapse the frame. Check that the canvas is parallel to the frame sides. Holding the frame firmly, anchor the canvas to the rail with the upholstery tacks, spacing them at about 2in (5cm) intervals along the rail and placing a tack at each end. Try to avoid the old tack holes when placing the tacks in the rail.
5 Set up the deck chair again. Wrap the canvas around the top rail, then around the bottom rail. Holding the canvas on the lower rail, collapse the chair and lay it flat on the floor with the wrong side of the canvas facing up.

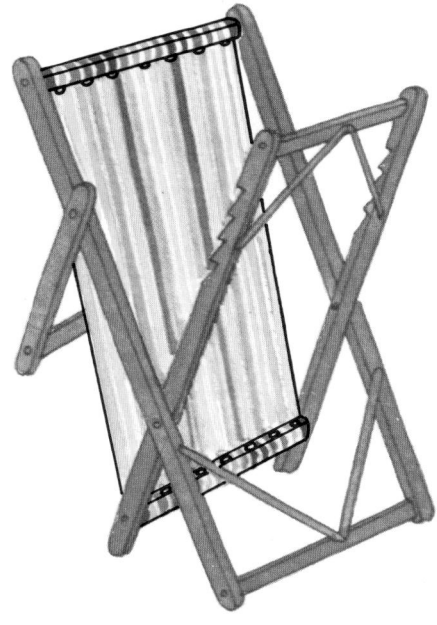

6 Pull the canvas taut. Turn under excess canvas. Anchor with upholstery tacks along the rail where the original cover was fastened. Space the tacks as on the top rail and avoid original tack holes.

7 If the lower rail is narrower than the top rail, simply fold the excess width to the wrong side, spacing the amount evenly between the two side edges, before tacking the canvas in place. Do not trim off this excess canvas.

Quilted hold-all/pillow for a deck chair

Materials
    1⅜yd (1.2m) of 45in (115cm)-wide *heavy cotton fabric*
    Piece of ½in (1.2cm)-thick foam 70×18in (180×46cm)
    3⅜yd (3m) of 1½in (4cm)-wide bias binding; matching thread

1 From fabric cut two pieces, each 47×18in (120×46cm). Cut a piece of foam the same size.
2 Place the foam between the two fabric pieces with wrong sides inside. Pin and baste around all four edges to hold the three pieces together.
3 Quilt the fabric as for the recliner cover, steps 2 and 3.
4 Finish the short ends with binding as recliner cover, steps 13 and 14.

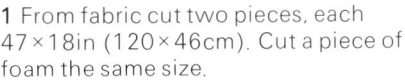

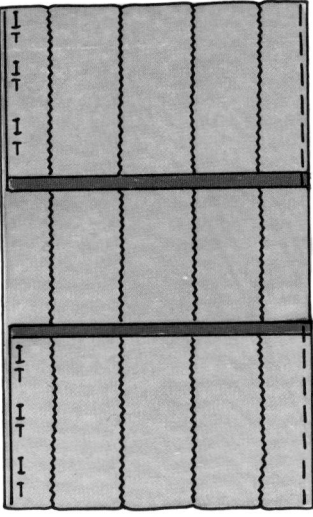

5 Fold each bound end toward the center for 10in (25cm). Pin and baste the side edges, forming two pockets.

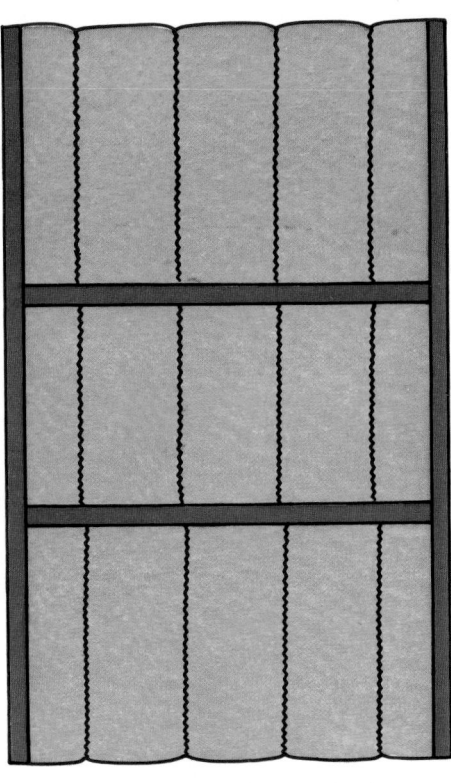

6 Finish both side edges with binding, as for short ends, step 4, turning in raw edges of binding at each end.

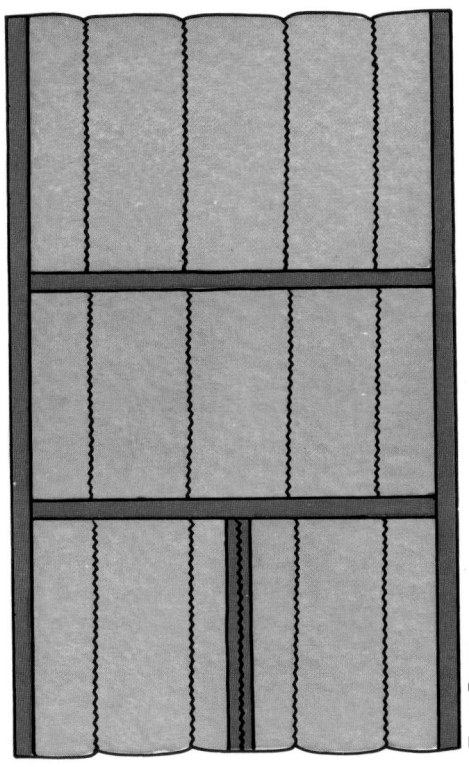

7 Cut a piece of bias binding 11in (27cm) long. Mark the center of one of the pockets at both top and bottom. Fold the binding in half lengthwise. Position it on pocket at center marks. Tuck under ½in (1cm) at each end. Pin, baste and stitch the binding in place through all layers to divide the pocket in two.

Terry Evans

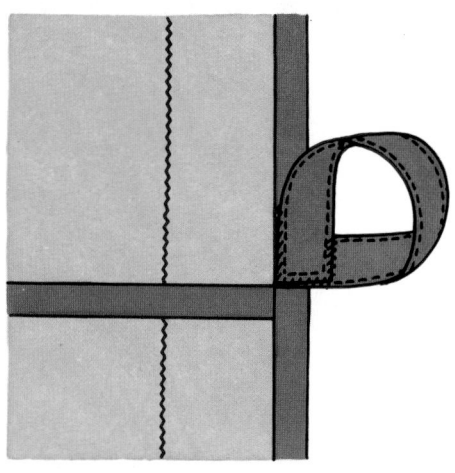

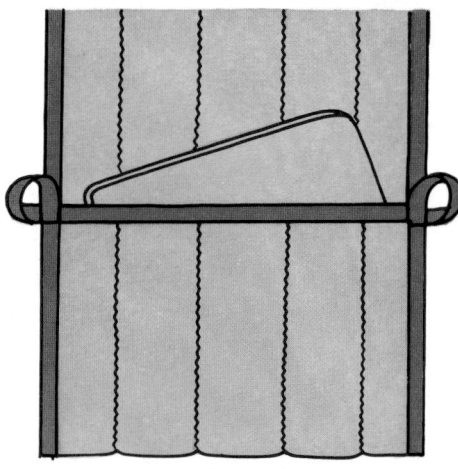

Fold one piece in half with wrong sides together, turning in short ends. Pin, baste and topstitch along the edges. Bring ends together to form a loop and place loop on binding at top of larger pocket as shown. Pin, baste and stitch loop firmly in place.

9 Repeat step 8 to make other loop in the same way.

10 For pillow, cut two pieces of fabric, each 13 × 9in (34 × 24cm).

11 Place the pieces together with right sides facing and edges matching. Pin, baste and stitch the edges, taking a $\frac{1}{2}$in (1cm) seam allowance and leaving an 8in (20cm) opening in one long side.

12 Trim seam and turn cover right side out.

13 Cut four pieces of foam, each $11\frac{1}{2} × 7\frac{1}{2}$in (30 × 20cm). Place the four pieces together and slip them inside the cover. Turn in the opening edges and slip stitch them together.

8 To tie the holder in place on the deck chair, make two loops. Cut two pieces of binding, each 16in (40cm) long.

14 Insert pillow into larger pocket to make head rest. Slip loops over each side of deck chair frame.